Praise for RFID Essentials

W9-BBW-964

"RFID is one of those rare 'change the world' technologies that will force a rethinking of many value-chain strategies. In that context, Bill and Himanshu's comprehensive expert-in-a-book creation should be on the must-read list for strategists and IT professionals who see RFID in their future. Unique competitive advantage erupts from enterprises that couple the RFID technologies laid out in *RFID Essentials* with modern business integration using service-oriented architectures. This is the book to read in order to understand this new landscape."

—MARK BAUHAUS, SVP: BUSINESS INTEGRATION, IDENTITY, AND APPLICATION PLATFORM SOFTWARE

"RFID, or Radio Frequency Identification, got legs with mandates from giants such as Wal-Mart and the U.S. Department of Defense; however, the use is going beyond the supply chain. Companies are seeing the benefits of RFID in other areas such as asset tracking and drug authentication. No matter what the need, the first step in any engagement is understanding the technology and how it can be used to gain business benefits. This book gives a good foundation on RFID fundamentals and is a must-read if you are considering adopting RFID for your business or applications."

—JULIE SARBACKER, DIRECTOR, SUN MICROSYSTEMS RFID BUSINESS UNIT

"The authors have done a commendable job of covering a lot of ground in the RFID space, including the infrastructure needed to share the volumes of data RFID will likely generate. While the short-term issues seem focused on read rates and hardware prices, in the end we may see yet another transformational use of the Internet in exchanging data about serialized assets and products."

—GRAHAM GILLEN, SENIOR PRODUCT MANAGER, VERISIGN

RFID Essentials

Other resources from O'Reilly

Related titles	Applied Software Project Management	The Art of Project Management
	Database in Depth	

oreilly.com

oreilly.com is more than a complete catalog of O'Reilly books. You'll also find links to news, events, articles, weblogs, sample chapters, and code examples.

oreillynet.com is the essential portal for developers interested in open and emerging technologies, including new platforms, programming languages, and operating systems.

Conferences

O'Reilly brings diverse innovators together to nurture the ideas that spark revolutionary industries. We specialize in documenting the latest tools and systems, translating the innovator's knowledge into useful skills for those in the trenches. Visit *conferences.oreilly.com* for our upcoming events.

Safari Bookshelf (*safari.oreilly.com*) is the premier online reference library for programmers and IT professionals. Conduct searches across more than 1,000 books. Subscribers can zero in on answers to time-critical questions in a matter of seconds. Read the books on your Bookshelf from cover to cover or simply flip to the page you need. Try it today for free.

RFID Essentials

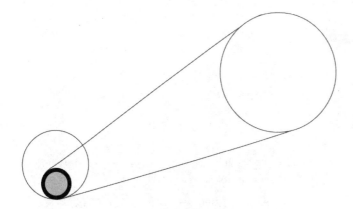

Bill Glover and Himanshu Bhatt

O'REILLY®

Beijing • Cambridge • Farnham • Köln • Paris • Sebastopol • Taipei • Tokyo

RFID Essentials
by Bill Glover and Himanshu Bhatt

Copyright © 2006 O'Reilly Media, Inc. All rights reserved. Printed in the United States of America.

Published by O'Reilly Media, Inc. 1005 Gravenstein Highway North, Sebastopol, CA 95472.

O'Reilly books may be purchased for educational, business, or sales promotional use. Online editions are also available for most titles (*safari.oreilly.com*). For more information, contact our corporate/institutional sales department: (800) 998-9938 or *corporate@oreilly.com*.

Editor:	Mary O'Brien	**Cover Designer:**	MendeDesign
Production Editor:	Colleen Gorman	**Interior Designer:**	Marcia Friedman
Copyeditor:	Rachel Wheeler	**Illustrators:**	Robert Romano, Jessamyn Read,
Proofreader:	Lydia Onofrei		and Lesley Borash
Indexer:	Angela Howard		

Printing History: January 2006: First Edition.

RepKover™ This book uses RepKover™, a durable and flexible lay-flat binding.

ISBN: 0-596-00944-5

[M]

CONTENTS

Preface

LIKE SO MANY OTHERS, THIS BOOK WAS WRITTEN BECAUSE WE COULDN'T FIND ONE LIKE IT. We needed something to hand to all of those people who have come to us asking for "a good book to read on RFID." When we looked for candidates we found some great books, but most were aimed at electrical engineers or top-level managers, with very little for those of us who are in between. This book is for developers, system and software architects, and project managers, as well as students and professionals in all of the industries impacted by Radio Frequency Identification (RFID) who want to understand how this technology works. As the title suggests, this book is about RFID in general and not just the most recent developments; however, because so much is going on in the area of RFID for the supply chain and especially the Electronic Product Code (EPC), we have devoted considerable space to these topics. Regardless of the type of RFID work you may be doing, we think you will find something useful here.

Who This Book Is For

This book is for developers who need to get that first RFID prototype out the door; systems architects who need to understand the major elements in an RFID system; and project managers who need to divide work, set goals, and understand vendor proposals. Students and instructors should find enough detail here to use this book as at least a supplementary text for a study of RFID. Even those with considerable experience in RFID should find this book a useful update on the latest developments, with enough of the fundamentals to serve as a reference. This book is probably not for anyone who wants either a cursory overview of the technology or a deep discussion of supply chain management, manufacturing, access control, or conspiracy theories. These are all interesting topics in their own right, but this is only one book!

Structure of This Book

There are 11 chapters, 2 appendices, and a glossary in this book. RFID is a broad subject, so while we think all of the sections of the book are necessary to tell the whole story, not every section will appeal to every reader. The book's structure divides neatly into two broad areas of interest: a general overview (the "Everyone" section), which should be of interest to any reader, and a section containing more-technical discussion ("Developers and Architects").

Everyone

Chapters 1 and 2 cover the basics of RFID and give readers a framework for further discussion. Most readers will also want to cover Chapters 9–11 for discussions of key topics in RFID.

Developers and Architects

Anyone who will actually be creating or interfacing with an RFID system or who wants to understand how all of the pieces work should read Chapters 3–8, where we get into the details of tags, readers, middleware, and the RFID information service.

What's in Each Chapter

The chapters proceed in what we hope you will find is a natural progression, starting with an introduction and overview, a chapter on architecture, and then a discussion of each component of that architecture. Following our discussion of all of the pieces, we take a look at the qualities of the entire system that deserve special attention, such as manageability, security, and privacy. We then wrap things up in the final chapter with a look at the future of RFID. Here's a brief tour:

Chapter 1, *An Introduction to RFID*
    Defines RFID and introduces some of the fundamental concepts

Chapter 2, *RFID Architecture*
    Describes the parts of an RFID system, their relationships to each other, and some of the functional and service-level requirements specific to RFID

Chapter 3, *Tags*
    Describes the tags that attach an identity to an item and communicate that identity to readers

Chapter 4, *Tag Protocols*
Examines how tags talk to readers

Chapter 5, *Readers and Printers*
Describes the readers that communicate with tags and connect RFID-tagged items to the network

Chapter 6, *Reader Protocols*
Covers how readers talk to middleware and applications

Chapter 7, *RFID Middleware*
Describes the middleware that manages RFID information and edge devices

Chapter 8, *RFID Information Service*
Examines the storage and use of RFID information

Chapter 9, *Manageability*
Discusses some of the specific concerns related to managing RFID devices on the edge of the network

Chapter 10, *Privacy and Security*
Discusses real concerns regarding the impact of RFID on security and privacy, as well as dispelling some of the myths

Chapter 11, *The Future*
Provides a look at where RFID may take us in the next few years

Appendix A, *EPC Identity Encodings*
Provides additional encodings to complete the discussion of EPC identity encodings introduced in Chapter 4

Appendix B, *References*
Lists resources available for those who want more information on RFID or who would like to become involved in defining the technology as it develops

Glossary
Includes key acronyms and terms to help you sort out some of the jargon used in this field

Conventions Used in This Book

The following is a list of the typographical conventions used in this book:

Italic
Indicates new terms, URLs, email addresses, filenames, file extensions, pathnames, and directories

`Constant width`
Is used for examples and the contents of files

`Constant width italic`
Shows text that should be replaced with user-supplied values

You should pay special attention to notes set apart from the text with the following icons:

NOTE

This is a tip, suggestion, or general note. It contains useful supplementary information about the topic at hand.

WARNING

This is a warning or note of caution, often indicating that your money or your privacy might be at risk.

Comments and Questions

Please address comments and questions concerning this book to the publisher:

O'Reilly Media
1005 Gravenstein Highway North
Sebastopol, CA 95472
(800) 998-9938 (in the U.S. or Canada)
(707) 829-0515 (international or local)
(707) 829-0104 (fax)

We have a web page for this book, where we list errata, examples, and any additional information. You can access this page at:

http://www.oreilly.com/catalog/rfid

The authors also maintain a site where you can find a list of RFID resources, along with news and updates:

http://www.rfidessentials.com

To comment or ask technical questions about this book, send email to:

bookquestions@oreilly.com

For more information about our books, conferences, Resource Centers, and the O'Reilly Network, see our web site at:

http://www.oreilly.com

Safari® Enabled

 When you see a Safari® Enabled icon on the cover of your favorite technology book, that means the book is available online through the O'Reilly Network Safari Bookshelf.

Safari offers a solution that's better than e-books. It's a virtual library that lets you easily search thousands of top tech books, cut and paste code samples, download chapters, and find quick answers when you need the most accurate, current information. Try it for free at *http://safari.oreilly.com*.

Acknowledgments

We would like to thank the many people who have provided both tremendous support and direct help to make this a better book. Much of what is good about this book is due to their diligence and care, and any mistakes or weaknesses are entirely ours.

We would like to thank our editors at O'Reilly Media, Inc.: Mike Hendrickson for getting us off to a great start; Andrew Odewahn for seeing this through; and Susan Brown Zahn, Marlowe Shaeffer, and Mary O'Brien for bringing it all together. Many people went out of their way to help by reading early drafts and providing detailed advice and reviews. We would like to thank Chuk Biebighauser, Jeff Coffin, Bryan Helm, Ravi Kalidindi, Brendan McCarthy, Ben Menasha, and Tim Seltzer. We were also lucky enough to have some very challenging technical reviewers critique our penultimate draft, and this is a much better book because of their help. Many thanks to Kevin Ellison from Sun Microsystems, Inc.; Graham Gillen from VeriSign, Inc.; John Hill, Jim Both, and Dennis Dearth from ESync; Mark Johnson of RFID Tribe; Steve Lazar of Texas Instruments; Mark Palmer from Progress Software; Ken Traub from ConnecTerra; Bryan Tracey from GlobeRanger, Inc.; and Marc Linster of Avicon. A special thanks goes to Paul Bodifee of the "Signals Collection 40-45." We did not use his photos in the final draft, but his information about WWII-era RF technology was a great inspiration (see Appendix B for a link to the Signals Collection web site). We would also like to thank the entire RFID team at Sun Microsystems for their passion for this space and for their support.

Bill would also like to thank his family for tolerating a sleepless, grumpy, and sometimes overwhelmed husband, father, and son for these past months. Thanks to Janise and Rhian, and thank you to Bill's parents, Janet and Bill.

Himanshu would like to thank his wife, Teju, for her encouragement and support through the writing of this book. He would also like to thank his little ones, Rohan and Ritu, for their innocence, boundless energy, and enthusiasm. Finally, thanks to his parents, Vinod and Yashavati, and his siblings, Rajendra and Jigu, for their lifelong love and guidance.

CHAPTER ONE

An Introduction to RFID

IN **TWELFTH NIGHT, SHAKESPEARE WROTE**, "Some are born great, some achieve greatness, and some have greatness thrust upon them." RFID is one of the more recent four-letter abbreviations to have greatness thrust upon it in a flurry of industry mandates, governmental legislation, and hyperbole. RFID stands for Radio Frequency Identification, a term that describes any system of identification wherein an electronic device that uses radio frequency or magnetic field variations to communicate is attached to an item. The two most talked-about components of an RFID system are the *tag*, which is the identification device attached to the item we want to track, and the *reader*, which is a device that can recognize the presence of RFID tags and read the information stored on them. The reader can then inform another system about the presence of the tagged items. The system with which the reader communicates usually runs software that stands between readers and applications. This software is called *RFID middleware*. Figure 1-1 shows how the pieces fit together.

Much of the recent interest surrounding RFID has arisen from mandates and recommendations by government agencies such as the U.S. Department of Defense (DoD) and the Food and Drug Administration (FDA), and from a few private sector megacorporations. For instance, in an effort to improve efficiency, Wal-Mart called for its top 100 suppliers to begin providing RFID tags by early 2005 on pallets shipped to its stores. This mandate caused the companies in Wal-Mart's supply chain to focus on implementing RFID

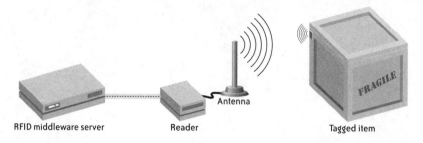

FIGURE 1-1. An RFID system

solutions. Companies worked to decide which tags and readers to use, how to attach tags
to (or embed them in) containers or products, and how to test the read rates for RF tags on
pallets as they moved through doors and onto trucks. Several companies have announced
their support for what are now commonly known as *tag and ship* applications, which tag a
product just before shipping it somewhere else, but few of these companies have moved
beyond minimum compliance with the mandates to using the information on RFID tags to
increase efficiency in their own internal processes.

The mandates have also focused most of these early implementations on tagging, and thus
on the physical side of the RFID systems. However, while it is important to both select tags
and readers and find just the right arrangement of antennas to recognize tags as they
move through docks and conveyor belts, the true benefit (and complexity) of RFID systems doesn't come from reading the tags, but from getting the information from those
reads to the right place in a usable form. The first 100 were only the beginning of the Wal-
Mart RFID rollout. Many more suppliers will be tagging pallets and cartons and some individual items by the end of 2006. Meanwhile, the biggest news in RFID may surround the
ePedigree initiatives aimed at reducing counterfeiting and improving efficiency and safety
in the distribution of pharmaceuticals. By then, many more new initiatives will have been
launched to apply RFID to other industries in ways we can hardly predict (although we'll
try in Chapter 11).

In the pages to come, we explain the essentials of an RFID system, and in order to put
these concepts in perspective, we will also briefly discuss the history, current status, and
future of the technology. This book will give you the information and understanding you
need to take on your first RFID project, but we hope you'll find it just as useful once you
become a seasoned veteran in the field.

The Case for RFID

RFID technologies offer practical benefits to almost anyone who needs to keep track of
physical assets. Manufacturers improve supply-chain planning and execution by incorpo-
rating RFID technologies. Retailers use RFID to control theft, increase efficiency in their
supply chains, and improve demand planning. Pharmaceutical manufacturers use RFID
systems to combat the counterfeit drug trade and reduce errors in filling prescriptions.
Machine shops track their tools with RFID to avoid misplacing tools and to track which

tools touched a piece of work. RFID-enabled smart cards help control perimeter access to buildings. And in the last couple of years, owing in large part to Wal-Mart and DoD mandates, many major retail chains and consumer goods manufacturers have begun testing pallet- and case-level merchandise tagging to improve management of shipments to customers.

Part of what made the growth in RFID technologies possible were the reductions in cost and size of semiconductor components. Some of the earliest RFID tags were as big as microwave ovens, and the earliest readers were buildings with large antennas, as described in Chapter 3. Figure 1-2 shows a modern RFID tag (in the clear applicator) and a reader.

FIGURE 1-2. A tag and reader (image courtesy of Merten G. Pearson, D.V.M.)

Note how the bar code on the applicator matches the code read on the reader. The tag is inside the applicator in this picture and is about the size of a grain of rice. It's very similar to the glass capsule tag shown in Figure 1-3.

FIGURE 1-3. The VeriChip is smaller than a dime (image courtesy of Applied Digital)

Like RFID tags, the size of tag readers is shrinking. While most tag readers are still the size of a large book, smaller and less expensive readers may open up opportunities for many new RFID applications that, over the coming years, could become a normal and mostly unnoticed part of our lives. Figure 1-4 shows one of the smallest readers currently available.

As individuals, we must consider what impact this technology will have on our lives. Such an efficient and unobtrusive tracking mechanism can be used in ways that raise concerns about individual privacy and security. As citizens, we must understand the benefits and

FIGURE 1-4. SkyeTek's SkyeRead M1-mini (image courtesy of SkyeTek)

costs of this technology and its impact on us. Conversely, as developers, we know that "unobtrusive" is a euphemism for "works correctly because a great deal of effort went into design, implementation, and testing." It is our job as managers, architects, and developers to make the technology work so well that it disappears. The following pages will provide an introduction to how RFID works.

Advantages of RFID over Other Technologies

There are many different ways to identify objects, animals, and people. Why use RFID? People have been counting inventories and tracking shipments since the Sumerians invented the lost package. Even some of the earliest uses of writing grew from the need to identify shipments and define contracts for goods shipped between two persons who might never meet.* Written tags and name badges work fine for identifying a few items or a few people, but to identify and direct hundreds of packages an hour, some automation is required.

The bar code is probably the most familiar computer-readable tag, but the light used to scan a laser over a bar code imposes some limitations. Most importantly, it requires a direct "line of sight," so the item has to be right side up and facing in the right direction, with nothing blocking the beam between the laser and the bar code. Most other forms of ID, such as magnetic strips on credit cards, also must line up correctly with the card reader or be inserted into the card reader in a particular way. Whether you are tracking boxes on a conveyor or children on a ski trip, lining things up costs time. Biometrics can work for identifying people, but optical and fingerprint recognition each require careful alignment, similar to magnetic strips. Facial capillary scans require you to at least face the camera, and even voice recognition works better if you aren't calling your passphrase over your shoulder. RFID tags provide a mechanism for identifying an item at a distance, with much less sensitivity to the orientation of the item and reader. A reader can "see" through the item to the tag even if the tag is facing away from the reader.

RFID has additional qualities that make it better suited than other technologies (such as bar codes or magnetic strips) for creating the predicted "Internet of Things."† One cannot,

---

* Lawrence K. Lo, "AncientScripts.com: Sumerian," *http://www.ancientscripts.com/sumerian.html.*

† This term was originally attributed to the Auto-ID Center. We will discuss both this term and the Auto-ID Center in more detail later in this book.

for instance, easily add information to a bar code after it is printed, whereas some types of RFID tags can be written and rewritten many times. Also, because RFID eliminates the need to align objects for tracking, it is less obtrusive. It "just works" behind the scenes, enabling data about the relationships between objects, location, and time to quietly aggregate without overt intervention by the user or operator.

To summarize, some of the benefits of RFID include the following:

Alignment is not necessary
A scan does not require line of sight. This can save time in processing that would otherwise be spent lining up items.

High inventory speeds
Multiple items can be scanned at the same time. As a result, the time taken to count items drops substantially.

Variety of form factors
RFID tags range in size from blast-proof tags the size of lunch boxes to tiny passive tags smaller than a grain of rice. These different form factors allow RFID technologies to be used in a wide variety of environments.

Item-level tracking
Ninety-six-bit RFID tags provide the capability to uniquely identify billions of items (more about this in Chapter 3).

Rewritability
Some types of tags can be written and rewritten many times. In the case of a reusable container, this can be a big advantage. For an item on a store shelf, however, this type of tag might be a security liability, so write-once tags are also available.

The Promise of RFID

As previously mentioned, the capability to attach an electronic identity to a physical object effectively extends the Internet into the physical world, turning physical objects into an "Internet of Things." Rather than requiring human interaction to track assets, products, or even goods in our homes, applications will be able to "see" items on the network due to their electronic IDs and wireless RF connections.

For businesses, this can mean faster order automation, tighter control of processes, and continuous and precise inventories. Business partners will finally be able to share information about goods end to end through the supply chain and, just as importantly, to instantly identify the current location and status of items. For example, pharmacists will be able to track how long perishables have been out of refrigeration.

Military personnel, law enforcement officers, and rescue workers may soon use RFID tags to help build and configure complex equipment based on rules enforced by tag readers. RFID already tracks expensive and sensitive assets used in each of these fields.

For individuals, RFID could provide more effortless user interfaces—so-called "smart" systems that could tell you, for example, which clothes in your closet match. Smart medicine cabinets could warn you against taking two drugs that might interact negatively. It's even conceivable that supermarkets of the future may not have checkout stands—you may fill your cart with goods that a reader in the cart will scan and add to your total. Video monitors on the shelves will offer specials on complementary products; they may even offer to guide you to all of the ingredients for a recipe, based on some of the items you've already chosen. As you walk out the door, you will place your thumb on a pad on the cart handle to approve payment. A shoplifter, however, wouldn't make it very far before the readers recognized unpurchased items passing beyond the sales floor.

Some of these applications are already running in pilot stages. Libraries and video stores use RFID to thwart theft. Some shoppers in Japan use RFID-enabled cell phones to make purchases from vending machines. Businesses use RFID to track goods, and animal tracking has been around for years.

RFID will enter the home and the supermarket aisle when the prices of readers and tags become low enough and when the information infrastructure to use and maintain the new technology is in place. Some of these applications may seem far-fetched, but they are things we know we can do with a bit of engineering. What RFID promises most is to surprise us with uses we can't even imagine at this stage of adoption.

> **NOTE**
> For more on the future of RFID, see Chapter 11.

The Eras of RFID

The progress of RFID adoption divides naturally into eras: the Proprietary era, the Compliance era, the RFID-Enabled Enterprise era, the RFID-Enabled Industries era, and the Internet of Things era. In Figure 1-5, you can see when some of the capabilities of RFID technology became, or will become, available.

In the beginning, during the Proprietary era, businesses and governmental entities created systems designed to track one particular type of item, and this tracking information typically remained within the same business or governmental entity. In the Compliance era (the present era), businesses implement RFID to meet mandates for interoperability with important customers or regulatory agencies but often don't use the RFID data themselves. The future will bring the era of the RFID-Enabled Enterprise, where organizations will use RFID information to improve their own processes. The era of RFID-Enabled Industries will see RFID information shared among partners over robust and secure networks according to well-established standards. The final RFID era that is currently foreseeable is the era of the Internet of Things. By this time, the ubiquity of RFID technology and other enabling technologies, combined with high standards and customer demand for unique products based on this infrastructure, will lead to a revolutionary change in the way we perceive the relationship between information and physical objects and locations. More and more,

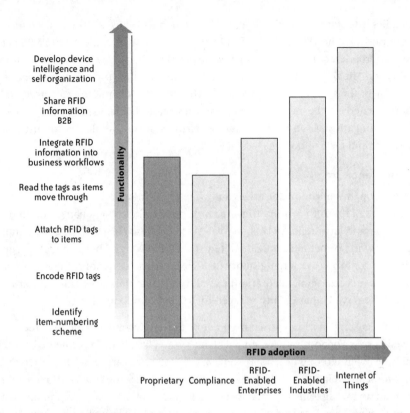

FIGURE 1-5. New capabilities will come with deeper adoption

we will expect most objects in our daily lives to exist both in a particular place, with particular properties, and in the information spaces we inhabit. For instance, a park bench has a particular shape, color, and location, but with a tag, it can also have a list of notes left by people who have stopped there to rest. The list is just as real as the color of the paint, and just as much an attribute of the bench. This is now a green metal bench on the north end of Shaker Park with "a great view of the sunrise," according to "pigeon-guy."

Companies, regions, and even individuals will move through these eras at different paces. Even now, some users of RFID are touching on the RFID-Enabled Industries era as emerging standards make this possible, while others are still in the Proprietary era. In many other areas, RFID has not been adopted at all.

The Proprietary Era

For almost 60 years now (triggered by the development of transistors in 1947), businesses and governmental entities have used RFID to track items and provide access control to facilities. The smaller size and greater durability of transistors made it possible to attach transmitters to valuable items, and over time developments such as improved batteries, integrated circuits, and microchips reduced the cost of the transmitters (tags), allowing tracking of less valuable items. Some of the applications in this era included the tags used to track rail cars and the chassis tags that have been used since the 1980s to track automobiles through an assembly line. In the 1970s and 1980s, RFID was used for tracking dairy cattle. In the 1990s, the beef industry began tracking cattle using $5.00 ear tags. Expensive, proprietary RFID tags, which were usually recycled, were a major characteristic of this era. The reuse spread the cost out, such that a single use might cost only a few cents. Some of the systems developed during this era were technically advanced and tightly integrated into business processes, but they were characterized by both poor support for sharing information between trading partners (incompatible IDs, for instance) and costly reader and tag components.

The Compliance Era

The steep drop in semiconductor prices and widespread adoption of broadband networking at the end of the 20th century triggered an era we call the Compliance era. In this era, the U.S. DoD and large retailers such as Wal-Mart and Tesco began asking their suppliers to tag pallets (and sometimes individual items) with RFID tags. Their mandates required that the tags conform to emerging standards. The anticipated volume of tags that will be purchased to meet these mandates has pushed these same standards much closer to universal adoption, which has greatly reduced the cost of components.

Because this tagging effort has arisen from efforts to comply with a mandate rather than a perceived business opportunity for suppliers, many suppliers have implemented so-called tag and ship applications, which apply RFID tags to pallets or cartons as they leave the supplier's control and ship to a retailer or government customer. The supplier then uses the information on the tag to fill out an advanced shipment notification (ASN), notifying the recipient to expect goods tagged with particular identifiers. The supplier does not tag the goods early enough in its own cycle to take advantage of tracking to improve its processes.

In short, some of these suppliers currently may see RFID as an added expense and burden. They are driven almost entirely by cost efficiency in complying with the mandates, and we do not see applications that integrate RFID into internal business processes or extensive sharing of RFID information between partners in this era. Also, the new, less expensive tag technology is still prone to manufacturing defects, and, due in part to early implementation of the tag standards, often Compliance-era tags do not perform as well in practice as the tags in the Proprietary-era systems. Thus, while adoption of RFID is on the rise, there has actually been a slight slump in its capabilities (in the sense of how the technology is used, if not the purposes to which it is applied). Fortunately, new, more efficient standards and rapid improvement in both tag quality and throughput are quickly closing the gap.

The RFID-Enabled Enterprise Era

As standards stabilize and component costs fall, many organizations will begin to implement RFID tracking within their internal processes. This will allow them to measure the pulse of their distribution systems for materials, assets, and products and to keep real-time inventories of items, such as the location and age of perishable goods. During this era, declining costs will inspire a steady transition from tracking shipping units to tracking individual items. Other types of sensors will join RFID to monitor information such as the highest temperature to which an item has been exposed or whether gases produced by spoilage are present. Labor-intensive bar code inventories will, in many cases, be replaced with scan-by inventories, allowing someone simply to walk down the aisle with a hand-held reader. Similarly, portal readers at the door will record the entry and exit of every item in a shop or warehouse.

In response to demand, more manufacturers will begin tagging items with standards-compliant tags at the point of origin, taking over from the suppliers and distributors who performed this role in the Compliance era. Business integration products and inventory tools will begin to fully support individual item tracking.

However, even with widespread internal adoption and tagging at the origin of the supply chain, it will take time for businesses to develop the agreements and security to allow organizations to share RFID information with one another (so-called business-to-business, or B2B, communication). While businesses will continue to share whatever B2B information they have shared in the past, the new RFID information will be used largely within the enterprise.

The RFID-Enabled Industries Era

In this era, RFID standards, RFID information networks, business agreements, and comprehensive security and privacy policies will solidify to the point where entire industries and supply chains can share appropriate information reliably, trusting that only authorized users can see any sensitive information. This will probably include a redefinition of what constitutes sensitive information, as unexpected revelations are likely to arise from the study of detailed instance data (where only aggregates and estimates were available before). Safety overstock inventories will drop, along with fulfillment times and costs, due to theft and error. Simply knowing "what was where when" provides a powerful tool for applications that we have only begun to realize. Expect to see new products, partnerships, and even whole cottage industries develop by harnessing the advantages of this new flow of information.

For many years, pundits have predicted that businesses will begin to share information much more freely, but it hasn't yet happened on the scale they predicted. Why might RFID information be different? The key is that RFID information is very concrete. It can be difficult for partners to agree on what an item description should contain, but RFID information can be as simple as a universally standardized ID code, a timestamp, and a universally standardized location code. (For more information on ID and location codes, see Chapter 4.)

While we will realize all of these advantages, significant challenges will also arise as managing all of this information, including the sensors and software that produce it, becomes more difficult. Ad hoc or dated architectures will creak and even fail under the load.

The Internet of Things Era

This final era will be triggered by widespread adoption of RFID technology and the associated demand for easier management of distributed sensor networks, as well as by a reduction in the cost of smart devices and tags. Lower costs and greater demand for information will commercialize existing technologies already in use so that military and manufacturing applications can create self-organizing networks of cheap, expendable components with extremely low incremental maintenance and management costs. This technology will finally make it possible to adopt RFID technology on retail floors, in farm fields, and in homes. It will expand the group of businesses adopting the technology to include even the smallest entrepreneurs. RFID tags will cease to simply be labels applied to items and will more often be added as integral parts at the time of manufacture or as part of the packaging. At this stage of development, the idea that an item has a digital identity will become as basic as the idea that an item has a color or weight or size.

In this era, physical objects will be tied to the Internet through their digital identities. Just as we expect to be able to do a quick Internet search to find the answer to an obscure trivia question, we will expect to be able to wave a soda bottle past a cell phone and find out where and at what specific time the soda was manufactured and, if we like, the last known location of every other bottle of that soft drink manufactured within the same hour at a particular location. Invisible digital graffiti associated with identities attached to physical objects will surround us in the form of messages posted to the Internet. But this could go far beyond messages like "Joey was here"—for example, a how-to video for using a piece of equipment could be associated on the Internet with the equipment's tagged ID. By this era, we probably won't think about RFID technology any more than we think about electrical technology today. We will simply expect it to work.

Application Types

Certain broad types of RFID applications characterize whole approaches to this technology and are different enough in considerations and implementation to warrant a separate discussion. The tree in Figure 1-6 shows RFID's relationship to other identity systems, as well as the relationships between different types of RFID.

The term "autoid," short for automatic ID, describes any automated system for attaching an identity to an item. Real-Time Location Systems (RTLSs) are automated systems for tracking the location of an item. Notice that RFID is related only indirectly to RTLSs and that RFID is only one type of automated identity system. We will discuss RTLSs and how they can complement RFID in Chapter 11.

Obviously, we can't fit all of the possible uses of RFID into five simple categories, so we've left out a few applications. For example, while we don't directly discuss payment systems, pay-at-the-pump systems based on RFID raise some (but not all) of the same concerns as access control systems. Refer to the "Access Control" section for information on considerations and implementation; although payment systems don't always have issues with

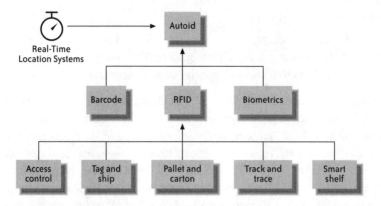

FIGURE 1-6. Relationships among the various types of RFID applications

tailgating, both types of system must overcome counterfeiting and require strong audit procedures. We've also left out some unique applications, such as using RFID tags on compatible pieces of equipment to coordinate assembly of mobile structures in the field for military deployments and trade shows. However, these five categories are inclusive enough to provide at least some sense of the issues and considerations involved in typical RFID applications. The future will bring even more varied applications, but they will raise many of the same concerns as the applications in these categories.

Access Control

Access control applications are RFID systems used to selectively grant access to certain areas—for example, RFID tags attached to an automobile or held in a person's hand as a card, key chain, or wristband may allow access to a road, building, or secure area.

Considerations

Primary considerations for this type of application are:

Anti-counterfeiting
   Counterfeit tags must be recognized and attempts to use or manufacture them discouraged.

Tailgating
   Tailgating occurs when an unauthorized person or vehicle enters just behind an authorized person or vehicle before the gate or door can close.

Emergency access
   In an emergency, the access control system must allow emergency personnel or vehicles access to secured locations. It must also allow nonemergency personnel to evacuate without getting in the way of the emergency response team. Yet emergency access provisions must not provide an attractive "exploit" that allows unauthorized persons to defeat the system by staging a false emergency.

Implementation

To address tailgating and emergency access considerations, most access control implementations include a barrier to entry such as a gate or door. The timing of the door and additional sensors can "singulate" vehicles or persons who enter, restricting access to one at a time.

The anticounterfeiting consideration is the most difficult to address. Many existing systems try to keep the construction and programming of their tags a secret in hopes that no one will reverse-engineer them, but several of these systems have already proven vulnerable to such attacks. Fortunately, most of these systems were noncritical or were backed by audit procedures that caught reverse-engineering attempts. Strong encryption of both a randomly generated challenge message and digital signatures might reduce the opportunity for counterfeiting in cases where the added cost of more complex tags is acceptable, but in general, a human guard, video camera, or police interceptor vehicle is sufficient to discourage all but the most incorrigible. The lesson is that RFID systems do not operate in a vacuum, and effective systems often involve supporting automation, other sensors, and manual processes to ensure success.

Tag and Ship

Tag and ship applications are minimal RFID systems that allow a user to associate an RFID tag with an item, apply the physical tag to the item, and then verify that the tag operates properly while attached to the item. In some cases, these systems even use pre-encoded tags to further reduce cost (see the "Implementation" section for a warning about this practice).

Considerations

Primary considerations for this type of application are:

Cost
Because the drivers for this sort of application typically comply with a mandate, keeping cost low is the primary concern of the end user. This includes initial cost and the total cost of ownership (TCO) over time, from upgrades and repairs to monitoring and maintenance.

Isolation
Tag and ship systems are in some cases the first automated system to be deployed at a given location. The support and maintenance infrastructure needed for such systems, and even the floor space they take up at the dock or shipping area, often aren't readily available.

Tag failure
Manufacturing defect rates are still high for the smart labels (paper tags with embedded RFID antennas and chips) used in this type of application. Since the logistics of trying to reorder missing numbers would be difficult, the system may have to discard one or more labels before finding a functioning label to apply to the item. For pre-encoded labels, this means discarding serial numbers.

Because this type of application is typically implemented in response to an external mandate rather than a perceived internal need, the application's impact on the throughput of what may be a finely tuned manual process can be an important issue. RFID labels appear as only an added cost from this perspective, and each extra second spent attaching labels raises that cost.

Implementation

To implement a tag and ship system, the first requirement is to create or purchase a tag and ship device with a low TCO. A self-contained appliance that operates as simply and reliably as possible should be the best fit. Repairs and maintenance should be no more difficult than changing a light bulb. This means it is often cheaper to buy a few spare devices than to maintain and manage a single device or pair of devices. Owning spare devices can, for example, lower the costs of maintaining and supporting the device in harsh environments where visits from IT personnel are rare.

For the device to resolve the other primary considerations, it should operate simply and quickly and impact manual processes as little as possible. This means there cannot be a complex workaround for failed labels or a multistep process for applying the labels. The simplest way to implement this system is to use labels that are encoded by the appliance itself rather than those pre-encoded by a tag vendor. This enables you to simply skip a failed label and write the same identity to successive new labels until one succeeds. Wherever possible, a tag and ship system should also use an automated "print and apply" device that encodes the label, prints human-readable and bar code information in ink on the surface of the label, and either presses the adhesive label onto the item or blows it on with compressed air. When items are too awkwardly shaped for this approach, the system should provide a visual prompt to indicate how the tag should be applied manually (position and orientation) to reduce errors by the operator.

Pallet and Carton Tracking

One of the most commonly mentioned forms of RFID, pallet and carton tracking, essentially puts a "license plate" on a shipping unit made up of one or more individual items.

Considerations

Primary considerations for this type of application are:

Pallet or carton integrity

This type of tracking works best with a shrink-wrapped pallet that contains only one type of item; the pallet ID is then associated with a simple item count. It also works well with a mixed pallet that has a more complex manifest, describing counts for more than one item. Pallet and carton tracking can be ineffective if there is a possibility that the pallet or carton may be broken down and reconstituted. In this case, the counts or manifest may become invalid.

Pallet orientation

Pallets have six sides. Given that the bottom is typically inaccessible, we still have five choices when deciding where to attach the tag. Because most dock doors are roll-ups, placing a reader overhead can be difficult, so few implementations tag the top of the pallet. Most pallets have an orientation, and shippers typically place pallets with a certain side facing out, so in most cases it isn't necessary to put tags on all four sides. Even if putting a tag on each side seems reasonable, this means creating and reading a whole set of duplicate tags, which can cause problems for both printers and readers. The front of a pallet is blocked by the forklift, although it is possible to place a reader there. (We talk more about antenna placement in general and forklift pitfalls in particular in Chapter 5.) The back of the pallet is blocked from the readers by the pallet itself and then by the forklift upon passing through the portal. This leaves the left and right sides available for tagging. No strong consensus exists on which to use, so most implementations place readers on each side but tag only one side of the pallet.

Interfering contents

You might expect that a tag on the outside of a box would be easily visible to a reader, regardless of its contents, but this is not so. Imagine the reader as a bright light and the tag as a small mirror. Could you see a small mirror attached to a larger mirror, even if the light of a 300-watt floodlight illuminated it? A tag on a box of metal cans can be just as difficult for a reader to distinguish. If the product contains metal, have mercy and put the tag on a thin foam backing. The added distance will usually create enough space between the tag and the reflected signal to greatly improve read rates.

Implementation

Because the considerations for pallet and carton tracking have to do with implementation, we have already covered several implementation ideas in the preceding section. To sum things up:

- Track wrapped pallets with known contents.
- Place tags on the left or right side (as seen from the forklift) but not on both sides.
- Put a foam backing on the tag to raise it a bit if the contents of your pallet are high in metals or liquids.
- Check Chapter 5 for antenna alignment tips and warnings about forklifts.

Track and Trace

One of the earliest uses of RFID was to track dairy cattle. Now, companion animals and livestock of all types are routinely tagged with injectable glass capsules or button ear tags. These tags are used to identify lost pets and to sort, care for, and track the history of livestock. In recent years, RFID has also been increasingly used to track produce and pharmaceuticals. Information from livestock, produce, or pharmaceutical tracking can be critical in the event of a public health threat.

Considerations

Primary considerations for this type of application are:

Information sharing

By definition, track and trace applications require information sharing. One of the key requirements when merging information is coordinated identification. If one producer claims this flat of strawberries should be called 12345 and another claims that a different flat of strawberries should be called 12345, how can the inconsistency be reconciled? What if one producer reuses numbers and sends a flat 12345 this week and another flat 12345 next week? In any track and trace system, each identity must be unique across all producers and for as long a period as the information must be maintained. This can be accomplished in several ways, but the simplest method is either to assign a prefix to each producer to put at the beginning of their identities or to assign blocks of identities to each producer from a central authority (which accomplishes the same thing). Whatever method is used must be universally enforced—otherwise, the integrity of the data in the system will be suspect.

Role- and instance-based access control

Sharing information includes pooling information with competitors. Track and trace systems must have a provision for role- and instance-based control over access to information. In simplest terms, a role is a job, such as veterinarian or retailer, while an instance is a particular person. For example, a retailer may need general information but should not be able to view sensitive information about individual producers or manufacturers. A veterinarian should be able to view detailed information, but only for clients with whom she has a professional relationship. A government inspector should be able to see which animals or produce might have been commingled with a certain suspect lot, but might not need to see any other information.

Implementation

Rather than "rolling your own" identity management system ("identity" meaning user identity for role- and instance-based access control), when implementing a track and trace system you should buy an off-the-shelf identity management and access control solution in the form of an integrated software stack. Several enterprise software vendors offer these. Likewise, you should not create a completely new and proprietary system for provisioning identities. Because so many entities need to share track and trace information, you should ensure that your system makes use of the emerging identity standards (such as those described in Chapters 2 through 9).

Smart Shelf

A smart shelf system is a set of shelves, or some other container (such as a refrigerator), that constantly keeps track of the individual items it contains. If an item is removed or added, the shelf immediately updates the inventory. By tying the identity of an item to its attributes, such as expiration date or lot number, a system using smart shelves can immediately locate all expired products and products from a certain lot. An example of a smart shelf system is a system that contains indicators such as horns or lights that warn users if a product has been removed from refrigeration for too long and should therefore be discarded. Similarly, if the user removes two drugs at the same time that are known to interact negatively, the system signals a warning.

Considerations

Primary considerations for this type of application are:

Item-level inventory support
> The most important consideration in a smart shelf system is the necessity of resolving inconsistencies between existing applications and a system that handles individual inventory. Most inventory systems currently deal only with tuples made up of stock keeping unit (SKU) codes and a count.

Physics and hardware
> Developing a reliable smart shelf system from readers, antennas, and standard shelving is a daunting task due to the complexity of choosing components, placing antennas, and modeling the possible side effects.

Handling spurious reads
> A reader may sometimes fail to recognize a tag. This can be due to interference or absorption of the RF signal. For instance, someone may reach for one item and briefly block the signal response of several others. Also, passing carts full of items by the reader at once may cause false positives to appear on a shelf. The systems must be able to deal with these reads in a manageable way.

Implementation

Several vendors provide prebuilt smart shelf units. Such units are expensive, but the cost may be justified when compared to the TCO of creating your own version. To handle spurious and intermittent reads, many readers can perform "smoothing," in which the reader configuration sets a threshold number of reads to which a tag must fail to respond before the reader marks its absence. A similar threshold can require several reads before an item is added to a shelf, so tags in a passing cart have a smaller chance of being around long enough to cause confusion. With this kind of threshold in place, tags will likely have weaker signals, which could alternatively cause them to be ignored.

Interfacing with existing inventory systems can be complicated; however, you can greatly simplify things by using middleware to handle individual item events and sending inventory changes only to backend systems. Again, you should compare the TCO of custom middleware to the cost of buying a commercial product.

Challenges

Any new technology introduces both costs and benefits, and RFID is no exception. Let's begin with the challenges it presents:

Cost

The most-discussed cost element for RFID systems is the cost of individual tags. However, this is just a part of the overall cost. Successful adoption of RFID will require changes to business processes and information systems, personnel training, and, in some cases, customer education.

Accuracy

Many of today's RFID systems are far from robust. Most of the projects we surveyed in early 2005 reported a read accuracy rate of between 80 and 99 percent. What this means is that if we move a pallet carrying 100 tagged boxes past an RFID reader, the reader will fail to recognize anywhere from 1 to 20 tags. There are many reasons for this, but most stem from the inherent challenges in moving liquids and metals using RF communications.

Implementation

Introducing RFID will invariably change your business processes, from how items are labeled to how they are selected, palletized, cycle counted, and so on. For each step in the business process, you will need to incorporate capabilities for exception processing—that is, what to do if the RFID technologies are not working properly. For example, if an RFID reader stops working or a label falls off, how will you continue? Apart from the RF side, there are many challenges to overcome in integrating the RFID data and procedures into your existing systems and the business processes they support.

RFID Adoption Guidelines

With things changing so quickly, it can be difficult for organizations to decide where, when, and how much to commit to any particular RFID product or standard. The following guidelines offer a strategy for approaching RFID. Simple as the steps may seem, ignoring any one of them can lead to lost opportunities at best, and failure at worst.

Determine the business need.

The current process exists for a reason. Before you even think about changing it, make sure you know its strengths, weaknesses, and reasons for being. Don't start from the premise, "Where can I use RFID?" Instead, start by asking, "How can I improve this process?"

Evaluate potential changes.

Carefully assess the costs and benefits of any potential changes. For example, if you want to automate a manual process, ask yourself a few questions about the change. Would a bar code work better than the manual procedure? Could the process be changed in some way to take more advantage of RFID, or conversely, to eliminate it from your process? How will you handle equipment failures or other types of failure? Note that RFID is sometimes mistakenly referred to as a "replacement for bar codes." Bar codes are actually better than RFID for some applications, and they're considerably less expensive. Also, with RFID there is a temptation to develop automated systems with minimal human oversight. But what happens if someone puts a box full of RFID tags on a pallet and accidentally runs it through the reader? Will your systems believe you've shipped 100 pallets? With bar codes, someone would probably scan each pallet manually, which would prevent this error.

Develop a long-term roadmap.

Instead of implementing RFID systems in an ad hoc manner, develop a long-term business justification for adopting RFID and formulate a vision of how your business processes will look in an RFID world. Follow this up by developing a master plan that shows which systems will need to change and how. Show what your application and infrastructure architecture will look like after deploying RFID. Doing the design up front will give you a clear goal and will also promote the necessary discussions between you and your business units, end users, operations staff, IT staff, and business partners. Don't underestimate how much RFID will impact these stakeholders.

Start small.

Develop a proof of concept (prototype) to validate your assumptions. It's better to fail small and learn early than to fail large and have to recover. Don't be afraid to revise the roadmap and architecture based on mistakes in your prototype, and be ready to start the cycle over again, learning more each time and managing risk as you progress.

Run in parallel with existing systems.

Take a lesson from mountain climbers—don't let go of the last toehold until you are sure the new one won't crumble away beneath you. Not only is it more responsible to run the new system in parallel with the old system for a while, but it can also lead to valuable insights that were invisible when looking at either system in isolation. Don't forget to test the workarounds and recovery strategies you identified earlier. You might be surprised to discover that all of the RFID readers in the building fail when you turn on the exhaust fan for the first time. Only when everything runs smoothly should you begin to depend on the new technology.

Be flexible.

Now that you've made these changes, you have a brand new process. The old process took time to develop, and the new one will take time to mature. While this is happening, be ready to take advantage of new capabilities. Readers with new features and smarter controllers will come out; meanwhile, your personnel should be looking for innovative ways to make use of the new equipment. Watching carefully how people use a piece of equipment can provide important clues for streamlining the process.

Share with partners.

You have a great system in place, but your suppliers are still sending signals by carrier pigeon. Work with your less-enlightened trading partners and show them how to improve their own processes. RFID is an evolving technology, so taking a leadership role will allow you to define the agenda and the standards for future integration. Wal-Mart is an example of a company that has approached a potentially disruptive technology by choosing to lead in its development. As Dr. Alan Kay said, "The best way to predict the future is to invent it." If you keep it all to yourself, you'll just have to change your system when one of your partners chooses a completely different approach.

Summary

In this chapter, we discussed the following:

- RFID is a technology that allows a small radio device attached to an item to carry an identity for that item.

- RFID has been around a while—long enough that we can divide its history into eras and begin to predict future trends.

- In the current era (Compliance), cheap semiconductors and fast Internet connections have encouraged retailers and governmental agencies to require suppliers to place RFID tags on shipping units such as pallets and cartons. However, most suppliers are just tagging pallets and shipping them without using the information internally, and even retailers are simply breaking down the pallets on receipt.

- As the components get cheaper and the information infrastructure becomes more defined and robust, RFID will be used for an increasingly broad array of tasks.

- There are five main categories of RFID applications. Knowing the type of application in question can tell us quite a bit about special considerations and implementation.

- This is a volatile time for RFID, so we must take a disciplined approach to both acquiring knowledge about it and adopting the technology within our organizations. Keep an eye on key players and standards as we move through this era to see which way the technology will shift.

CHAPTER TWO

RFID Architecture

FOR OUR PURPOSES, AN ARCHITECTURE MAY BE DEFINED AS A DECOMPOSITION of a particular computer system into individual components to show how the components work together to meet the requirements for the entire system. With this definition in mind, we can confidently say that there is no such thing as a single, universal RFID architecture that fits all requirements for all systems. Likewise, there is no set number of variations on a single theme. Because of a recent confluence of technologies, RFID systems now offer some key functionalities that have a distinct and predictable impact on the architectures of systems that use it. In this chapter, we describe the components that RFID adds to the architectures of these systems and how RFID affects systemic qualities (i.e., nonfunctional requirements of the system, such as performance, security, scalability, and manageability). From these observations we will derive some architectural guidelines for systems that incorporate RFID.

A Confluence of Technologies

RFID may be seen as the next logical step in the progression of tracking systems and sensor networks because of technological advances in several fields. Let's look at some of the developments that have made RFID possible.

HYPE AND REALITY

Every so often a new technology is introduced that seemingly promises to solve a myriad of problems. In 2001, one of the authors was invited to participate in a technology roundtable on web services hosted by the Chief Technology Officer (CTO) of a Fortune 500 company. Each of the panel members was asked to make an opening remark about the very much hyped web services technologies. One of the vendor participants began by declaring web services "revolutionary" and likening their effects on the IT ecosystem to those of a tsunami. The CTO immediately interrupted and stressed that he wanted to have a pragmatic discussion about web services and did not want anyone to indulge in hype. Declaring web services revolutionary would mean that all learning thus far, including sound software development and architectural principles, does not apply to them.

We have found that, in the early adoption phases of emerging technologies, the amount of caution, past learning, and pragmatism applied to projects that make use of those technologies is inversely proportional to the amount of hype that surrounds them.

History teaches us that hype is generally more profitable for sellers than buyers. We have all seen our share of failed projects in which caution and past learning were abandoned in the name of a new wave. The CTO's comment in 2001 about web services rings very true today for RFID systems. Therefore, instead of indulging in hype and issuing heady promises, we'll take a look at how today's RFID technologies have evolved from the advances we have seen over the past five decades in device, platform, and software technologies.

Advances in semiconductor technologies

RFID would have remained a niche technology if it was not for Moore's law and the ability of the semiconductor industry to produce chips that package processing power at a level that makes it affordable for the mass RFID market.

Intelligent devices

Advances in semiconductor technologies haven't just brought down the cost of RFID chips—they are also the primary drivers behind the development of intelligent devices, including sensors such as RFID readers. Smarter devices and virtually ubiquitous bandwidth have opened up a host of mobility and edge-based applications. RFID is one implementation of the general idea of a "Network of Things" connected together to provide automation beyond the edges of corporate data centers. Smart homes, smart cars, and other smart objects are additional applications that require processing at the edges. Current implementations of smart home systems incorporate a variety of IP-enabled household devices connected to residential gateways that are in turn connected to the Internet. Figure 2-1 depicts the vision of intelligent devices connected to the Internet.

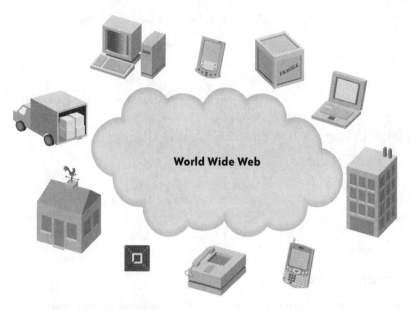

FIGURE 2-1. Network-enabled life

Broadband wired and wireless networks and cheaper edge processing servers

The availability of pervasive broadband data networks, coupled with affordable yet powerful servers, has led to the development of architectures that move processing to where the business processes are carried out. This means that it is now easier to deploy pieces of enterprise applications in edge locations such as warehouses and stores.

Edge processing capability

Edge processing capability derives from having powerful yet low-cost personal computers and servers deployed at the edges of the enterprise network as well as a broadband connection to the data center. RFID systems put greater computing, data management, and bandwidth requirements on these edges. This is not a unique phenomenon, however, but a continuation of the overall trend. By "edge," we mean any location where business processes are carried out that is outside the data center or central office (for example, on production lines, in warehouses, or at retail locations). Figure 2-2 illustrates this.

Service-oriented architecture

Successful adoption of RFID technologies in your enterprise will depend on how well you integrate the RFID data into your business processes. RFID readers can generate a lot of data. If it is exposed unfiltered to downstream applications, it can overwhelm them. To prevent applications from being flooded with RFID data and to isolate them from physical devices such as readers and antennas, you can use sophisticated middleware components such as event managers. Service-oriented architectures allow us to develop and deploy loosely-coupled modules that interface with each other using web services–based standards. As we will see later in this chapter, many of the RFID middleware components are based on web services standards, and the overall RFID system architecture follows the principles widely accepted today as the underpinnings of service-oriented architectures.

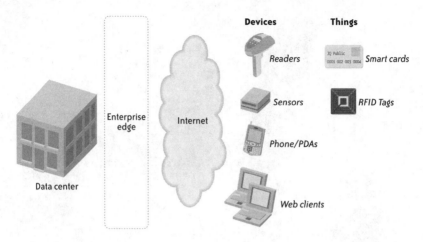

FIGURE 2-2. The enterprise edge

Key Functionalities

What does an RFID system look like? Because there are many possible uses for RFID systems, there will naturally be differences in their architectures. For instance, as described in Chapter 1, a typical tag and ship application implemented by a consumer packaged goods manufacturer would focus primarily on automating RFID tagging of products and ensuring that the tags can be read by the specified readers at higher than the minimum acceptable read accuracy. Generally speaking, these systems focus on the physical side of the implementation, and outside of generating fairly simple reports such as advanced shipment notifications (ASNs), they tend to have minimal data management/exchange requirements. (The ASN is a manifest indicating what items the receiver of a shipment should expect and what the identities of those items will be.) On the other hand, a pharmaceutical company that wants to track the movement of drugs from manufacturing plants to distributors to retail pharmacies would want up-to-the-minute information, including details on where a particular product is at any point in the process, how and where it was manufactured, and where it has been. It is very likely that both the manufacturer and the retailers will also need some of this tracking information. Thus, such a system will require not only item-level tracking capabilities, but also some degree of business-to-business (B2B) information exchange.

Figure 2-3 lists the five eras of RFID described in Chapter 1 and shows the corresponding capabilities required of the RFID systems in each.

As you can imagine, RFID systems will continue to evolve to meet a wide spectrum of needs and thus will require various architectures. As we stated at the beginning of this chapter, it would be impossible to define a general-purpose RFID system architecture or implementation suitable for all the uses of RFID. However, certain capabilities are required of almost every RFID system. In this chapter, we'll focus on those broad underpinnings. Once we've covered the basics, we'll provide some guidelines for developing architectures that will help you get started.

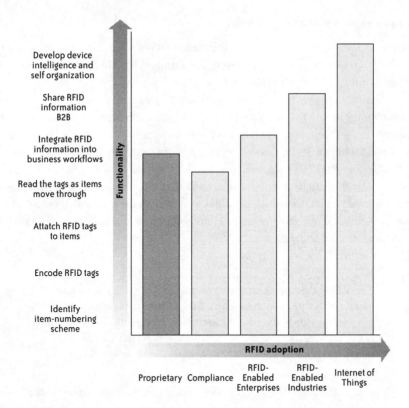

FIGURE 2-3. Capabilities required of different types of RFID systems

Generally speaking, an RFID system must provide some, if not all, of the following features and capabilities:

- The ability to encode RFID tags
- The ability to attach encoded RFID tags to items
- The ability to track the movement of tagged items
- The ability to integrate RFID information into business applications
- The ability to produce information that can be shared between businesses
- The ability to develop self-organization of intelligent devices

Let's take a closer look at each of these items.

Encoding RFID Tags

Encoding RFID tags is a two-step process. The first step is to select an identification scheme to uniquely track the items in question. Once this is done, you can attach those identities to the RFID tags. Let's look at both steps in greater detail.

Deciding on an item-numbering scheme

Identification is the act of recognizing the identity of an object or item. But what is an identity? In RFID, an *identity* is a string of letters and numbers attached to an item to allow a person or an automated system to recognize either that item's type or even the unique item itself. As an analogy, consider the system used to identify books in a library. When you visit a library to find books on RFID, you can determine from the card catalog or computer database that these books will be in the 600s—that is, that each will be labeled with a code starting with a 6 in the Dewey Decimal System (or, more likely, the Universal Decimal Classification (UDC) system, which grew out of Dewey's older system). UDC numbers beginning with 6 all deal with technology. Using the UDC number, we can find all of the copies of a particular book, film, or audio recording in the same place on a shelf or digital storage medium. For example, Klaus Finkenzeller's *RFID Handbook* (John Wiley & Sons) has the number 658.7'87 in UDC.

> **NOTE**
>
> Notice how UDC uses characters beyond the Arabic digits to create identities. For this reason, calling a UDC identity a "number" can be misleading. This is also true of identity schemes we discuss later in this book. Yet many of these codes are called numbers in formal usage; where it is necessary for clarity, we will retain this usage.

Under this system, 100 copies of the same title would each have the same UDC code. The code, then, cannot tell us which copy of the book we are holding. To include that information we would have to add another identifier: a serial number. For example, we might create our own serialized UDC identity with a space separating the serial number from the UDC code. In such a scheme, copy 5,023 of *RFID Handbook* would be numbered 658.7'87 5023, allowing us to confidently refer to an individual book rather than a title or a printing.

> **NOTE**
>
> Individual identity schemes used and proposed for actual libraries and bookstores are slightly more complex than what we've described here. We are not proposing "space and a number" as a new encoding, but this discussion serves as a good example of how you might provide for individual item tracking.

Consider the need to uniquely identify entities, be they products, containers, physical assets, animals, or even human beings. For a large enterprise, there could be millions of items moving through the supply chain at once. A numbering system could be used to uniquely identify these items, but its value would be limited if no one outside of your company could understand it. An industry or universal standard can help.

MULTIPLE IDENTITIES

An object can have multiple identities. Consider the *RFID Handbook*. In addition to its UDC identifier, the same edition of the same book has the U.S. Library of Congress code TS160.F5513 and the International Standard Book Number (ISBN) 0-470-84402-7. Different identifiers are required by different organizations. The Library of Congress uses the Library of Congress Number, and to that organization the ISBN is just another attribute of the book, like its title. To a bookseller, the ISBN is the identity. It's even printed on the back as a bar code. If the local library uses UDC, it views the ISBN and the Library of Congress Number merely as attributes. Likewise, to our families, we may be known by our names, but to the Social Security Administration, we are known by our Social Security Numbers (SSNs). How can we keep up with all of this? The answer lies in what happens during the event known as the "birthing of an identity." When an item first receives its identity, the attributes of that item are associated with the identity in some directory or database. For a book, the title, author, publisher, and printing date—as well as all of the various codes for identifying it—are associated with the new key identity. Similarly, paperwork for registering a baby's name and applying for an SSN is typically completed immediately after the birth, and this information is recorded in government databases.

In 1999, a group of universities—M.I.T. (US), Cambridge (UK), Adelaide (Australia), Keio (Japan), Fudan (China), and St. Gallen (Switzerland)—formed the Auto-ID Center along with industry partners such as Sun Microsystems and Gillette. Their hope was that they could develop standards that would reduce the cost of individual tags—the component that has long been the primary expense of RFID applications—and that standard identifiers could facilitate information-sharing among industry partners. In October of 2003, EPCglobal, Inc. took over managing the standards, and a group now called the Auto-ID Labs continued as a separate research organization. EPCglobal is a joint venture between European Article Number International (EAN International; now GS1), the Uniform Code Council (UCC; now GS1 US), and industry partners that aims to reproduce the success of EAN.UCC standards for bar codes in the area of RFID. EPCglobal is developing standards that describe the components and architecture for what it calls the "EPCglobal Network." The idea is that this network of compatible tags, readers, and information systems will allow systems over an entire supply chain to integrate, from manufacturers to distributors to retailers. The work of EPCglobal centers around what is known as the Electronic Product Code (EPC).

EAN.UCC bar codes currently track things, so why can't we use the same system in RFID? In fact, we can, and some bar code encoding systems are already being used to make RFID tags. These systems are designed, for the most part, to track product categories, not individual items, but with the addition of a serial number, optical codes such as bar codes and two-dimensional "scatter codes" could track individual items. Item-level tracking and RFID are converging, and the point at which they are converging is the EPC. In EPCglobal's Version 1.1 Tag Data Standard, one general identity type is defined: the General Identifier (GID). Five specific identity types derived from EAN.UCC product codes are also defined. These specific identity types add individual asset references or serial numbers to existing EAN.UCC identifiers such as the Serialized Global Trade Item Number (SGTIN) and the Serial Shipping Container Code (SSCC). (The GID and the five System Identifiers are discussed further in Chapter 4.)

An example GID can be expressed as a uniform resource identifier (URI) in the form:

    urn:epc:id:gid:GeneralManagerNumber.ObjectClass.SerialNumber

An example GID might look like this:

    urn:epc:id:gid:00012345.054322.4208

As you can see, the urn:epc:id:gid: part of the GID is static and serves as a header that indicates the type of identifier as well as what fields should follow based on the specifications defined by EPC. This header is followed by value fields, the number and length of which are determined by that header. These three segments respectively identify the *General Manager Number*, the *Object Class*, and the *Serial Number* for the GID.

The General Manager Number identifies the organization (usually a company or trading group) responsible for assigning the numbers in the two succeeding fields. The Object Class identifies the product family or type. Finally, the Serial Number identifies the specific instance of the Object Class being tagged. This approach of delegating ownership of a particular range of numbers to a General Manager provides the flexibility to allow organizations to manage their own product numbers without having to submit changes to a central authority while ensuring that multiple organizations will not produce the same identities for different items.

Encoding identities on RF tags

Once you have chosen an item identification method, you must consider where and how this identification is going to be encoded onto an RFID tag. *Encoding* is the process by which rules are used to turn a human-readable message into machine-readable code. Each type of identification tag, from bar codes and optical scatter codes to magnetic stripes and RFID tags, has a particular encoding that allows it to represent an identity.

Theoretically, once an identity is established for an item, we could simply write the identity on a label and place it on that item. Other people would then be able to identify the item without difficulty (depending on our handwriting). However, an automated system might have more trouble. Printing the identity in a particular font might make the job easier for the system, but if the identity only needs to be read by the automated system, why not print the identity in a form that it can read very easily?

The ubiquitous bar code is the result of this reasoning. In a bar code, lines of specific thicknesses indicate particular letters or numbers. Bar codes come in different types, and each one has rules that describe how it can be formed from a particular kind of identity. The rules that determine both how we turn numbers and letters into bars and which other numbers and letters we can add to make a valid tag are called the *tag encoding*, or simply the encoding. Thus, the bar code may contain the item's identity, a number to indicate what type of bar code it is, and, in many cases, a number that represents the organization that assigned the identity. Figure 2-4 shows a bar code for the ISBN discussed in the sidebar "Multiple Identities."

FIGURE 2-4. An ISBN shown as a bar code

In Figure 2-4, the callouts A, B, and C indicate the sections of the bar code. The section marked A contains the digits 978, a prefix indicating the book industry. Callout B indicates the ISBN number itself. Often bar codes also have a *check digit*, which is a value used by the automated reader to verify that it didn't misread the tag. Callout C marks the check digit, which happens to be 1 in this case. If you have sharp eyes, you may have noticed that the original ISBN ended with a 7. This was the check digit for the original 10 characters of the ISBN, but since we added the industry prefix, we had to recalculate the check digit. Even when we are writing an ISBN as text we must follow the appropriate encoding rules.

In order to select the proper encoding to write an identity to an RFID tag, you must know both the type of identity you want to write and the memory capacity and type of the tag itself. We will discuss EPC encoding in greater detail in Chapter 4 and in Appendix A, but for now, we will use the example GID code introduced previously. As a "pure identity," a GID cannot be written to a tag of any type without some sort of encoding. For our example, let's assume we want to write this to a 96-bit Class I EPC tag—that is, a tag that can store a 96-bit ID and conforms to EPC standards for tags that can be written by end users. First, we take the parts of the GID and arrange them in the right order for the tag, leaving out any fields that are not part of the tag encoding. Fortunately, GIDs contain only relevant fields that are already in the right order. We then add the additional information necessary for the tag type and produce an appropriate URN that can be understood by the reader or event manager. The format of this URN for a GID in a 96-bit tag is:

    urn:epc:tag:gid-96:*FilterValue.GeneralManagerNumber.ObjectClass.SerialNumber*

For our example GID, the URN would look like this:

    urn:epc:tag:gid-96:0.00012345.054322.4208

The Filter Value indicates the logistical type of whatever is being
tracked (e.g., a pallet or carton). We left it as zero for this example.
Chapters 4 and 6 discuss encoding and filter values in detail.

If your application talks directly to a reader, you may need to produce these tag-specific
URNs. If your application talks to some sort of RFID middleware or to a smart reader that
incorporates some elements of RFID middleware, you may be able to use a pure identity
URN like the one mentioned previously. The reverse is also true: a reader may give you a
tag-specific URN, while middleware can give you a pure identity on a read. However,
more and more readers have begun to support the reporting of pure identities.

Attaching RFID Tags

Attaching tags to items is a process that requires time. As with many other processes,
attaching tags manually is the most obvious but least efficient method. Bar codes are often
applied using print-and-apply machines that press or blow an adhesive tag onto an item as
it passes by on an assembly line, and similar devices exist for smart label RFID tags. Many
of these devices also write both a bar code and human-readable information to the paper
tag before applying it. (Of course, the devices, techniques, and issues involved in attaching
other form factor tags to items are different, and almost any style of tag is more durable
and less prone to manufacturing defects than a smart label. We'll discuss other types of
tags in Chapter 3, but we'll use smart labels as an example here to point out some of the
considerations for attaching tags.)

One important consideration when weighing the cost of adopting an automated method
for attaching smart labels is the relatively high defect rate of these RFID tags due to their
delicacy and sensitivity. Any automated or manual system must take into account the
likelihood that many tags on a roll may be defective. Some manufacturers mark any tags
on the roll that test as defective, but often they miss some, while others fail after the test.
Rolls typically have some unmarked bad tags, which means that tags must be verified
before they are printed and applied to the items, and then again after they are applied.
This means that if you purchase pre-encoded tags, you cannot associate an item with its
tag (known as "birthing the tag") until this second verification is complete (although as tag
durability improves by means of new application methods and packaging technologies,
the benefit of birthing pre-encoded tags late in the process will diminish). Many informal
studies claim an insignificant rate of failure for tags that pass this second verification.
Attaching these paper tags to more rigid items seems to help protect the delicate antenna
from breaking even under considerable abuse.

Tracking the Movement of Items

Attaching a tag at the point an item is shipped out the door benefits receivers because they
can track the movement of the item from the sending dock to their receiving dock. The
shippers benefit only in that they have complied with the wishes of the receivers. If an

READING RFID TAGS

An RFID tag communicates with the outside world by sending and receiving electromagnetic signals. *Active* tags have batteries that power their communications, while *passive* tags reflect back a signal generated by another device known as a *reader*. *Semi-passive* tags have a built-in power source so that they can perform certain functions independently, but they still use the reader's radio signal to power communications.

Just as rules define the process of encoding information on a tag, rules also define the way a tag talks to a reader. This set of rules is called an *air interface*, because the tag and reader interface with each other "over the air." An air interface describes the frequencies the tag and reader use to communicate, as well as a communications protocol. This protocol defines which commands the tag understands and how a tag responds to the reader. The protocol also includes rules for communicating with one tag among many and for inventorying all tags present.

---

item is tagged earlier—for example, on receipt from the manufacturer or during its production—more of the supply chain can benefit from knowing how and when the item moved through the chain. It can be valuable to know that a particular shipped item arrived on the dock at 2:05 p.m. Consider how much more valuable it could be to know that a particular item sat in storage bay 11 of the warehouse for six weeks while newer stock shipped from storage bay 10, emptying that bay twice? Or being able to ask your system for the locations of all of the purple widgets made on Friday the thirteenth of May between 9:30 and 10:30 a.m. (the time when the purple widget jabber was misaligned). The cost of this knowledge is the widespread deployment of readers throughout your business in addition to changes to processes to ensure that readers see tags when they arrive at a new step in your process.

Using RFID Data in Business Applications

At the time of writing, the majority of the work being done with RFID systems is focused on the physical side—the tags and readers. It is important to ensure that the right tags, readers, and antennas are selected and that they are configured and aligned to achieve the required read rates. You will realize the true benefits of RFID technologies, however, only when you integrate the tracking information from RFID components into your business applications. Most likely, using RFID information will require integration with, and modifications to, your existing applications. Integrating RFID information with your enterprise applications is no different than integrating other data sources. Architectural approaches, technologies, and products available for application integration apply equally well to RFID solutions.

Sharing RFID Data B2B

Once companies integrate RFID data internally and adapt their business processes to leverage that data, they will find reasons to share it with their business partners and will begin to provide business-to-business services based on the data. Consider an RFID-enabled pharmacy. A pharmacist working in such a pharmacy might be able to retrieve up-to-the minute FDA warnings or other relevant information about a drug just by carrying its container close to an information terminal. The pharmacy's point of sale (POS) system could request a web service provided by the drug manufacturer or some other information intermediary. The drug company could obtain complete tracking information on every drug that it has manufactured and shipped to a particular region by enabling the distributors, shippers, and pharmacies to transfer this information to its tracking systems.

Any of these scenarios assumes the capability of these respective companies to share information. Of course, "one-off" solutions exist to enable these B2B workflows, but long term, these are not the most cost-efficient, the most flexible, or the quickest ways to share information. Sharing information and workflows across enterprise boundaries is not a new phenomena. As we will see later in this chapter, a host of options are available for accomplishing it. In addition to the technology options that are generally available, industry bodies such as EPCglobal are proposing mechanisms for standardizing how we exchange this information. Chapter 8 describes some of these options in more detail.

Self-Organization of Intelligent Devices

As an increasing number of devices are connected to the Internet, the task of provisioning, configuring, monitoring, and managing them poses an ever-growing challenge. An average retail outlet might a dozen servers connected to a couple of dozen POS terminals, at most. However, when the same retail outlet adds RFID-enabled smart shelves and POS terminals, a couple of hundred antennas and readers could be connected to the infrastructure fabric. RFID middleware standards such as application-level events (described later in this chapter) help decouple the enterprise applications from readers and antennas, but configuring those components to work with RFID middleware can be a time-consuming task. Technologies such as Jini and mesh networks, and old standbys such as SMTP provide dynamic configuration and self-healing characteristics so that RFID middleware can adapt to changes in the physical configuration of readers and other sensors. Chapter 9 describes these and other RFID system management issues and options.

RFID System Components

Figure 2-5 shows the primary components of an RFID system. We will explain each of these components in detail soon, but first let's look at the big picture, starting with the components typically present at the edges.

Figure 2-5 shows the typical components found in a retail store. In the bottom-left corner of the diagram, there is a set of RFID tags that represent the tagged merchandise. The store

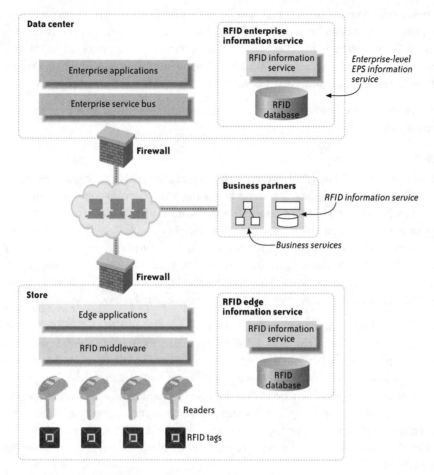

FIGURE 2-5. RFID system components

also has readers stationed within the shelves and at the checkout lanes. These readers may read tags hundreds or even thousands of times per minute, but most of these reads will not be interesting to our application. The readers must also be configured and managed and must know how to work together to cover blind spots should a reader fail. The box marked RFID middleware represents one or more software modules that handle these responsibilities. The box marked Edge applications represents any enterprise applications that have components running inside the store—for instance, POS system components. The box marked RFID information service represents a mechanism to store RFID events and related data at the edge. As you can see, we are showing similar RFID information service boxes in the enterprise's data center and in its business partners' data center. This is because RFID information is stored at various points in the infrastructure: at the edges, within the data center, and with business partners. We will provide more detail on what this information looks like later in this section. For an in-depth discussion of RFID information networks, see Chapter 8.

The two other components shown inside the enterprise data center in Figure 2-5 are the enterprise service bus and enterprise applications. The enterprise service bus is any mechanism that your company may have selected for application integration. Standards-based products that facilitate this are now available. Enterprise applications are any applications that are clients of, or are otherwise affected by, RFID data in your enterprise.

With this basic introduction complete, let's look at the primary RFID components in greater detail.

Tags

As we discussed in Chapter 1, the term "RFID" is typically used to describe systems wherein a base station of some sort (a reader) is able to recognize another electronic device (a tag) using one of several possible wireless transmission mechanisms. These mechanisms may include microwave but not infrared or visible light systems. Since a reader is able to identify a particular tag, the system can claim to have identified the object to which that tag is attached. Tags may be housed in small plastic buttons, glass capsules, paper labels, or even metal boxes. They may be glued to a package, embedded in a person or an animal, clamped to a garment, or hidden in the head of a key.

To understand how an RFID tag notifies a reader about its presence and identity, consider the simple scenario depicted in Figure 2-6. In this figure, the RFID reader transmits radio signals at a preset frequency and interval (usually hundreds of times every second). Any radio frequency tags that are in the range of this reader will pick up its transmission because each has a built-in antenna that is capable of listening to radio signals at a preset frequency (as we'll see in Chapter 3, the size and shape of the antenna determine what frequencies it will pick up). The tags use energy from the reader's signal to reflect this signal back. Tags may modulate the signal to send information, such as an ID number, back to the reader.

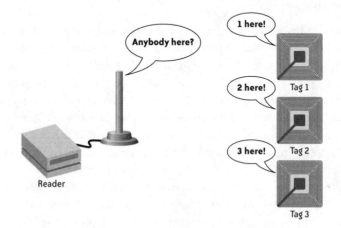

FIGURE 2-6. Communication between RFID tags and a reader

Different kinds of tags and readers fit different applications and environments. Deciding which tag or reader to use involves determining the best fit for your needs. The tag you choose can greatly affect the cost of the system. Readers also have a wide range of prices and features.

Important characteristics of RFID tags include the following:

Packaging

As noted previously, tags may be housed in PVC buttons, glass vials, paper labels, or plastic cards. They may be combined with jewelry, hung from key chains, or built into the heads of keys. The DIN/ISO 69873 standard defines a standard for tags that may be inserted into holes built into machining tools. Some tags used in auto assembly lines are designed and packaged to survive the intense heat of paint-drying chambers. In short, the ways in which tags can be packaged are remarkably varied. Figure 2-7 shows two tags: the quick-payment tag in the key fob is exposed to show the antenna and chip, and the head of the key also contains a vehicle immobilization chip.

FIGURE 2-7. *Two RFID tags (image courtesy of Texas Instruments)*

Coupling

Coupling refers to the means by which the reader and tag communicate. Different coupling methods allow for different strengths and weaknesses. Coupling choices especially affect the range of communications, the price of tags, and the conditions that might cause interference.

Power

Many RFID tags use some sort of "passive" system, wherein an electromagnetic field or a pulse of radio frequency energy emitted by the reader powers the tag. In other ("active") tags, a battery powers a microchip or additional sensors. However, active tags still use power from the reader for communications. The third type of tag is the so-called "two-way tag," which powers its own communications and may even be capable of communicating directly with other tags without a reader.

Information storage capacity

Tags provide varying amounts of storage capacity. Read-only tags are set to store a particular value at the factory. Users can set a value to write-once tags one time, while the value stored by a write-many tag may be changed many times. Some tags are also able to gather new information, such as temperature or pressure readings, on their own. Tags range in storage capacity from the 1-bit tags used for theft prevention to tags used in auto assembly lines, which may store thousands of bytes.

Standards compliance

Many types of RFID systems conform to particular national and international standards. A developer working on "an ISO 11785 system" is actually working on a system compatible with that standard. Some standards, such as the Class system used by EPCglobal, specify frequencies, coupling type, information storage capacity, and more.

Selecting tags

Many considerations are involved in selecting tags. They include the following:

Required read range

Active tags provide a longer read range than passive tags. For retail applications, the read ranges offered by passive tags are usually sufficient.

Material and packaging

Different materials have differing RF characteristics. For example, liquids may impede the flow of radio waves. Metal containers also pose interference challenges to the readers.

Form factors

RFID tags come in different sizes. The form factor for the tags used for individual products will depend on the packaging used for these products.

Standards compliance

It is important to consider whether most of the readers that are generally available will understand the RF tag you select. EPCglobal and the International Standards Organization (ISO) provide standards for communications between RFID tags and readers.

Cost

The cost of a single RFID tag plays an important role in its selection because most applications use many tags.

Chapters 3 and 4 provide more information about RFID tags and how they work.

Readers

RFID readers, also called *interrogators*, are used to recognize the presence of nearby RFID tags. An RFID reader transmits RF energy through one or more antennas. An antenna in a nearby tag picks up this energy, and the tag then converts it into electrical energy via induction. This electrical energy is sufficient to power the semiconductor chip attached to the tag antenna, which stores the tag's identity. The tag then sends the identity back to the reader by raising and lowering the resistance of the antenna in a kind of Morse code. This is only one scenario, and different tags can work in slightly different ways, but this is typical of the way readers and tags interact. We describe methods of communicating between tags and readers in more detail in Chapter 3.

Readers come in many shapes and sizes and can be found in stationary, as well as portable, handheld varieties. For our purposes, you can think of readers as the point at which tags connect to the network. Figure 2-8 shows how a reader fits between tags and the outside world and illustrates the components of a reader.

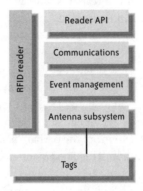

FIGURE 2-8. Parts of a reader

A reader is a system comprised of four distinct subsystems:

Reader API
   The reader API is the application programming interface that allows programs to register for and capture RFID tag read events. It also provides capabilities to configure, monitor, and otherwise manage the reader.

Communications
   Readers are edge devices, and like any other RFID device, they are connected to the overall edge network. The communications component handles the networking functions.

Event management
   When a reader sees a tag, we call this an *observation*. An observation that differs from previous observations is called an *event*. The analysis of observations is called *event filtering*. Event management defines what kinds of observations are considered events and determines which events are interesting enough to merit being either put in a report or sent immediately to an external application on the network.

Antenna subsystem
   The antenna subsystem consists of one or more antennas and the supporting interfaces and logic that enable RFID readers to interrogate RFID tags.

Selecting readers

Your selection of a reader is constrained by the tag you select. Some readers are compatible with certain types of tags but not with others. Readers, as powerful radio transmitters, must also conform to local regulations concerning frequency, power level, and duty cycles (how often the reader is actually transmitting). When selecting a reader, also pay close attention to the physical environment in which it will be operated. The reader must be small enough to be out of the way of personnel and equipment and tough enough to withstand exposure to dust, shock, humidity, or temperature extremes. Finally, an often-overlooked consideration in selecting a reader is how well it will cooperate with your current IT monitoring and management tools.

RFID Middleware

Choosing the right tags and readers and determining where to put the antennas is only the first step in building a working RFID system, because identifying items is only the first step in managing them. The capability to read millions of tags as they move through the supply chain and the need to tie tag codes to meaningful information will generate large amounts of data with complex interrelationships. One of the primary benefits of using RFID middleware is that it standardizes ways of dealing with the flood of information these tiny tags produce. In addition to event filtering, you also need a mechanism to encapsulate the applications so as to prevent them from knowing the details of the physical infrastructure (readers, sensors, and their configurations). Ideally, you want a standards-based, application-level interface to the RFID infrastructure that applications can use to request meaningful RFID observations.

Figure 2-9 shows the primary components of RFID middleware.

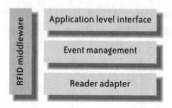

FIGURE 2-9. Components of RFID middleware

Motivations for using RFID middleware

There are three primary motivations for using RFID middleware: providing connectivity with readers (via the reader adapter), processing raw RFID observations for consumption by applications (via the event manager), and providing an application-level interface to manage readers and capture filtered RFID events.

Let's start with a simple approach to processing data collected by the readers, as shown in Figure 2-10. The sheer inadequacy of this approach will help to illustrate several points. In this figure, we expose the output of the readers directly to our applications. Today's readers provide minimal event filtering. From the perspective of the enterprise applications, using this approach for anything but a very small deployment or a proof of concept would be akin to trying to shove a bowling ball through a keyhole.

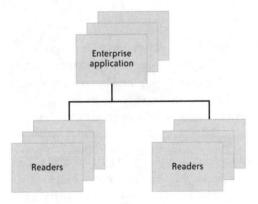

FIGURE 2-10. *Exposing applications directly to RFID readers*

In Figure 2-11, event-processing middleware is introduced between the readers and the applications. This approach is suitable for small-scale deployments using the capabilities provided by application integration products.

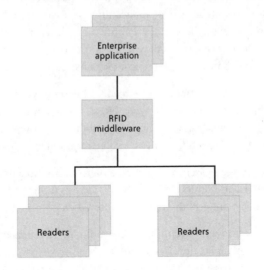

FIGURE 2-11. *Using RFID middleware*

The reader adapter

Several dozen types of RFID readers are available in the marketplace today, and each has its own proprietary interface. It would be impractical to expect application developers to learn different types of reader interfaces. Reader interfaces, as well as data access and device management capabilities, differ widely, so you should try to use middleware that shields you from having to learn the idiosyncrasies of individual readers. The reader adapter layer encapsulates the proprietary reader interfaces so that they don't come in contact with the application developers.

The event manager

A fully deployed, RFID-enabled supply chain for an enterprise could have hundreds or even thousands of readers scanning at hundreds of reads per minute. Most of these observations would be too fine-grained to be meaningful to applications, so you want to encapsulate the reader interface to keep the applications from being bombarded by raw data. Enterprises will thus need to deploy special-purpose RFID middleware near the edges of their IT infrastructures.

Readers are less than 100 percent accurate at picking up tags in their vicinity. Suppose 100 items were present near a reader that was set to scan a couple of hundred times a minute. Chances are that each scan of the reader would pick up anywhere from 80 to 99 of these items. The fact that item 2, for instance, is sensed by the reader 80 percent of the time across multiple read cycles would be a good indication that it is still around. However, this scenario demonstrates why RFID scans from readers are considered "raw" and require further processing to derive meaningful business events. Suppose this reader was positioned for a smart shelf system. Would you want to expose unfiltered reader observations to your enterprise applications? For all but trivial applications, you would probably want these observations to be processed further before sending them downstream. One example is a "smoothing" filter that can take a series of reader scans and aggregate the results in a way that accounts for the less-than-perfect read accuracy of some of the RFID technologies.

If you think exposing the observations of one reader directly to your enterprise applications would be a bad idea, consider that a typical RFID implementation incorporates at least a few dozen RFID readers. Imagine the amount of data that would be generated by all of these readers and how much filtering would be required!

An RFID event manager aggregates raw RF read data from multiple data sources (such as readers) and consolidates and filters it based on previously configured application-level event filters. Most event managers then feed the filtered data to the backend systems.

Let's take a closer look at how an event manager would be used in a smart shelf scenario. Imagine that for a certain application, each reader scans shelves around 10 times a minute. Each scan returns a set of observations, and each observation might look like the following:

```
Reader Observation
timestamp, reader code, antenna code, RF tag id, signal strength
```

To get a sense of the volume of data generated by the smart shelf readers, consider the following example. An electronics retailer called Nirvana Electronics wants to implement a smart shelf system. The store averages 25 items per shelf and 4 shelves per rack, for an average of 100 items per rack. Each of Nirvana's 10 stores has 20 isles, each containing 20 racks (10 on each side). So, a Nirvana store has 400 racks, which means the average total inventory would be around 40,000 items. Table 2-1 recaps these totals. (Aren't you glad we didn't start with a grocery store or warehouse example?)

TABLE 2-1. Average inventory (items)

Location	Average inventory (items)
1 shelf	25
1 rack (4 shelves)	100
1 store (400 racks)	40,000
All 10 stores	400,000

Now consider the volume of data generated as the RFID system reads this data:

- Each scan returns observations that contain information on all the items that were recognized to be on the targeted shelves.

- 25 items per shelf x 4 shelves per rack x 10 scans per minute = 1,000 observations per minute, per rack.

- 1,000 items read per minute x 400 racks = 400,000 observations per minute.

- 400,000 items read per minute x 60 minutes per hour = 2,400,000 observations per hour.

- Let's say the store is open 10 hours a day. 10 hours x 2,400,000 items read per hour = 24,000,000 observations per day, per store.

- 10 stores = 240,000,000 observations between all the stores.

This data is summarized in Table 2-2.

TABLE 2-2. Average number of observations

Location	Number of observations
1 rack per minute	1,000
1 store per minute	400,000
1 store per day	24,000,000
All stores per day	240,000,000

Wow! That's some serious volume, and we haven't even counted the observations that would be coming from the checkout lanes—but you get the point. Processing all these observations will require some serious architectural planning. But before we start drawing boxes and arrows, we need to understand a little more about the quality and relevance of the information contained in the observations.

If you simply pass all these observations to the enterprise applications running in your data centers, you will not only overwhelm those applications but also possibly push the networks and other infrastructure elements to the limit. Also, the downstream applications will likely find the raw RF reader observations uninteresting. For instance, say a customer picks up a DVD from a shelf and puts it on another shelf. This would generate a series of observations from the readers on the respective shelves. However, if we look at this in the context of Nirvana's order management system, this information would be uninteresting because the store inventory has not changed. In fact, even if the customer buys that DVD, the order management system might not care about this event if the store inventory for that DVD does not fall below a certain level, as established by the store's business rules.

This example illustrates the need for mechanisms to aggregate observations over time and across multiple readers. It also illustrates the need to filter, consolidate, and transform raw RF reader observations. This is why your RFID system needs middleware that runs inside the edges of your enterprise data centers. This way, only the observations that are important to your corporate applications are sent to those applications. The rest of the data is filtered out by the RFID middleware.

So, what sorts of things must be filtered out? Since the antennas are in close proximity (two per rack), their read ranges will overlap. Therefore, the observations coming from them will need to be filtered to remove duplicate reads. Also, as individual scans tend to be less than 100 percent accurate, these observations need to be aggregated over several read cycles to smooth them out. (As explained in Chapter 5, the inexact nature of reads is the product of several factors, including the nature of radio frequency transmissions, alignments of the RFID labels, obstructions, and environmental factors.) As customers move along the aisles with products in their hands or in shopping carts, the nearby readers might pick up these items, too. We should filter out any such spurious observations to avoid sending a flood of inaccurate observations to the inventory control system. Figure 2-12 illustrates a filtering and smoothing system devised to address typical scenarios experienced in retail stores.

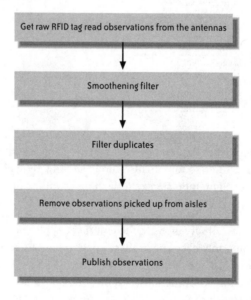

FIGURE 2-12. Event filters

Each element of the system is explained further in the following list:

Get raw observations (EPC reads)
The readers pick up raw event data (observations).

Smoothen observations
Today's readers are less than 100 percent accurate in picking up RF tags with a single scan, so we analyze the raw reader data over several scans and pick up observations based on averages. For example, if 70 percent of observations tell us that an RCA cable box is on a counter, we accept that information.

Filter out duplicates
Duplicate observations caused when more than one antenna identifies an item should be filtered based on relative signal strengths.

Filter out observations from aisles
Observations of items moving through the aisles will generally have lower signal strengths and be transient in nature. They should be filtered out.

Publish observations
After the necessary filtering, our data is ready to communicate downstream.

RFID readers already provide some filtering capabilities, and as readers become smarter, they will take over more and more of the filtering tasks themselves. So why do we need to do additional filtering in the middleware? As we've seen, some filtering requires information from multiple readers, other sensors, or even other systems (such as the inventory system, in the case of comparing stock levels). This higher-level filtering will always need to occur in a system located above the readers in the event hierarchy.

The application-level interface

The application-level interface is the top layer in the RFID middleware stack. Its primary purpose is to provide a standardized mechanism that enables applications to register for and receive filtered RFID events from a set of readers. In addition to this, the application-level interface also provides a standard API for configuring, monitoring, and managing RFID middleware and the readers and sensors it controls. Many RFID middleware vendors provide proprietary interfaces designed for these purposes. More recently, EPCglobal has published the Application Level Events (ALE) specification for standardizing the event management portion of RFID functionality. We cover the ALE specification in greater detail in Chapter 7.

Finally, note that RFID middleware comes in various shapes and sizes. What we just presented was a logical breakdown of what middleware is and what it does. In practice, you might find that various middleware vendors provide modules that you can deploy on particular reader types for specific types of applications.

Relevant EPCglobal standards

There are a number of EPCglobal standards that are important to RFID middleware. Two of these standards are:

Reader protocols

There are efforts underway within EPCglobal to create standards for the reader and printer network protocols. (We cover reader protocols in Chapter 6.) RFID middleware vendors plan to support these standard protocols as they become available. We expect that within the foreseeable future, custom drivers will continue to be required for most device types.

Application Level Events (ALE)

ALE is an upcoming EPCglobal standard that provides a declarative interface so that applications can interact with the filtering and collecting engine. The ALE standard supports request/response and pub/sub-style programming. This approach has proven to be vastly simpler than the early real-time workflow model of Savant, and it has replaced all Savant efforts within EPCglobal.

The RFID Service Bus

An enterprise service bus (ESB) is a distributed integration platform designed for application connectivity, data transformation, guaranteed transactions, and messaging. An RFID service bus is a type of ESB used to integrate applications using RFID data. Depending on the implementation you choose, ESB products offer web services, messaging, business process orchestration, and other capabilities. Generally, ESBs orchestrate business processes across application, or sometimes enterprise, boundaries.

As we know, RFID systems will not function in a vacuum. They have to coexist with and extend the capabilities of enterprise applications such as warehouse management systems (WMSs), enterprise resource planning (ERP) systems, or point of sale systems. Do not underestimate the importance of adapting these applications and systems to utilize RFID-enabled data. Extending the capabilities of your existing applications is an important activity that must be carefully thought out before you begin any RFID adoption process.

Many companies use ESB architectures, which are also referred to as *integration servers*, to enable disparate applications to collaborate with each other. At a minimum, such software provides interfaces that enable you to integrate various systems that use differing technologies. It provides adapters to understand input coming from these systems, and then it translates that input into a common format (usually XML). Integration servers also provide capabilities that enable you to define and execute business processes. It is possible that the RFID event manager product you use provides rudimentary integration server capabilities.

The primary purpose of an RFID service bus is integrating application-level events captured by event managers into workflows that occur at the enterprise's edges (edge workflows). Specific vendor implementations may vary (some RFID middleware vendors provide scaled-down versions of ESBs), but an RFID service bus is essentially an integration server that runs the relevant edge workflows and provides integration capabilities with modules of enterprise applications such as POS or WMS packages. The RFID service bus also integrates into the ESB and can be configured to supply specific events and observations. Because a typical ESB product can be complex and expensive, it's common to see simpler application server–based custom implementations designed to serve this need.

The RFID information service

It is important to realize that an EPC, or for that matter, any other item identification system, is just a unique identifier and by itself does not provide any product details. EPCglobal envisions that collaborating businesses and industries will set up a network of EPC Information Service (EPCIS) servers to provide an on-demand repository of information related to individual EPCs. Information made available using the EPCIS servers could include the last observed location of an item carrying an EPC (based on an RF reader observation), as well as pricing information and product manuals, if appropriate. While it will take years to realize the vision of an industry-wide network of EPCIS servers, a necessary intermediate step would be to implement a database that maps the identifiers used in RFID tracking data to a richer set of information relevant to business applications. An example might be mapping product reference information to its identifier. Even small and non-EPC applications will need to tie the EPC codes to product tracking information (or other reference data related to the product type or instance) and so may need to use and update information managed by an RFID information service.

EPCglobal intends to leverage existing and evolving data sources for the RFID information service. For example, the Serialized Global Trade Item Number (SGTIN) has been proposed as the unique EPC identifier for the consumer packaged goods and retail industries.

The RFID information network

As RFID-tagged products move through the supply chain, various participants in the supply chain will need standards-based means to share their tracking information and to get reference information on products based on their product tags (EPCs). EPCglobal envisions a mesh of networked B2B EPCIS systems collaborating to provide a comprehensive reference source for EPCs. The EPCglobal Network is a vision coupled with an evolving set of standards that aims to provide a standard framework for product information exchange. Centered around EPC RFID technologies and the existing Internet infrastructure, the EPCglobal Network will offer the potential for increased efficiency and accuracy in tracking products between trading partners. Since the details of the EPCglobal Network are still emerging, we'll focus here on the principal features that might characterize an RFID information network.

Figure 2-13 shows one vision of the RFID information network. As a product flows from
its manufacturer to a distributor and then to a retailer, each of these parties captures its
tracking information. How, you might ask, is the tracking information the distributor
captures tied to the tracking information originally supplied by the manufacturer and
then supplemented by the retailer? This is where the Object Naming Service (ONS) and
the EPCIS come in. As shown in Figure 2-13, the manufacturer, distributor, and retailer
maintain local EPCIS instances. The local EPCIS instances are tasked to maintain the
EPC tracking information generated by the constituent, and they also help interface
with other EPCIS instances that maintain relevant and desired EPC information. An
EPCIS server can host, as well as facilitate access to, serialized product information generated by EPC-tagged products. This means a distributor's EPCIS server can be configured to interface with a manufacturer's EPCIS server to access and/or aggregate related
EPC data.

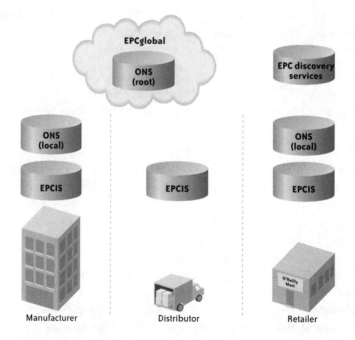

FIGURE 2-13. The RFID information network (image courtesy of VeriSign)

The ONS is a centralized, authoritative directory that routes requests for information
about particular EPCs; it follows the architectural underpinnings of the Domain Name

System (DNS). VeriSign maintains the root ONS server for the EPCglobal Network. The EPC Discovery Service is an authoritative registry of every EPCIS server that has information about a particular product. The EPCIS thus works with the ONS and the EPC Discovery Service to realize the vision of a distributed information network.

The RFID information network provides five principal services:

Assigning unique identities

Tracking items is not possible without the capacity to uniquely identify them. This is where the EPC comes in. Like the UPC or bar code, the EPC is an identification system for products. However, unlike the UPC, the EPC allows item-level tracking by identifying not only the manufacturer and product type, but also the serial number.

Detecting and identifying items

The identification system consists of EPC tags and readers. Each tag contains a microchip attached to an antenna. The EPC is stored on this tag. At the most basic level, the EPC provides a coding scheme for RFID tags that helps identify an item's manufacturer, product category, and unique serial number. The tag is applied to an item either during the manufacturing process or somewhere down the supply chain. The EPC readers use radio frequency waves to interrogate the EPC tags, which then communicate their EPCs back to the readers. EPC readers deliver information to local business information systems using EPC middleware.

Collecting and filtering events

EPC middleware provides specifications for services that enable data exchange between EPC readers and business information systems. Much of the raw EPC observations coming from the readers would be noise to the enterprise applications. Event management middleware is needed to facilitate the collection of observations from the readers and to filter and group them for consumption by the applications.

Storing and querying events

The EPCIS enables users to exchange data with trading partners based on EPCs. The EPCIS specification (not available at the time of writing) aims to provide standards to allow disparate applications to share EPC data. The specification provides standards for capturing and querying EPC data between trading partners.

Locating EPC information

To enable trading partners to share EPC observations, it is necessary to provide lookup or discovery services that can locate repositories for the required EPC data. For authoritative data from the manufacturer, this role is handled by the ONS. The ONS provides the means to look up service resources that provide further information on an EPC. The ONS is very similar to, and is in fact implemented on top of, the DNS technology that handles the billions of domain name queries on the Internet today.

As we noted earlier, the EPCglobal Network specifications are still being defined by the EPCglobal architectural committee and will be published under the EPCIS specification.

EPCglobal has already published the standards for the ONS. In Chapter 8, we'll look at some of the alternatives for sharing RFID information across enterprise boundaries.

Before we move on to the systemic quality considerations for an RFID system, remember that successful implementations of business-to-business information-sharing networks are only partially dependent on technology. Data ownership and liability, business processes, security, and legal considerations all need to be addressed before you begin setting up such a network. We anticipate that the technological underpinnings of the EPCglobal Network will initially be developed around two-party, and then later multiparty, vendor relationships before any sort of industry-wide or global EPC information network is successfully implemented.

Systemic Quality Considerations

As we know, a system's requirements come in two flavors: functional and nonfunctional. The functional requirements define what the system does, while nonfunctional requirements involve systemic qualities such as privacy and security, performance, scalability, manageability, extensibility, and maintainability. RFID systems demand vastly increased data-processing capabilities at the edges of corporate environments. The volume of raw RFID data that is captured and available for filtering, coupled with the need to automatically monitor and manage RFID devices (such as antennas and readers), requires a level of sophistication that was generally absent from the bar code–type systems that RFID systems replace.

Some of the most important systemic qualities for RFID systems are covered in the following sections.

Privacy and Security

Privacy and security considerations are a core part of the design and architecture of any RFID solution. Ironically, even though RFID solutions are sometimes offered as enhancements to security, the technology itself presents certain vulnerabilities. As in any enterprise system, security considerations for an RFID system—ensuring the authenticity of the information stored on the tags themselves, securing the transmission of information between tags and readers, and ensuring overall application and infrastructure security—permeate the various layers of its architecture.

Physical security measures involve efforts to prevent both corruption of tag data and interception of communication between tags and readers. For instance, a malicious tag reader that is not part of an RFID system can attempt to read tags in its vicinity. Wireless security focuses on securing the communication pipe between readers and tags since this communication can be intercepted using wireless sniffing and spoofing devices. Any security-sensitive application must carefully weigh the risks of both interception or alteration of tag-to-reader and reader-to-tag communications.

Of course, security considerations vary depending on business needs. For example, using an RFID-enabled credit card to purchase goods can be done securely as long as the fulfillment systems on the backend are prepared to handle and detect fraudulent data (as credit card systems are), but a ticketing system that depends on the authenticity of every tag read might be more easily compromised.

In addition to security considerations, individual privacy is a very important consideration in implementing RFID systems and introducing them to operators and users. We have dedicated Chapter 10 to a discussion of privacy and security.

Performance

Performance is measured in terms of time taken to perform a unit of activity. Depending on the layer of the RFID system at which you're working, the performance considerations will vary. For instance, for the physical layer, the time required to recognize a tag is an important performance consideration. As with the performance metrics for other systems, this measure would be taken at peak throughput and averaged over a period of time appropriate to system usage. We might be tempted to state requirements in the form of scans per second, such as: "Each loading dock must recognize a newly arrived tag within 10 seconds on average at peak periods and 2 seconds on average at nonpeak periods." Because of the simultaneity of RFID inventories, however, it is much more common (and useful) to state RFID performance requirements in the throughput form, such as "The loading dock must recognize 96 tags per minute on average during peak load periods and 23 tags per minute on average during nonpeak periods."

As you move up to the RFID event manager and other application-level components, the performance characteristics you'll be most concerned with will be based on the time taken to perform a unit of application-level activity. For a tag and ship application, you could define this as the time taken to retrieve an EPC and print it. When building any application, performance considerations and requirements for various uses of the system should be defined and tested early on.

Scalability

Scalability has to do with how small a system may start and how quickly it must be ready to grow. For RFID systems, scalability involves much more than "CPU headroom." RFID scalability requirements are often stated like so: "The shipping system should be able to handle 12 loading docks initially and be able to scale to 60 loading docks in 3 years with no more than a 2-week cycle to install a group of 4 new loading docks and bring them online." However, one of the qualities of RFID systems that may be especially unfamiliar to IT personnel is the need to plan for site surveys and RF tuning as well as the installation of new equipment and software. The RF environment of an area 10 feet from the last install cannot be considered "just the same" as before the install, and there is no guarantee that an earlier site survey of that area is still valid if, for instance, the forklift for certain docks now parks in a different spot when not servicing a load. Once readers are in place, changes to the RF environment can usually be spotted quickly due to changes in performance, but during an install, the environment offers enough variables without adding unexpected signal absorption and reflection.

Manageability

RFID information servers are typically housed in a data center or server room. Operations staff can monitor and manage the servers using procedures developed for any other application server. Event managers and readers are found in loading bays and warehouses, in truck trailers and train yards, and even in corrugated tin shacks in the middle of fields. A reader may be just as complex as a server, requiring software or firmware upgrades, monitoring, and management. An event manager is likely to be located on server hardware but deployed close to the readers. These are edge systems and must be managed as such. One of the primary management differences between edge systems and other systems is that they are likely to be less accessible and more prone to environmental extremes such as heat, dust, and vibration. Furthermore, because a reader has a fixed location, if it should fail, another reader in a different location cannot be assigned to take over unless it is physically close to the failed reader. These characteristics of edge systems require both new practices and training for operations personnel and management software capable of managing these relationships. Manageability requirements are often stated in terms of human resource utilization—for example, "The entire shipping system should be able to operate and meet all availability and performance requirements with only one help desk technician on duty."

Adding sensors introduces additional opportunities for both automation and error. If RFID allows you to push a pallet of boxes onto a truck without stopping to scan bar codes manually, it also allows you to push the wrong pallet onto the truck if the right pallet is close enough for the reader to see it. This could be a problem especially if backup readers have powered up to cover a dead spot from a failed reader. Because RFID allows you to automate a process to the point of obviating human interaction, a failed reader could result in serious errors or lost information if there is no equally automated way to monitor the system's status.

We have dedicated Chapter 9 to this topic. For now, though, note that real-world RFID deployments will not succeed without automated provisioning, monitoring, and management of the RFID infrastructure.

Extensibility and Maintainability

For most organizations, RFID readers are the first step into a new space at the edge. Some industries—especially within the areas of manufacturing, agriculture, and defense—have worked with distributed sensors for some time, but a company new to RFID may falsely assume that once it gets the RFID readers talking to the management applications, it's done. Mandates and contracts that today require RFID compliance could easily require temperature, humidity, shock, or magnetic field exposure tracking tomorrow. RFID systems are in a state of flux as technology advances and standards only begin to solidify. An RFID installation of any size must be prepared to plug in readers with different mounting requirements, different management interfaces, and even different manufacturers depending on what is available this week. Requirements in this area are often stated thus: "The receiving system should be able to use any EPC Class I reader from any vendor, with less than three person-days of configuration for a new type."

Architecture Guidelines

The infrastructure for RFID edge components must be incredibly robust. Ideally, the readers, RFID middleware, and so on should support effortless plug-and-play functioning. In other words, they should be the edge equivalents of telephones in terms of ease of use, provisioning, monitoring, and management. A human operating a bar code scanner will be able to tell if the scanner goes down, but you'll need to employ automated means to monitor and manage RFID readers. Also, you'll want to shield your applications from the large number of readers deployed in a store or other location. To support all this, your edge architectures will need to be more flexible, scalable, robust, secure, and manageable than ever before.

As is always the case in a technology's early adoption phase, RFID standards and products are rapidly evolving. It is very likely that you will encounter a highly heterogeneous infrastructure, whereas types of RFID tags, readers, and other sensors will vary. Event managers based on standards such as ALE will have to coexist with other vendor-specific extensions to vertical applications such as point-of-sale and warehouse-management systems. When developing your RFID architecture roadmap, it is very important to take a close look at both your business and systemic quality requirements and how they might evolve over time. RFID systems are no different than any other distributed system in that you should plan for performance, scalability, security, manageability, maintainability, ease of use, and failover early on. The following section cover some important principles to consider when devising an RFID architecture roadmap for your company.

Begin with Business Requirements

While researching this book, we approached many experts in RFID technologies and asked them what aspect was most overlooked when designing RFID systems. The almost unanimous response was business processes. In our experience as system architecture consultants, which has spanned several new waves of technologies, we have often seen people forget that technology's ultimate purpose is to solve business problems. This is the case even more so with promising new technologies, as the newness and buzz surrounding these technologies drive a bottom-up way of thinking. While you're defining the business requirements and capturing functional requirements, pay careful attention to accounting for exception processing. These are the "what if" situations, such as what to do if a reader goes down, or a tag falls off a package, or you are not able to read a particular tag. The exception scenarios should provide capabilities to use alternate means to accomplish the task. For example, if a read registers only 50 packages of a product when an operator visually determines that the number should be closer to 100, you could create alternate workflows to obtain the inventory count manually.

Don't Forget Your Existing Infrastructure

More often than not, RFID systems will have to coexist with bar code systems, providing alternate, more automated capabilities. When planning the architecture of your RFID system, pay careful attention to your existing systems and business processes.

Process Data at the Edge Where Possible

Process as much data as possible at its source. This means that the raw RFID observations collected by readers should be filtered at the edge before sending only what is meaningful to applications. Develop a data-management architecture that keeps data needed for the workflow at the edge on the edge. If RFID data gives you enough information to sort items at the factory into different bins based on their models, then don't make that decision at corporate headquarters. Have the edge server make the call based on an understanding of which item types go in which bins. The list of which item types go in which bins can be updated from time to time via an automated process.

Track Items to the Level Your Business Processes Will Support

The item-level tracking ability offered by RFID systems can come in handy for many applications. You might wonder then why we are listing it as a challenge. The real challenge is not in identifying an RF tag uniquely, but in figuring out what you are going to do with that information. More information is not always better. Weigh the cost of generating, storing, and processing this information against the business benefits. Tracking items at instance level greatly increases the data that is generated as the items move through the supply chain. Returning to our earlier example, consider that each Nirvana store stocks 20 Samsung P725 cell phones. With item-level tracking, each store inventory will have a unique record for each instance of the phone. Similarly, each instance of the phone will be separately tracked as it moves through Nirvana's supply chain. In addition to adjusting to the increased volume of information, this finer-grained tracking data would need to be incorporated into the business processes and thus the systems that support them.

System Management

The level and scale of automation for some RFID systems poses significant challenges for system administrators and managers. As stated earlier, if a manual bar code scanner is down, a human operator will immediately pick up on it and call for service. The automated processing capabilities that RFID technologies offer make automated detection of system faults and stoppages indispensable. Similarly, we need to provide novel solutions for provisioning, monitoring, and managing our silently ticking antennas, readers, and other RFID infrastructure components.

Think ease of configuring, provisioning, managing, and monitoring when deciding on infrastructure components such as readers, sensors, event managers, servers, storage, and networks. Build redundancy into the architecture. Have a plan in place for what should happen when an antenna, a reader, or an event manager malfunctions. Consider using

RFID middleware and other system management solutions to stay ahead of the difficulties that come with a fast-growing edge infrastructure.

Start with Architecture

Much of the time, enterprise architecture grows out of its selection of products. With minor exceptions, over time, a proprietary architecture that is locked into a particular product and vendor develops. Begin with well-defined interfaces between different layers, such as event managers, applications, and integration servers, and then choose products that fit your architecture. Later, this will pay in greater flexibility and independence.

Use RFID Middleware

As explained earlier in this chapter, you will find it necessary to use RFID middleware for all but trivial implementations. RFID middleware helps decouple your enterprise applications from the physical architecture of your RFID systems; those applications don't need to know about the reader vendors, their APIs, or the physical configuration of readers and antennas. In addition to this, RFID middleware provides the important function of filtering the highly fragmented data that comes from the readers. By cutting down the volume of data that passes over wide area networks, event filtering also allows you to define application-level events and pass more meaningful information to your enterprise applications.

Summary

RFID and other, similar technologies are pushing increasingly more network intelligence toward the network's edge, where RFID readers, temperature and light sensors, and smart middleware manage events without requiring guidance from massive, central servers. This movement toward edge computing is changing the way companies think about their data and computing resources. We shouldn't underestimate how disruptive this will be to the way we design, deploy, and manage our enterprise systems. In large part, how we design systems for RFID now will shape the way we deal with other edge devices for many years to come.

In this chapter, we covered the following important points about RFID:

- A confluence of factors has led us to the tipping point, where RFID seems primed for widespread adoption. Technological factors include advances in semiconductor technologies, the advent of intelligent devices, widely available broadband networks, and web services standards available under the umbrella of service-oriented architecture. Non-technological factors include the interest of leading government agencies such as the FDA and the DoD, coupled with megacorporations such as Wal-Mart and Tesco, in RFID technology.

- When planning the architecture of an RFID system, the key processes include selecting an item numbering scheme, encoding RFID tags, attaching RFID tags to items you want to track, reading the RFID-tagged items as they move through the physical environment, integrating RFID information into enterprise applications and business processes, and, finally, sharing RFID information within and between companies.

- As with most enterprise systems, RFID systems are multi-layered. The physical layer components include RFID tags, antennas, readers, and sensors.

- RFID middleware provides many important services, including decoupling the physical layer components from the application layer components, managing and monitoring physical layer components, and filtering raw RFID observations and generating high-level events that are more meaningful to applications. The Application Level Events (ALE) standard is the EPCglobal standard that is gaining momentum for RFID middleware. There are already several vendor products available that implement ALE. (ALE is explained in detail in Chapter 7.)

- An RFID service bus is a type of enterprise service bus that serves to integrate application-level events captured by event managers into edge workflows.

- As companies deploy RFID systems, they will want to share some of the tracking information and other relevant information about the items being tracked. Various options are available for RFID information services. The EPCglobal Network (discussed further in Chapter 8) is a vision of RFID information services proposed by EPCglobal.

- As with any enterprise application, it is paramount to understand systemic quality requirements before designing an RFID system. Important RFID system qualities include privacy and security, performance, scalability, manageability, flexibility, and maintainability.

The intent of this chapter was to introduce you to the important facets of RFID system architecture. The remainder of this book discusses the individual components in further detail.

CHAPTER THREE

Tags

THE PURPOSE OF AN **RFID** TAG IS TO PHYSICALLY ATTACH DATA ABOUT AN OBJECT (ITEM) to that item. Each tag has some internal mechanism for storing data and a way of communicating that data. Figure 3-1 shows diagrams of several representative RFID tags.

Not every sort of RFID tag has a microchip or a built-in power source, but every RFID tag has a coil or antenna of some sort.

While it is important to realize what all tags have in common, classifying tags helps in understanding how they work. In this chapter, we will categorize RFID tags by those criteria most likely to affect the capabilities of the tag within our applications. We will divide tags based on their physical characteristics, their air interfaces (how they communicate with readers), and their information storage and processing capacity. With these criteria in mind, we will then explore some of the standards that define these variations and talk about guidelines for matching tags to applications. We'll start by looking at some basic tag capabilities before launching into the discussion of tag categories.

Basic Tag Capabilities

Many basic operations can be performed with an RFID tag, but only two of them are universal.

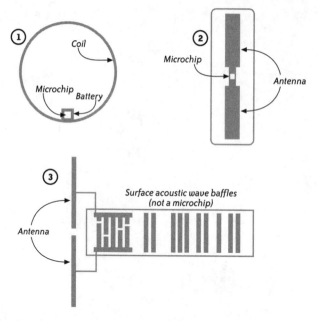

FIGURE 3-1. Typical RFID tags

Attaching the tag

Any RFID tag must be attachable to an item in some way.

Reading the tag

Any RFID tag must be able to communicate information over some radio frequency in some way.

Many tags also offer one or more of the following features and capabilities:

Kill/disable

Some tags allow a reader to command them to cease functioning permanently. After a tag receives the correct "kill code," it will never respond to a reader again.

Write once

Many tags are manufactured with their data permanently set at the factory, but a write-once tag may be set to a particular value by an end user one time. After that, the tag cannot be changed except, possibly, to be disabled.

Write many

Some tags can be written and rewritten with new data over and over.

Anti-collision

When many tags are in close proximity, a reader may have difficulty telling where one tag's response ends and another's begins. Anti-collision tags know how to wait their turn when responding to a reader.

Security and encryption

Some tags are able to participate in encrypted communications, and some will respond only to readers that can provide a secret password.

Standards compliance

A tag may comply with one or more standards, enabling it to talk to readers that also comply with those standards; or, in the case of standards for physical characteristics, a tag may fit in a particular standard receptacle.

With these basics in mind, we can begin to explore the various categories of tags.

Physical Characteristics

Because RFID tags must physically attach data to items of different shapes and sizes in different environments, they come in a wide assortment of shapes and sizes. Furthermore, they may be housed in many different kinds of materials. Some of the physical characteristics of various tags include:

- PVC or plastic buttons and disks, usually including a central hole for fasteners. These tags are durable and reusable.
- RFID tags shaped like credit cards, which are called "contactless smart cards."
- Tags made into the layers of paper in a label, called "smart labels." These may be applied with automated applicators similar to those used for bar code labels.
- Small tags embedded in common objects such as clothing, watches, and bracelets. These small tags may also come in the form of keys and key chains.
- Tags in glass capsules, which can survive even in corrosive environments or in liquids.

Figure 3-2 shows just a few types of tag housings.

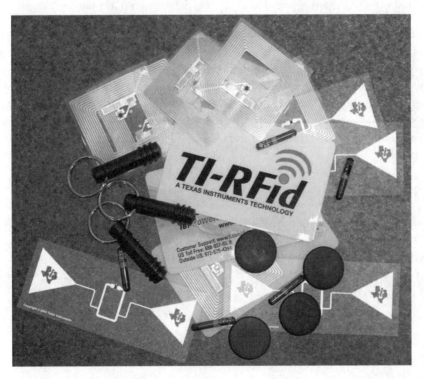

FIGURE 3-2. Tags come in many shapes and sizes (image courtesy of Texas Instruments)

Packaging may be the most obvious way to divide tags into categories, and this is the property of a tag that most directly affects how the tag can be attached to an item. We've already mentioned that buttons typically attach with a fastener through a central hole. Keys and key chains attach as you would expect, and smart labels attach with an adhesive backing. A plastic medicine bottle may contain a glass capsule in its lid or base, and smaller capsules can be injected for tracking pets and livestock.

> **WARNING**
>
> Any new RFID application should be tested in candidate systems, with tags in the same packaging and attached in just the same way as they would be in the production system.

Power Source

A common way of categorizing tags is by their source of power. This is also one of the main determining factors for the cost and longevity of a tag. *Passive* tags obtain all of their energy by some method of transmission from the reader. *Active* tags use an on-board battery to power communications, a processor, memory, and possibly sensors. Traditionally, tags that use battery power for some functions but still allow the reader to power communications have been termed "active" as well, but for clarity, we will use the more recent terminology for them: *semi-passive*. One additional type of tag is not only capable of supplying power for itself but is also able to initiate communications with other tags of its own kind without the aid of a reader. These tags are called *two-way* tags.

As you might expect, having a battery on board makes for a more expensive chip, but semi-passive and active tags have several advantages over passive tags. In the case of semi-passive tags, the read range may be longer because the passive communications can use all of the power provided by the reader for communications rather than sharing some of the power with the chip. An active tag may have an extremely long read range and may perform some functions in the absence of a reader—for example, using battery power for environmental sensors. This capability can be very useful for tags that identify items such as perishable goods.

Air Interface

The *air interface* describes the way in which a tag communicates with a reader. By knowing a tag's air interface, we can determine the tag's read range and identify readers compatible with the tag. The following sections describe the attributes that comprise the definition of an air interface. The major attributes include the tag's power source, operating frequency, communication mode, keying, encoding, and coupling.

RFID IN HISTORY

RFID has been in use longer than most people realize. It first appeared in the air war during WWII. British pilots noticed that sometimes, inexplicably, all of the German planes in sight would roll in unison. British intelligence later learned that German pilots were participating in a sort of manual RFID to help identify their planes to the newly invented German radar systems. By changing their radar images in response to a ground challenge, the pilots identified themselves as Luftwaffe.

The British later developed an automated system for their own aircraft that caused their planes to appear to pulse according to a preset rhythm when illuminated by the British "Chain Home" (CH) air defense radar. This new system was known as the MK I and was the predecessor of all Identify Friend or Foe (IFF) and aircraft transponder systems in use to this day.

Like RFID systems today, the most important components of the system were an *interrogator* and a *transponder*. In early IFF systems, the interrogator was the radar system itself and the transponder was an unwieldy box of tubes with dials and switches. The term "interrogator" gives us a clue as to how the system worked: the ground station sent out a radar signal, and the transponder receiving this signal reflected it back, causing the radar antenna to receive a stronger return than it otherwise would have. The transponder also "swept" the frequency of its return back and forth over a small range as it responded, causing the radar return to pulsate according to a specific rhythm.

Operating Frequency

The *operating frequency* is the electromagnetic frequency the tag uses to communicate or to obtain power. The electromagnetic spectrum in the range in which RFID typically operates is usually broken up into low frequency (LF), high frequency (HF), ultra-high frequency (UHF), and microwave (see Table 3-1). Because RFID systems broadcast electromagnetic waves, they are regulated as radio devices. RFID systems must not interfere with other, protected applications, such as emergency service radios or television transmissions.

TABLE 3-1. RFID frequency ranges

Name	Frequency range	ISM frequencies
LF	30–300 kHz	< 135 kHz
HF	3–30 MHz	6.78 MHz, 13.56 MHz, 27.125 MHz, 40.680 MHz
UHF	300 MHz–3 GHz	433.920 MHz, 869 MHz, 915 MHz
Microwave	> 3 GHz	2.45 GHz, 5.8 GHz, 24.125 GHz

In practice, this means that the actual frequencies available to RFID are limited to those frequencies set aside as Industrial Scientific Medical (ISM). Frequencies lower than 135 kHz are not ISM frequencies, but in this range RFID systems are usually using powerful magnetic fields and operating over short ranges, so interference is less of an issue than it might be otherwise.

Different frequencies have different properties. Lower frequency signals are better able to travel through water, while higher frequencies can carry more information. Higher-frequency signals are also typically easier to read at a distance. Table 3-2 shows the read ranges for the different frequencies and how they have been used in different applications.

TABLE 3-2. Read range by frequency

Frequency	Typical max. read range for passive tags	Some typical applications
LF	50 centimeters	Pet identification and close reads of items with high water content
HF	3 meters	Building access control
UHF	9 meters	Boxes and pallets
Microwave	> 10 meters	Vehicle identification of all sorts

The recent cost reductions in UHF tags have led to an increased use of these tags in applications where LF and HF tags were more common in the past. UHF is not likely, however, to replace LF in implanted tags or microwave in long-range (greater than 10-meter read range) applications.

Regulatory bodies have chosen different ranges for UHF in different parts of the world. In Europe, South America, and much of Asia, UHF RFID tags operate from 865 MHz to 868 MHz. In North America, they operate from 902 MHz to 928 MHz, and India recently adopted a range of 865 MHz to 867 MHz. China has not announced which range it will favor, but there has been some indication that the range it chooses will support global standards (see Chapter 11). One possible global standard is the EPCglobal Gen2 standard, described in more detail later in this chapter. Gen2 tags operate from 860 MHz to 960 MHz and at a range of power levels designed to match varying local regulatory requirements.

Communications Mode

Another way of distinguishing tags is by whether or not the tag and the reader can "talk" at the same time. This is known as the *communications mode*. As with wired communications, RF communications may be *full-duplex* (FDX) or *half-duplex* (HDX)—that is, the tag and reader may talk at the same time (FDX) or take turns (HDX). In most cases, for passive tags, the reader provides power throughout the conversation, but in one variation on HDX, power transmission stops while the tag responds. A capacitor or some physical property of the tag allows it to store energy and respond while the power transmission is off. We will call this communications mode *sequential* (SEQ), in keeping with Finkenzeller.*

---

* Klaus Finkenzeller, *RFID Handbook: Fundamentals and Applications in Contactless Smart Cards and Identification*, trans. Rachel Waddington (Chinchester, West Sussex, England: John Wiley & Sons, 2003).

Types of Keying

The term "keying" comes from the days of telegraphy, when an operator pressed a manual key to make long and short tones. Keying describes which attributes of an analog carrier—the analog carrier can be a wave or a field—may be modulated to represent the ones and zeros of a digital message. There are three main types of keying:

Amplitude-shift keying (ASK)
> A type of keying that sends digital data over analog carriers by changing the amplitude of a wave in time with the data stream

Frequency-shift keying (FSK)
> A type of keying that sends changes through the frequency of the wave (or how often a wave crest comes along)

Phase-shift keying (PSK)
> A type of keying that sends changes through the distance by which the waves lead or follow a reference point in time

Encoding

Encoding determines the way the tag and reader will interpret changes in the analog carrier to represent digital data. Thus, an encoding is an agreement between sender and receiver regarding what the keyed changes mean. Morse Code, one example of an encoding, uses long tones to represent "dashes" and short tones to represent "dots." If we substituted "0" for "dash" and "1" for "dot," Morse encoding would work for sending information over a serial bus.

It might seem odd to think of RFID as devices communicating over a serial bus, but even though the components are wireless rather than wired, most tags and readers use serial communication because of the limited frequency range available. RFID even uses some of the same encodings that many of us first encountered in Universal Asynchronous Receiver/ Transmitter (UART) chips. Various encoding schemes commonly used in RFID include:

Biphase Manchester encoding
> This encoding uses a negative transition in the middle of the bit cell to mean a "1" value and a positive transition in the middle of the bit cell to mean a "0" value. Transitions that happen at the bit cell boundary do not encode a value and are used to "reset" the encoding to send the same value again in the middle of the cell. Encoding is independent of the type of keying or modulation, so this could be an ASK, FSK, or PSK transition. Because transitions are synchronized with the clock, this method is said to have the clock in the data stream. A recipient can derive the clock signal from this encoding and so regain synchronization, which makes biphase Manchester encoding well suited for transferring large messages. ISO 18000-6 type B tags use biphase Manchester encoding to talk to a reader.

Pulse interval encoding
> This is similar to Morse Code, where values are encoded by the length of the pause, or interval between, short pulses. A pause of a specific length represents a "1," while a

pause twice as long represents a "0." This has the advantages of requiring less power and being resistant to noise. It may be a problem for longer transmissions, though, because the data stream does not contain a clock. ISO 18000-6 type A tags use pulse interval encoding to send messages to a reader.

Biphase space encoding

In biphase space encoding—a type of encoding that is often used for reader-to-tag communication—transitions happen at each clock tick (actually, at the edges of the bit cell, but it amounts to the same thing). If a transition occurs in between these "ticks" of the clock, it represents a "0"; no extra transition represents a "1." This encoding method contains the clock in the data stream and so is well suited for long messages. ISO 18000-6 readers use biphase space encoding.

Pulsed RZ encoding

This is a term we've coined to describe a type of encoding in which four short pulses in the first half of a bit cell represent a "1," while four short pulses in the last half of the bit cell represent a "0." The "RZ" means "return to zero," which is a term used to describe encodings in which the signal returns to a point that is neither high nor low (i.e., at zero) for some part of the bit cell. EPC HF readers use pulsed RZ encoding with four pulses for each symbol.

EPC Miller encoding

Miller encoding encodes a number by having a transition in either direction at the half-bit point. EPC UHF Gen2 uses a version of this encoding that can have several timing pulses in a bit, wherein a "transition" is actually represented by the lack of one of the timing pulses. The number of transitions to use as a timing pulse in a bit is called the "M" value. For example, for M=2 we would have 2 pulses per bit cell to mark the timing of the clock. If one of these pulses does not occur, this represents a "1"; otherwise, the bit cell represents a "0."

"1 of 256" and "1 of 4"

These two forms of encoding are used in tags that conform to ISO 15693. For "1 of 256," values from 0 to 255 may be encoded in the data stream by the timing of a pulse. There are 512 timing slots per frame during which a pulse may occur, and the value is encoded by multiplying it by 2 and then adding 1. This gives the slot location—for example, a value of 12 would be encoded by a pulse at slot 25. Only odd slots are used for data, as even-numbered time slots are used for End of Frame (EOF) signals. Counting the odd slots leaves 256—thus the name of this encoding and its capability to send an entire byte in each frame. "1 of 4" encoding works in a similar way but uses only eight total time slots, which allows for 2 bits to be sent at a time.

FSK subcarrier encoding

This is another term we've coined for want of a better one. This sort of encoding is the exception to our earlier claim that RFID communicates over a serial bus and that encoding and keying are different. In this type of encoding, two subcarriers represent "1" and "0," respectively, and the sender uses FSK to create pulses on these subcarriers in time with the data stream. EPC UHF tags use FSK subcarrier encoding to talk to a reader.

Coupling

A tag's coupling mechanism determines the way a circuit on the tag and a circuit on the reader influence each other to send and receive information or power. The type of coupling a tag uses directly affects the read range between the tag and reader. We can group the different read ranges loosely into those systems where the read range is *close* (within 1 cm), *remote* (1 cm to 1 m), or *long-range* (more than 1m). A synonym for remote coupling is "vicinity coupling." In this section, we will discuss backscatter coupling, inductive coupling, magnetic coupling, and capacitive coupling. Capacitive and magnetic coupling are examples of close coupling, inductive coupling is a type of remote coupling, and backscatter coupling may be remote to long-range.

Along with range, the choice of coupling mechanism strongly affects which frequency the tag should use. Inductive coupling typically works best in either the LF or HF range. Backscatter coupling works better with higher frequencies. Magnetic coupling is most efficient at 1–10 MHz, and capacitive coupling usually runs at about 10 MHz to provide a fast enough clock for communications and processing.

RFID coupling, especially in the case of passive tags, may seem a bit mysterious at first. How can a tiny tag with no battery participate in a radio conversation? Let's find out.

Backscatter coupling

Backscatter coupling provides an elegant solution to the puzzle of how to make an RFID tag without a battery. The name itself, "backscatter," describes the way the RF waves transmitted by the reader are scattered back by the tag. That is to say, the waves are reflected back to the source to send a signal. Imagine the reader as a flashlight and the tag as a signaling mirror with a cover, as shown in Figure 3-3.

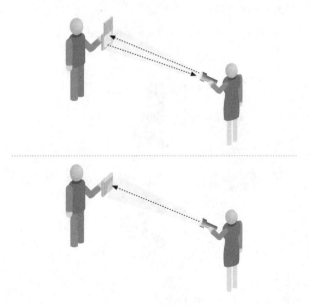

FIGURE 3-3. Backscattering an RF signal is like reflecting light with a signaling mirror

The person holding the flashlight sends signals by turning the beam on and off. When left on, the flashlight provides a signal carrier that allows the person holding the mirror to respond by exposing and concealing the mirror. In effect, this emulates a second, much weaker flashlight. A backscatter tag uses a similar trick to reflect or backscatter the RF signal generated by the reader.

So how can a reader actually power the tag's chip as well as its communication? Imagine for a moment that the shutter of the signaling mirror is controlled by a microchip. If a photovoltaic cell powered the microchip using energy from the light of the flashlight beam, our example would be very similar to a passive backscatter tag. If this microchip were powered by a small battery, but the device still used reflected light from the flashlight to communicate, it would be similar to what we referred to earlier as a "semi-passive" backscatter tag.

Notice that in our example, we are sending back the same frequency electromagnetic waves from the mirror as we receive from the flashlight. The term "backscatter" is used today to describe tags that reflect the same frequency emitted by the reader but change various qualities of that reflection to send information to the reader. Some tags do this via physical properties of the tags themselves, and others by switching a load connected in parallel to the tag's antenna that causes the antenna to reflect less efficiently when the load is applied. The distinguishing characteristic to remember is that backscatter tags reflect back the same frequency that the reader supplies to power them.

Because the reader and tag are each using the same frequency for communications, they typically take turns. As mentioned earlier, we call this a half-duplex (HDX) communications mode. The reader continues to power the tag even when the reader is waiting for the tag or receiving from it, so backscatter systems are not the kind of system we described as SEQ. In our flashlight and mirror example, we used ASK as the keying because we did not change the phase or frequency of the signal.

Components similar to those in our example are packaged in a more convenient form in Figure 3-4.

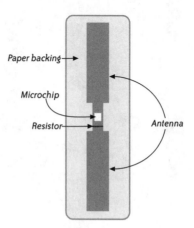

FIGURE 3-4. A modern "smart label"–style RFID tag

Besides reflecting power back to the reader for communications, the tag's antenna conducts some of that energy to provide power for a small chip. The chip controls a resistor between the two halves of the antenna. This resistor is like the shutter in our flashlight and mirror example. When the two halves of the antenna connect directly with low resistance, they reflect the reader's signal with a high amplitude. When the resistor separates the two halves of the antenna, they reflect the reader's signal with a lower amplitude. By switching the resistor in and out of the circuit, the chip is able to create a load-modulated ASK signal to transmit a unique ID number stored in the chip's memory.

Inductive coupling

Inductive coupling is a common type of remote coupling. Some of the most common types of tags in recent years have been various kinds of inductively coupled tags, including tags that follow the ISO 15693 standard for vicinity-coupled smart cards. A reader powers inductively coupled tags by using a coil antenna to generate a magnetic field. The field drives current through a coil on the tag by induction in much the same way that a transformer transfers energy between two coils. This is illustrated in Figure 3-5.

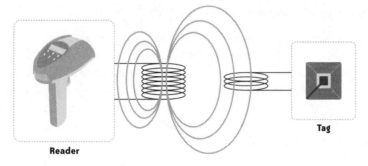

Reader

Tag

FIGURE 3-5. Inductive coupling uses transformer coils

For this reason, this type of coupling is sometimes called *transformer coupling*. The field provides ample energy to power a microchip, which may then communicate with the reader by load modulation in almost the same way as in the backscatter example. A resistor that is switched on and off in the tag causes fluctuations in the magnetic field, which create voltage changes in the reader's antenna. Unlike with backscatter coupling, however, the changes are so minute that designing a reader to recognize them directly would be prohibitively expensive. Thus, one of three methods is used to generate a tag response frequency.

In the *subcarrier* method, the tag switches its resistor on and off very quickly. Thus the tag seems to generate two new frequencies, one above the fundamental frequency and one below. For example, if the reader is operating at 13.56 MHz and the tag switches its resistor at 500 kHz, the two new frequencies will appear at 13.810 MHz and 13.310 MHz. These two new frequencies are called subcarriers. The reader can recognize them easily because they differ from the frequencies the reader itself generates. The tag sends information to the reader by modulating one or more of the subcarriers.

Another trick used with inductive coupling is the *subharmonic* method, which divides the fundamental frequency by an integral value—usually two—to produce a frequency for the tag to use in its responses. If, for instance, the reader generates a fundamental frequency of 128 kHz, a tag using a subharmonic based on one half of the fundamental frequency would respond at 64 kHz. (Division by other values is possible but rare.)

Both subcarrier and subharmonic inductive coupling use FDX mode to communicate, since the reader and tag transmit on different frequencies. Unlike with RF backscatter, there is no need to take turns. Any sort of keying can be used to encode the data, but the most commonly used keying is, again, ASK.

The remaining type of inductive coupling is sequential (SEQ) and uses FSK for modulation. Interestingly, it is also technically a variation on the backscatter method, since it uses the same frequency to send data from the tag and from the reader. In sequential operation, the reader field charges a capacitor on the tag and then shuts off. The tag then uses an oscillator to create its own magnetic field at the same frequency as the reader's (because the antennas on the reader and tag are both tuned to that frequency). The reader is able to detect this field because its own field is off. The tag encodes data using FSK, by accelerating and decelerating the circuit's oscillation.

Tags using inductive coupling are passive or semi-passive and have capacities of up to 2 kilobits. Read-only, write-once, and rewritable tags are all available with this type of coupling. Inductively coupled reader antennas are coils that generate a magnetic field, so this type of coupling has relatively large antennas and short read ranges. Typical read ranges can be as much as 25 cm with a 25-cm reader antenna and 40 cm with a 40-cm reader antenna, but 10-cm read ranges are the most common. This is far enough that inductive coupling may be classed as a remote coupling.

Magnetic coupling

Magnetic coupling is a close coupling that is similar to inductive coupling in that the reader and tag form a pair of transformer coils. The major difference is that the reader coil in magnetic coupling is a round or u-shaped ferrite core with windings, as shown in Figure 3-6. The tag must be within 1 cm of the reader and placed over the air gap in the core. Because the distance is so small and the coupling is so strong, magnetic coupling uses direct ASK with load modulation for simplicity.

This type of coupling can power complex chips. Close coupling systems usually require the tag to be inserted into the reader, so close coupling is ideal for smart cards. (ISO 10536 defines standards for magnetically coupled smart cards.)

Capacitive coupling

Capacitive coupling, another form of close coupling that works best with the tag inserted into the reader, is also usually used for smart cards (as defined under ISO 10536). Capacitive coupling dispenses with antennas and replaces them with electrodes. The reader and

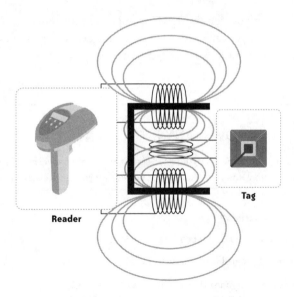

FIGURE 3-6. Magnetic coupling uses a ferrite core antenna

tag each have conductive patches that together form a capacitor when held exactly parallel to each other without touching. As Figure 3-7 shows, the circuit created is identical to one in which the reader and tag are directly connected through a capacitor and share a common ground. As with magnetic coupling, this type of coupling can easily power complex tags, and it may use simple ASK with load modulation to transfer data.

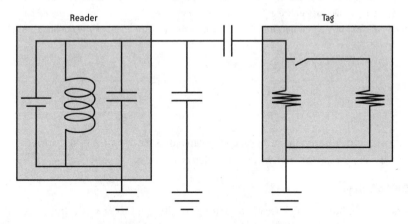

FIGURE 3-7. Capacitive coupling is akin to connecting the tag and reader through a capacitor

Information Storage and Processing Capacity

Information storage and processing capacity is the final major consideration when dividing tags into categories. RFID tags range widely in their capability to store information. The simplest tags store only 1 bit. Systems based on these tags, such as those commonly used in libraries and clothing stores for theft prevention, can only recognize the presence or absence of a tag; they cannot identify individual items. On the other hand, some tags may store kilobytes of data. Larger capacities usually require active tags, and even among passive tags, larger memory capacity directly increases the cost per tag.

HOW MANY BITS DO I NEED?

Some of the latest active tags ordered by the U.S. Department of Defense will be able to store as much as 256 bytes of information. How much storage do you need for your application? To get an idea, let's look at some numbers:

- Number of people on Earth: $6.3 * 10^9$

- Number of grains of sand on Earth's beaches: $7.5 * 10^{17}$

- Number of photons in the visible universe: $1 * 10^{88}$

This means we can count everyone in the world in 33 bits (2^{33} = 8,589,934,592). We can count all of the grains of sand on the world's beaches (not counting deserts) in 60 bits, and we can count every photon in the observable universe in 293 bits (less than 37 bytes).

For less tangible things such as license keys or electronic message IDs, there may be some value in going to a larger number, but probably not. A 256-byte RFID tag must be storing much more than a number. Larger capacities allow tags to store location IDs for every place they have visited, or sensor readings that have either come from on-board sensors or been sent to the tag by a reader. Electronic signatures or encryption keys might take up more room and so make use of larger memory sizes. At some point, tags may carry entire user manuals and item-care instructions for automated handling systems. But for now, to uniquely identify tangible items, most applications will not need more than 96 bits.

This section examines storage and processing capacities for 1-bit EAS tags, surface acoustic wave (SAW) tags, and state machines and microprocessors.

One-Bit EAS Tags

Electronic Article Surveillance (EAS) tags are typically used to prevent theft. Rented videos and library books typically have EAS tags attached in the form of thin strips or labels. Stores often tag clothing with EAS tags inside hard plastic clips or buttons that are difficult to remove without the correct tool. Some EAS tags are even designed to damage an item if removed incorrectly and so discourage theft.

EAS tags are often called "1-bit" tags because they are capable of communicating 1 bit of information. One bit may be used to store the answer to a yes or no question—in this case, the question is, "Is there a tag present?" If a tag is detected, the answer is "1" or "yes." If a tag is not present, the answer is "0" or "no." EAS tags are simple and inexpensive. At present, these are the most commonly used RFID tags.

Because of their simplicity, EAS tags often do not have microchips or memory storage and are always passive, using modulation appropriate to a given type of coupling to create a distinctive signature that may be recognized by a reader. The types of coupling available in EAS tags are as numerous as in other types of RFID tags—for example, EAS tags may use induction or backscatter coupling, as do the more complex tags. However, the way EAS tags generate a response is somewhat different.

Inductive EAS tags are simple, resonant circuits that cause a voltage drop across the reader's coil. The reader "sweeps" the frequency of its field to allow for minor tuning defects in the tags and thus further reduce their cost. Once an item is purchased, these tags may be deactivated by "burning out" the resonant circuit with a massive induced voltage.

In the case of backscatter, which is usually used at microwave frequencies, a diode generates a harmonic of the fundamental frequency—that is, a frequency some integral factor higher than the fundamental frequency, such as two or three times the fundamental frequency. This harmonic frequency is then modulated using ASK to create a distinct pattern. All of the tags of a particular type will have the same pattern, so this does not constitute a unique ID. The purpose is to differentiate between a responding tag and environmental noise of the same frequency. Once an item is purchased, these tags, which are slightly more expensive than inductive EAS tags, are removed and applied to other items in the store.

Frequency divider tags make use of a simple microchip and a coil. Powered at a fundamental frequency generated by the reader, the chip divides the fundamental frequency by two and modulates the subharmonic with ASK or FSK, creating a modulated wave that is detected by the reader. Like the tags mentioned earlier in this section, frequency divider tags use this modulation simply to help distinguish a tag from environmental noise. These tags are also usually removed and reused rather than being disabled.

Electromagnetic EAS tags use a strip of amorphous metal that causes a distinctively odd variation in magnetic flux when it is exposed to an oscillating magnetic field. This variation is at a harmonic of the oscillation frequency of the field (the fundamental). To differentiate between tags and environmental noise, the reader may also modulate the fundamental, thus causing a matching modulation in the harmonic returned by the tag. These tags are usually disabled at the point of purchase by magnetizing hard metal plates in the tags with a strong magnet. The plates will then keep the amorphous strip from reacting to the reader's field. Demagnetizing the hard metal plate will reactivate this type of tag.

Acoustomagnetic tags also contain an amorphous metal strip and a hard metal plate, but in these tags the hard metal plate is magnetized when the tag is active, and the amorphous strip is attached at only one end. When exposed to a reader's field, this strip begins to vibrate. The reader then shuts off the field, but the strip inside the acoustomagnetic tag continues to vibrate like a tuning fork, generating a weak alternating electromagnetic field that the reader can then detect without interference from its own field or reflections. This is very similar to sequential mode communications, although no information other than the presence of the tag is communicated. To disable this type of tag, the hard metal plate is demagnetized. These tags are somewhat more secure than electromagnetic tags in that disabling them is more difficult for a thief or prankster to accomplish without an expensive deactivator.

Surface Acoustic Wave (SAW) Tags

In between the 1-bit tags and other, more advanced RFID tags is an ingeniously designed oddity. SAW tags operate in the microwave range as backscatter tags and have no processors, but unlike 1-bit tags, a SAW tag can be encoded at the point of manufacture to contain a number.

Figure 3-8 shows what a SAW tag looks like. The antenna at the left receives the microwave pulse from the reader and feeds it to the interdigital transducer (the block on the left). The transducer contains a piezoelectric crystal, which vibrates when it receives the microwave pulse. This vibration creates an acoustic wave that travels through the tag, encountering reflector strips (shown on the right).

FIGURE 3-8. A SAW tag

The strips reflect back part of the wave, causing the crystal to vibrate again and creating a backscatter reflection. The number and spacing of the reflector strips determines the number and timing of the pulses sent back to the reader, and so determines the number represented by the tag. Since the number must be set at the time of manufacture, SAW tags are read-only, and because they have no logic circuit, many tags may respond simultaneously to a reader pulse without waiting their turn, causing difficulties in sorting out where one tag's response starts and another's stops. At the time of writing, practical size constraints also limit SAW tags to a 32-bit capacity.

Because there is a delay as the acoustic wave propagates through the tag and reflects back to the reader, SAW tags operate in the SEQ communications mode. The reader broadcasts its pulse and then waits, without needing to power the tag. The reader cannot really be said to communicate with the tag since its interrogatory pulse is always the same. Think of a SAW tag as if it were simply "shaped like" a particular number that the reader is able to "illuminate" so that it becomes visible.

State Machines and Microprocessors

Some tags have more complex logic circuits than others. Most 1-bit tags and all SAW tags have no logic circuits at all, while other types of tags have sophisticated state machines incorporated into custom chips. An on-board state machine allows these tags to participate in a complex anti-collision dance with the reader, which helps the reader to distinguish individual tags from a large group of similar tags (For more on anti-collision, see Chapter 4.)

More complicated processors can provide security through encryption or through control sensors built into the chip. Advanced smart cards even have powerful microprocessors that can be programmed and reprogrammed with new capabilities. As with memory capacity, more processing capacity means a higher cost, so finding the right balance for a given application can mean the difference between a profitable system and an expensive failure. The best guiding principle here is probably "don't buy more than you need." Fortunately, even the most advanced tags are dropping in price as production volume increases, so what might have been too expensive last year may be a good fit this year.

Standards

Some RFID applications need to interoperate only with the procedures and systems of a single company. Others must share information with a global consortium of partners. No matter where in this spectrum an individual application falls, standards will affect the choice of tags for that application—if only because large manufacturing runs of tags fitting a particular standard may make those tags less expensive than equivalent proprietary tags, even though the latter may be more simply designed. Choosing a tag is, to a large extent, choosing the type of RFID system you intend to build, and tag standards often involve much more than the physical characteristics and air interface of a tag.

EPCglobal Tag Types

EPCglobal, Inc., a collaboration between GS1 and industry partners, defines a combined method of classifying tags that specifies frequencies, coupling methods, types of keying and modulation, information storage capacity, and modes of interoperability. As described in Chapter 2, EPC tags are intended to carry EPC numbers, which are assigned by the specific management entities who own the object classes involved. (We will talk in detail in Chapter 4 about encoding and decoding EPC numbers from tag bitstreams.)

The European Article Number and Uniform Code Council groups, formerly known as "EAN.UCC," chose the new name "GS1" in 2005. "GS1" is not an abbreviation, but instead stands for "one global standard, one global system and one global organisation."* We will use "EAN.UCC" and "GS1" interchangeably in this and other chapters, as some of the specifications predate the name change.

Table 3-3 shows the different classifications of tags recognized by ECPglobal. These classifications, which began with the Auto-ID Center, have mutated as actual standards developed and vendors made suggestions. For instance, Class 0+ is a slightly modified (but still compliant) implementation of the Class 0 standard offered by a particular manufacturer. Version 1.1 of the EPC Tag Data Standard defines the contents and encoding for all EPC data carriers (tags) regardless of their class, but the air interfaces (that is, the coupling, frequencies, and communications protocols) are, at the time of this writing, specified only for Class 0 and Class I tags.

TABLE 3-3. EPCglobal tag classes

Class	Description
Class 0	Passive, read-only
Class 0+	Passive, write-once but using Class 0 protocols
Class I	Passive, write-once
Class II	Passive, write-once with extras such as encryption
Class III	Rewritable, semi-passive (battery-powered chip, reader-powered communications), integrated sensors
Class IV	Rewritable, active, "two-way" tags that can talk to other tags, powering their own communications
Class V	Can power and read Class I, II, and III tags and read Class IV and V tags, as well as acting as Class IV tags themselves

The EPC tag classes should not be seen as an attempt to create a taxonomy of RFID tags. Instead, these specifications are intended as a roadmap, with the goal of replacing installed tags with somewhat backward-compatible, higher-class tags as they become available. We say "somewhat" backward compatible because there have been suggestions that the intention is not to provide backward compatibility in the tags themselves, but instead to upgrade reader software or firmware to support both existing and new tags during a transition. ECPglobal has consistently promised to provide a reasonable migration path for early adopters. The standard defines an air interface from 860–930 MHz in the UHF range. Earlier Auto-ID Center working documents also defined an air interface for 13.56 MHz in the HF range.

* "EAN Australia—New Name, New Identity," 31 March 2005, *http://www.ean.com.au/news/_news_ details.asp?id=6299.*

EPC HF tags are inductive coupled FDX tags with read ranges of up to one meter. The encodings are not specifically named in the specification, but the reader-to-tag encoding seems to be biphase space encoding, whereas the tag uses pulsed RZ encoding to respond to the reader. These tags use a protocol called the Slotted Terminal Adaptive Collection (STAC) protocol, which allows a reader to select a single tag from among a group of tags. For this reason, this protocol is called a *singulation* protocol.

EPC UHF Gen2 tags use backscatter coupling and an HDX communication mode, allowing for read ranges of up to 10 meters with optimal orientation of the tag and reader. Reader-to-tag communications are ASK and pulse interval encoded, and tag-to-reader communications are encoded using FSK subcarriers with biphase space or Miller encoding. These tags use a different singulation protocol than the HF tags: the Slotted Random Anti-Collision (SRAC) protocol takes advantage of the faster turnaround time in UHF communications. Earlier EPC UHF tags used still another protocol, known as Adaptive Binary Tree (ABT).

> ### NOTE
> Don't be confused by the terms "Gen2" and "Class II." Class II is a particular class of tag functionality, as shown in Table 3-3. "Gen2" is short for Class I Generation 2, which is a new generation of tag protocols for UHF Class I tags.

All EPC tags must also support the permanent, remote destruction of an individual tag using a password. This password is 24 bits in Gen2. All tags also support a Cyclic Redundancy Check (CRC), which is stored in the tag. The CRC in Gen2 is 16 bits. EPC has defined tags for 64-bit and 96-bit memory capacity and is working on a standard for 256-bit. We will discuss tag communications, CRC, and anti-collision protocols including STAC, SRAC, and Slotted Aloha in more detail in Chapter 4.

ISO/IEC 18000 Tags

In the past, GS1 has backed both the EPC standards and the GTAG initiative, which includes the 18000-6 standard for UHF. This standard originally conflicted with the EPC UHF specification and the new EPC UHF Generation 2 specification, but tag manufacturers were already selling EPC Class 0, Class 0+, and Class I tags. Some have expressed concern that the 18000 air interfaces and command protocols are more complex than those defined by the EPC standards, which could lead to both more expensive tags and stall adoption of the standard. Chris Turner, who has worked on the development of the 18000 standards, disagrees.* He contends that the 18000 protocols are flexible enough to support an EPC on an ISO tag for a price equivalent to that of an EPC tag.

---

* Chris Turner, "EPC and ISO 18000-6," *RFID Journal*, 3 March 2003, *http://www.rfidjournal.com/article/articleview/325/1/2/*.

In late 2004, EPC and ISO announced a plan to adopt EPC Gen2 as the standard for 18000-6C tags, but at the time of this writing (in the summer of 2005), ISO has not formally adopted Gen2. Table 3-4 lists the individual 18000 standards.

TABLE 3-4. ISO/IEC 18000 standards

Standard	Title	Description
18000-1	Generic Parameters for the Air Interface for Globally Accepted Frequencies	Principles and architecture for an RFID standard
18000-2	Parameters for Air Interface Communications below 135 kHz	LF, two tag types, optional anti-collision Tag type A: FDX 125 kHz Tag type B: HDX 134.2 kHz Passive, inductive coupling
18000-3	Parameters for Air Interface Communications at 13.56 MHz	HF, two modes (both require a license from the IP owner) Mode 1: 105.94 kbps from tag to reader Mode 2: 423.75 kbps from tag to reader Passive, both use inductive coupling, FDX
18000-4	Parameters for Air Interface Communications at 2.45 GHz	Microwave, two modes Mode 1: Passive Mode 2: Semi-passive, tags talk first Passive, backscatter, HDX
18000-5	Withdrawn	Withdrawn (was for 5.8 GHz)
18000-6	Parameters for Air Interface Communications at 860 to 930 MHz	UHF, two tag types Type A: Pulse interval encoding, Aloha anti-collision Type B: Manchester encoding, Binary Tree anti-collision Passive, backscatter, HDX Reader to tag uses biphase space encoding for both tag types (Type C: ISO may adopt EPC Gen2 as the type C tag in late 2005)
18000-7	Parameters for Air Interface Communications at 433 MHz	UHF, long range Read/write, active, HDX

ISO 15693 Vicinity Smart Cards

The ISO 15693 standard was originally intended as a specification for "vicinity cards." These contactless smart cards are typically used for access control but have also been used for many other applications, including supply chain and asset tracking. This standard defines one type of tag, which should be the size and shape of a credit card, inductively coupled, using ASK from reader to tag and ASK or FSK from tag to reader. ISO 15693 also defines an anti-collision procedure called the Slot Marker Method (more on that in Chapter 4) and two encoding methods. The method intended for fast reads is called "1 of 4," and the method intended for long range is called "1 of 256." Some vendors sell unique IDs, but these are unique only to the vendor; they are not globally unique as in ISO 18000 or EPC.

The new EPC Gen2 standard uses ISO 15693 IDs to identify tags. Think of the tag for a moment as an electronics product from a manufacturer rather than as a data carrier—this Tag ID (TID) is assigned by the tag manufacturer to identify its product. The tag then carries an Object ID (OID), which is the EPC for the object to which the tag is attached.

Summary

If you have an understanding of the different types of tags, choosing a tag for a particular application becomes easier. Tags with durable physical characteristics are available for harsh environments, and paper tags are available for controlled environments where the application calls for rapid, automated tag application. The air interface determines which tags may communicate with which readers, and the type of coupling defined for that air interface determines how far away a reader can be and still read a tag. Tags come in a variety of data storage capacities, and some even have additional information processing capabilities, but these additional capabilities come at a cost. By studying the standards, we also now know what EPC and ISO tags are and why (for now) they may need different readers.

With these characteristics and capabilities in mind, we can talk about guidelines for selecting the best tag for your application. We've only covered the essentials in this chapter, and the actual process of selecting tags for a given application still usually requires extensive testing and the help of a skilled RF engineer. However, here are some general rules of thumb to help match tags to applications:

- Use smart labels for automated application in a warehouse, but use PVC or glass for tougher environments.

- Use passive tags for the lowest cost, and semi-passive or active tags only as necessary for additional capabilities or greater read range.

- Use LF/HF tags for individual items.

- Use UHF tags for shipping units such as pallets.

- Use microwave tags for vehicles and long-distance reads.

- Where possible, to reduce cost, store only an identifier on the tag and look up the rest of the information. More storage capacity is more expensive.

- Follow the standards where you can, and watch what the largest adopters are doing.

- As always, don't reinvent the wheel!

This has been a complex chapter because the tag options are so numerous. As the Compliance era matures, the options in RFID systems will stabilize to the point where we can choose from a limited number of options with confidence that the elements will match.

CHAPTER FOUR

Tag Protocols

IN THE PREVIOUS CHAPTER, WE DISCUSSED THE "AIR INTERFACE," the bedrock of tag communications, and the circuit designer's view of tag and reader interaction. In this chapter, we'll examine the protocols readers and tags use to exchange messages over that air interface as well as take a more detailed look into the information stored on tags.

The Jargon File,* a dictionary of technical jargon, defines a *protocol* as:

> A set of formal rules describing how to transmit data, especially across a network. Low level protocols define the electrical and physical standards to be observed, bit- and byte-ordering, and the transmission and error detection and correction of the bit stream. High level protocols deal with the data formatting, including the syntax of messages, the terminal to computer dialogue, character sets, sequencing of messages, etc.

By this definition, the air interfaces described in Chapter 3 would be low-level protocols, while the protocols described here are the high-level protocols that define the actual syntax of messages and the structure of the dialog between a reader and a tag. The first part of

---

* Eric S. Raymond, "The Jargon File," v3.0.0.0, July 1993, *http://catb.org/~esr/jargon/*.

this chapter covers some important terms and concepts for understanding tag protocols and explains more about the relationship between bar code standards and tag encodings, which should be helpful for developers building EPC applications. (These same encodings appear again in the APIs in Chapters 6 and 7.) We then discuss various types of singulation and anti-collision procedures in depth to illustrate how a reader can recognize a tag across a crowded room. The chapter closes with sections on tag features for security and privacy and some tips on troubleshooting tag communications.

The singulation protocols may seem esoteric at first, but they have been the focus of heated debate during recent months and are in many ways responsible (for better or worse) for critical decisions on the timing of technology purchases and for adoption of RFID technologies across many industries. In particular, the publication of the Gen2 specification in early 2005, was one of the most anticipated events in RFID in early 2005.

Protocol Terms and Concepts

Technical jargon develops around any new technology, and RFID is no exception. Some of these terms are quite useful, serving as a convenient way to communicate concepts needed to describe other concepts that will appear in the pages that follow. These terms include:

Singulation
> This term describes a procedure for reducing a group of things to a stream of things that can be handled one at a time. For example, a subway turnstile is a device for singulating a group of people into a stream of individuals so that the system may count them or ask them for access tokens. This same singulation is necessary when communicating with RFID tags, because if there is no mechanism to enable the tags to reply separately, many tags will respond to a reader at once and may disrupt communications. Singulation also implies that the reader learns the individual IDs of each tag, thus enabling inventories. Inventories of groups of tags are just singulation that is repeated until no unknown tags respond.

Anti-collision
> This term describes the set of procedures that prevent tags from interrupting each other and talking out of turn. Whereas singulation is about identifying individual tags, anti-collision is about both regulating the timing of responses and finding ways of randomizing those responses so that a reader can understand each tag amidst the plethora of responses.

Identity
> As we discussed in Chapter 1, an identity is a name, number, or address that uniquely refers to a thing or place. "Malaclypse the Elder" is an identity referring to a particular

person. "221b Baker Street London NW1 6XE, Great Britain" is an identity referring to a particular place, just as "urn:epc:id:sgtin:00012345.054322.4208" is an identity referring to a particular widget.

How Tags Store Data

The high-level tag communications protocols know about the ID types that can be stored on a tag and so know, at a general level, how data is stored on the tag. However, since a reader only communicates with a tag via the air protocol, the actual physical layout of memory on a tag is left to the tag manufacturer. A discussion of the physical layout is beyond the scope of this book, but the logical or apparent layout of tag memory is specified in the EPC Class 0 and Class I (Generation 1) standards. Figure 4-1 shows that layout.

FIGURE 4-1. Tag data layout

The CRC is a checksum (described in more detail in the sidebar "CCITT-CRC"), the EPC is the ID on the tag, and the password is the "kill code" to disable the tag. Note that for a tag to be EPC-compliant under Class 0 and Class I Generation 1 standards, it must never transmit the password under any circumstances—not even in response to proprietary diagnostic commands used only by the manufacturer.

This password is the same password described previously as a means of disabling (destroying) tags. (Under Gen2, this changed; we will describe Gen2 in more detail in the "EPC UHF Class I Gen2" section of this chapter.)

Version 1.1, Revision 1.26 of the EPC Tag Data Standards describes EPC as a "meta-coding scheme" because it allows existing identifiers to be encoded as EPC identifiers, as well as allowing for the creation of completely new identifiers. This standard defines one encoding for General Identifiers (GIDs), which is intended for creating new identification schemes, and five specific encodings—called System Identifiers—for particular uses. The System Identifiers are based on existing GS1 (EAN.UCC) identifiers.

Table 4-1 describes each of these special encodings and gives examples of their use. The application identifier is a number that can be used as a prefix in a bar code to indicate which identifier the number represents.

CCITT-CRC

A Cyclic Redundancy Check (CRC) is a way of verifying that a block of data has not become corrupted. The sender of the data block calculates a value by treating the whole block as one large number and dividing it by a number called the *CRC polynomial*. The remainder of this operation is the CRC. The sender sends this CRC along with the data, and the recipient uses the same method to calculate a CRC over the data block for comparison. If the CRC from the sender doesn't match the CRC calculated by the recipient, the recipient may request that the data be resent. To generate CRCs, EPC protocols use the CCITT-CRC polynomial, which happens to be the same polynomial used for error detection in most disk drives and in the venerable XMODEM file transfer protocol. This protocol is a 16-bit CRC that uses the polynomial $x^{16} + x^{12} + x^5 + 1$. It catches about 99.998 percent of errors and can more or less be easily implemented. The pseudocode for calculating CRCs is as follows.

First, calculate the hex value for the polynomial. We do this by counting down from 15 (because this is a 16-bit CRC) and marking a 1 for each power that appears in the polynomial. For each power that does not apply in the polynomial, we mark a zero. This means we have a 1 at the 2^{12} position and a 1 at the 2^5 position. Since the polynomial ends with a +1, we then add a 1 to the end of our number, yielding 0001000000100001, or 1021 hex. We will call this number CCITT in the Java-like pseudocode below:

```
CCITT = x1021;
bytes[] = toBytes(x30500046501CC50000001070);
crc = 0xFFFF; // Set it to ones to start
i = 0;
while(i < bytes.length) {
  if (1 == (crc & 0x80) xor bytes[i])) //MSB of crc
    crc = (crc << 1) ^ CCITT;
  else
    crc = crc << 1;
  }
print crc;
```

This is, of course, a terribly inefficient way of doing the calculation. The EPC also uses a CRC-5 for short queries, but a CRC-5 would be too small to work for the tag IDs. The Gen2 specification includes example code and a circuit diagram for implementing CCITT-CRC and CRC-5 in hardware. For a clever, fast CCITT-CRC software implementation, see Ritter.[a]

---

a. T. Ritter, "The Great CRC Mystery," *Dr. Dobb's Journal of Software Tools*, 11 no. 2 (1986): 26–34, 76–83. *http://www.ciphersbyritter.com/ARTS/CRCMYST.HTM*.

TABLE 4-1. Application identifiers

Application identifier	Identifier	Name	Intended use	Example
(21)	SGTIN	Serialized Global Trade Item Number	Item tracking	Individual tires
(00)	SSCC	Serial Shipping Container Code	Shipping containers	An ISO/intermodal container
(414)	GLN	Global Location Number	Locations	An individual antenna in a warehouse
(8003)	GRAI	Global Returnable Asset Identifier	Rental and library items	A rentable hand-truck
(8004)	GIAI	Global Individual Asset Identifier	Asset tracking	An office chair
	GID	General Identifier	Individual IDs	New identification schemes

The GID is a special case. Unlike the System Identifiers, it does not simply adapt an existing identifier to work with EPC tags. The GID defines a header and three fields: the General Manager Number, the Object Class, and the Serial Number. The General Manager Number is assigned by EPCglobal to some company or entity and is guaranteed to be unique. An entity granted a General Manager Number is then responsible for assigning unique values for the dependent Object Class and Serial Number fields. These dependent fields only need to be unique for a particular General Manager; different General Managers can use the same Object Class numbers and Serial Numbers without conflict.

The GS1 System Identifiers each serve a particular purpose in identifying portions of the global trade network, as you can see in Figure 4-2. Imagine a pallet of automobile parts bound overseas from the factory. Separate Serialized Global Trade Item Numbers (SGTINs) might identify each individual part, while yet another SGTIN identifies the pallet composed of those parts. A railway dock door through which the pallets travel at the factory might be identified with a specific Global Location Number (GLN). The shipping container, identified with a Serialized Shipping Container Code (SSCC), would contain this pallet (among others), as well as a set of reusable shipping braces that belong to the factory. Each brace could be identified using a Global Returnable Asset Identifier (GRAI) number. Having standards for all of these pieces of information allows for unprecedented information sharing among trading partners throughout the supply chain. For example, there are currently hundreds of different standards for location information alone, so the benefits and challenges of moving to a single system, such as GLNs, are equally great. None of the global identity schemes (such as the GTIN) are strictly or even chiefly concerned with RFID, but their existence and momentum are important to the successful adoption of RFID on a massive scale.

Remember that "identity" has a special meaning here, as described in the previous section "Protocol Terms and Concepts." EPC defines three layers of identity: the Pure Identity Layer, the Encoding Layer, and the Physical Realization of an Encoding. A *pure identity* is an abstract name or number used to identify something. This identity remains the same

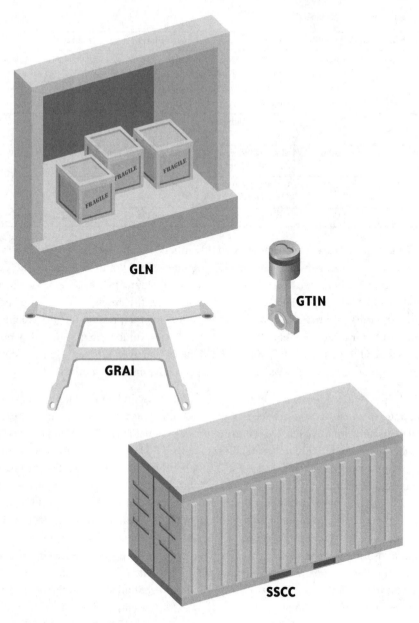

GLN

GTIN

GRAI

SSCC

FIGURE 4-2. Some system identities in use

regardless of the technology used to attach it to an item. An *encoding* is a procedure for combining the pure identity with syntax-specific information, such as a filter value or checksum, and then rendering that information into the syntax. A single pure identity could be rendered as a bar code encoding, an RFID tag encoding, or an EPC Uniform Resource Identifier (URI) printed on a piece of paper. The physical realization of an encoding is a particular transformation of that encoding that allows it to be stored as a bar code, written into a tag's memory, or physically realized through some other technology. Figure 4-3 gives an example of encoding a pure identity as a bar code or an EPC tag.

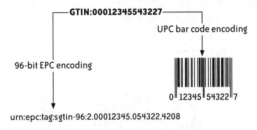

FIGURE 4-3. Encoding a pure identity

Notice that the GID is used as the fundamental encoding for EPC tags. Other encodings take an identity, which might be encoded in another form (such as a bar code), and convert it to a form that fits into a GID with a syntax similar to "Header.GeneralManager-Number.ObjectClass.SerialNumber." This requires the EPC to take some liberties with the GS1 SGTIN. For example, while the guidance from GS1 is that the GTIN should never be parsed and treated as separate fields, an EPC must have a General Manager Number and an Object Class for the Object Naming Service (ONS) to work, so the EPC-SGTIN divides the GTIN. In this case, an SGTIN is an example of a pure identity. The EPC-SGTIN is the encoding, and the bits on an EPC tag representing the EPC-SGTIN are the physical realization of that encoding.

GS1 SGTIN Encoding

EPC readers and RFID middleware present tag data according to its EPC encoding. Interfacing with a reader or middleware requires at least a cursory understanding of tag encodings for debugging code. An understanding of these encodings is also required to define the events and filters introduced in Chapter 2, which we will describe in more detail in Chapters 6 and 7. The SGTIN is a good example of an identity and its encoding, so we'll use it as an example in this chapter.

> **NOTE**
> For details on GLN, GRAI, and other encodings from Table 4-1, please see Appendix A.

EPC-SGTIN is an extension of the GS1 GTIN that assigns Company Prefixes and Item References for use in identifying particular classes of object. The common 12-digit UPC and 13-digit EAN bar codes are a subset of the GTIN. These types of codes are being merged with the 14-digit GTIN in 2005 by prepending zeros to the existing codes. The GTIN doesn't have an individual item serial number, so the SGTIN appends a serial number, the value of which is assigned by the General Manager.

Figure 4-4 shows a typical UPC bar code. To convert this UPC into an EPC and store it on an RFID tag, we must first convert it to a GTIN. This bar code has an Indicator Digit (0), a Company Prefix (12345), an Item Reference (54322), and a check digit (7). To convert this to a GTIN, we take the entire code as a string and add two zeros to the beginning, yielding a GTIN of 00012345543227. Notice that our Company Prefix has now become 00012345, an 8-digit number. We will then convert the GTIN to an SGTIN—which allows us to track individual items—by adding a Serial Number (4208).

FIGURE 4-4. UPC bar code

To represent a pure identity, the EPC uses a URI expressed in the URN notation. For an SGTIN, this notation is:

    urn:epc:id:sgtin:*CompanyPrefix.ItemReference.SerialNumber*

This notation includes only the information necessary to tell one item from another; it does not include the GTIN check digit or a filter value. The Item Reference here is actually the Indicator Digit plus the Item Reference from the GTIN (Figure 4-5). Our example would thus be encoded as:

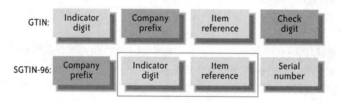

FIGURE 4-5. Conversion of GTIN to SGTIN

    urn:epc:id:sgtin:00012345.054322.4208

To express an identity encoded as SGTIN-96, a value dependent on the tag type, the EPC uses a different format for the URN:

    urn:epc:tag:sgtin-96:*FilterValue.CompanyPrefix.ItemReference.SerialNumber*

Using this notation, our example would be encoded as:

    urn:epc:tag:sgtin-96:2.00012345.054322.4208

The steps to encoding a 96-bit EPC to a binary string are:

1. Find the appropriate header for the identity type.

2. Look up the partition value based on the length of the Company Prefix.

3. Concatenate the 8-bit header, 3-bit filter, and 3-bit partition fields.

4. Append to this the Company Prefix and other fields appropriate to the identity (Item Reference and Serial Number for an SGTIN).

5. Calculate the CRC and append the EPC to the end of the CRC.

Find the header

A header identifies each type of identity and its specific encoding. Table 4-2 shows examples of encodings for SGTIN for 96-bit tags and 64-bit tags. Notice how the 64-bit header starts with a one and is only two bits. Only 64-bit headers start with one.

TABLE 4-2. SGTIN header values

Type	Header
SGTIN-96	0011 0000
SGTIN-64	10

Find the partition

We have 96 bits to work with. Of these bits, the encoding designates 44 for the Company Prefix and Item Reference. Different companies have prefixes of different lengths. The partition number tells us how many bits we have left for the Item Reference field based on how many bits the Company Prefix takes up. To see how many bits Company Prefixes of various lengths take up, look at the Company Prefix section in Table 4-3. Our example of the Company Prefix of 00012345 (eight digits long) corresponds to partition 4 in Table 4-3. From the other columns in this row, we know that we will need 27 bits to encode the Company Prefix on the tag and will have 17 bits to encode the Item Reference.

TABLE 4-3. SGTIN-96 partition values

Partition	Company Prefix		Item Reference	
	Bits	Digits	Bits	Digits
0	40	12	4	1
1	37	11	7	2
2	34	10	10	3
3	30	9	14	4
4	27	8	17	5
5	24	7	20	6
6	20	6	24	7

Concatenate the header, filter value, and partition

Notice the field name "Filter Value." This is not a part of the SGTIN, but is instead a way of quickly selecting EPCs based on common logistical types. For example, a filter value of 1 might be used for smaller individual items, while 3 might be used for something large that ships individually, such as a refrigerator. Table 4-4 lists the SGTIN filter values. We will use a filter value of 2 in our example, to indicate a "Standard Trade Item Grouping" such as a pallet or carton. All encodings support a filter value of 0, and SGTIN and SSCC also support a 1, meaning "undefined." SSCC defines 2 as "Logistical/Shipping Unit." More filter values may be defined in the future.

TABLE 4-4. SGTIN filter values

Filter value	Binary code	Meaning	Example
0	000	Unspecified	Unspecified
1	001	Retail Consumer Trade Item	A single shaving razor
2	010	Standard Trade Item Grouping	A carton or pallet of razors
3	011	Single Shipping/Consumer Trade Item	A refrigerator (large, shipped alone)
4	100	Reserved	Reserved for future use
5	101	Reserved	Reserved for future use
6	110	Reserved	Reserved for future use
7	111	Reserved	Reserved for future use

Since we are building an SGTIN-96, the standard header value is 0011 0000, or 30 hex. Building the SGTIN-96 is simply a matter of concatenating bits, starting with the header as the most significant bit (MSB), followed by the bits for the filter (3 bits) and the partition (3 bits). This yields the following (shown in 4-bit nibbles, with the last incomplete):

    0011 0000 0101 00

Append the Company Prefix, Item Reference, and Serial Number

We now append the Company Prefix to the previous bits by specifying the 27 bits available for it so that they represent the appropriate value. This yields:

    0011 0000 0101 0000 0000 0000 0001 1000 0001 1100 1

which can be represented in hex as 305000181C, with an extra bit set to 1.

We then append the Item Reference in 17 bits to the end of this number, which yields 305000181C B50C plus two bits set to 10.

Now we append the Serial Number, which is 38 bits long. This yields 305000181CB50C8000001070, which is a 12-byte, or 96-bit, number.

Calculate the CRC and append the EPC to it

This value is then stored in the tag along with a 16-bit CRC (CCITT-CRC), which would be FFF1 in this case. The value with the CRC would be FFF1305000181CB50C8000001070.

Figure 4-6 shows the parts of the encoding again.

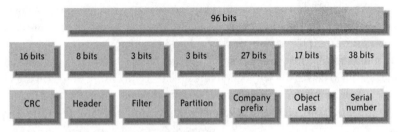

16 bits	8 bits	3 bits	3 bits	27 bits	17 bits	38 bits
CRC	Header	Filter	Partition	Company prefix	Object class	Serial number

FFF1305000181CB50C8000001070

FIGURE 4-6. Encoding for an SGTIN-96 with a partition value of 4

For each system identity, the specification describes an alternative encoding for 64-bit tags. To help fit the identity into a 64-bit encoding, the Company Prefix is removed and a Company Prefix Index takes its place in the encoding. This index is an offset into a Company Prefix table. A Company Prefix Index is supplied as needed by GS1 to those entities that intend to use 64-bit tags. This table is limited to 16,384 entries, and this encoding scheme is intended as a temporary solution until the industry universally adopts tags that are 96 bits or larger. Note that the SGTIN-64 encoding is the only currently defined header that contains a 1 in the MSB, allowing it to be only two binary digits long (11 is reserved for other 64-bit encodings).

For headers, partition tables, and field types of the other EPC-defined 96-bit encodings, see Appendix A.

Singulation and Anti-Collision Procedures

Our next topic concerns the way a reader and a tag use the air interface. There are many different ways for readers and tags to communicate, but the different methods can all be broadly categorized as Tag Talks First (TTF) or Reader Talks First (RTF). Logically, it would seem simplest for a tag arriving on the scene to announce its presence to all concerned. In practice, however, this is difficult unless tags are able to negotiate among themselves which tag will speak first. Some high-end active tags use TTF communications protocols, but the new crop of inexpensive smart labels and other passive tags exclusively use RTF protocols. In this section, we'll examine the most common of these protocols for RFID—Slotted Aloha, Adaptive Binary Tree, Slotted Terminal Adaptive Collection, and the new EPC Gen2 specification. In the later section "Tag Features for Security and Privacy," we'll look at how features of these protocols can affect security and data integrity in an application.

Slotted Aloha

Slotted Aloha is derived from a procedure known simply as "Aloha," which was originally developed in the 1970s by Norman Abramson of Aloha Networks in Hawaii for packet radio communication. Aloha was the inspiration for the Ethernet protocol, and a variation of this procedure is still used for satellite communication as well as for ISO 18000-6 Type B and EPC Gen2 RFID tags.

Aloha itself is as simple as an anti-collision procedure may reasonably be and doesn't really include the concept of singulation in the usual sense. With this procedure, tags begin broadcasting their IDs as soon as the reader's field energizes them. Each tag sends its entire ID and then waits for a pseudorandom period of time before broadcasting again. The reader simply receives the IDs, depending on chance to ensure that each tag will eventually broadcast during a period when all other tags are quiet. The reader doesn't respond to the tags in any way. The advantages of this procedure are speed and simplicity. Tag logic is minimal, and with such a low protocol overhead, this is the top performer for read rate where only a few tags are present.

However, adding tags means reducing the chances that any given tag will happen to transmit during a quiet moment. This means waiting for tags to transmit again and again until a clear transmission comes through—an approach that, depending on the length of transmission, becomes unworkable for most item-tracking implementations at about 8 to 12 tags. Fortunately, Slotted Aloha greatly improves the scalability of the protocol by adding the concept of singulation and requiring tags to broadcast only at the beginning of a particular time slot, which cuts the chances of collision considerably. This along with comparisons of received signal strength by the reader, has led to a protocol that some have claimed is capable of reading almost 1,000 tags per second. The cost of this optimization is, as usual, increased complexity.

Slotted Aloha uses three commands to sort out tags: REQUEST, SELECT, and READ. The first command is a REQUEST, which provides a timing mark to any tags currently in range. The REQUEST command also indicates how many slots are available for use by the tags. The tags each select one of the offered slots—that is, based on a number of options offered by the reader they randomly select a length of time to wait before responding to the REQUEST. The tags then broadcast their IDs at their chosen slots. The reader, upon receiving a clear ID with no collisions in a particular time slot, issues a SELECT containing that ID. Only the tag whose ID matches this ID responds. The reader then issues a READ command, to which the tag responds by sending whatever data it has to share with the reader. (In a nonsecure system, there may be no further data .) With that conversation over, the reader then sends another REQUEST command. Figure 4-7 shows the state transitions of the reader during this conversation, while Figure 4-8 shows the state transitions of the tag.

Fewer slots means faster reads, but with many tags, more slots means fewer collisions. Various implementations of Slotted Aloha optimize the number of slots in different ways. The reader may increase the number of slots in a REQUEST following a collision and continue to increase them in successive REQUEST commands until a clear ID transmission occurs without collision. A reader may also use a BREAK command to inform waiting tags that a clear transmission has occurred and that they should not transmit. In some implementations, a tag will enter a SLEEP (also called DORMANT or MUTE) state for some period following a successful read, thereby allowing any remaining tags more of a chance to be selected. The dramatization in the following sidebar may help further your understanding of the Slotted Aloha protocol.

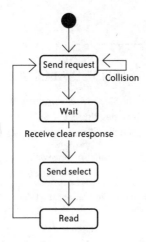

FIGURE 4-7. Slotted Aloha reader state diagram

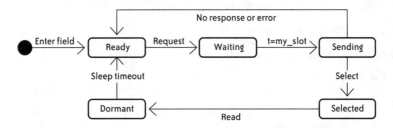

FIGURE 4-8. Slotted Aloha tag state diagram

Tag 5 puffs out his cheeks and sits in silence as Tags 1 and 2 roll their dice…. Rather than using timed intervals, the reader may indicate the end of a slot using a signal, called a "slot marker." Anti-collision protocols that use these signals are called Slot Marker protocols. A Slot Marker implementation of the Slotted Aloha protocol works much the same as that described above, except that the end of a slot is indicated by a signal rather than by the expiration of a set time. This allows some slots to be longer than others so that there is a better chance of a read in each slot.

Adaptive Binary Tree

EPC Class 0 and Class I Version 1.0 (Generation 1) UHF tags use a slightly more complicated approach to singulation and anti-collision known as an Adaptive Binary Tree procedure. As the name implies, this procedure uses a binary search to find one tag among many. Most of us are familiar with binary trees from other domains, but for the sake of clarity, we will revisit the basics here. Then we'll explain some of the nuances of doing a binary tree search using a query/response approach similar to the previous description of Slotted Aloha. Unlike with Slotted Aloha, with this protocol tags respond immediately. The EPC specification for the air interface of UHF tags uses two separate subcarriers for 1s and 0s in tag responses. Because the protocol doesn't care how many tags responded with a 1 or a 0 and only cares that one or more tags responded, this protocol neatly sidesteps

SLOTTED ALOHA

A dramatization may help to explain the Slotted Aloha protocol. In this case, we have a single reader and three tags using a protocol that includes BREAK and SLEEP commands. Imagine you have four actors: one plays the role of Reader, and the others play Tag 1, Tag 2, and Tag 5.

We begin in an empty room. A large clock hangs on one wall, showing the current time in milliseconds. Reader stands on a podium and tags enter from a door, stage left.

Reader: Is anyone there? It is now time t. I have slots at t+10, t+20, t+30, t+40, and t+50. Please respond.

(Tags 1, 2, and 5 enter.)

Reader: Is anyone there? It is now time t. I have slots at t+10, t+20, t+30, t+40 and t+50. Please respond.

Tag 1: (rolls percentile dice and selects t+40)

Tag 2: (rolls percentile dice and selects t+20)

Tag 5: (rolls percentile dice and selects t+10)

(The clock chimes t+10.)

Tag 5: Five!

Reader: Quiet, all of you! I hereby select Five.

(All tags except 5 shake their heads in disgust but remain silent. Five grins foolishly.)

Tag 5: That's me! I'm Five!

Reader: Have you any data to share, Five?

Tag 5: FFF1305000181CB50C8000001070, I'm Five!

Reader: Yes, well shut up now, Five… Is anyone there? It is now time t. I have slots at t+10, t+20, t+30, t+40, and t+50. Please respond.

---

most tag response collisions. The protocol does require that only one reader be involved, though, which may require careful configuration of readers that are near each other.

An easy way to imagine traversing or "walking" a binary tree is to imagine trying to guess a number made up of 1s and 0s by making guesses for each digit. When we start we have no information, so we ask, "Is the first digit 1?" If the answer is "yes," we can add that to our string of digits and ask, "Is the next digit 1?" If the answer is "no," we can add a 0 to our string of numbers. This question and answer repeats for each digit until we know the whole number. Figure 4-9 shows the "tree." The arrows show the correct digits at each step.

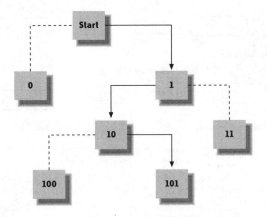

FIGURE 4-9. A binary tree

Now apply this strategy to finding one tag among many by the bits in the tag's ID. As before, we start with no information. The reader sends out a query that amounts to asking, "Does any tag have an ID with a 1 as the most significant bit?" All of the tags that answer "no" then cease to respond, while tags that answered "yes" are asked a similar question about the next bit. The tags continue to be narrowed down in this fashion until only one tag answers. In this way, a reader can typically narrow down the possibilities to one tag without going through the entire ID, although in the worst case—a population of sequential IDs—each search will necessarily go to the least significant bit (LSB).

This "worst case" would be a frequent problem, since in most cases tags are applied sequentially, but the EPC standard allows for three different IDs for a tag: ID0, ID1, and ID2. ID2 is the EPC code, ID1 is a pseudorandom number that is set at the factory, and ID0 is a pseudorandom number that is generated as needed. If a reader asks each of the tags to generate a new ID0 and then singulates based on that ID, the probability of sequential IDs becomes very small.

With the Adaptive Binary Tree protocol, the interaction between the reader and tag is necessarily more complex than it is with Slotted Aloha. The protocol uses a state machine made up of four interdependent sections. The first is a set of states associated with global commands, including the all-important Dormant state. The next section is a state for calibrating communications—specifically, synchronizing the time-keeping oscillators on the tags with the timing of the reader. Differences in manufacturing, age of components, and even temperature can affect timing of circuits enough that this calibration is critical to achieving reasonable read rates. The next set of states is concerned with walking the binary tree, and the last set of states is used for communicating with a tag once it has been singulated. Figure 4-10 shows the state machine.

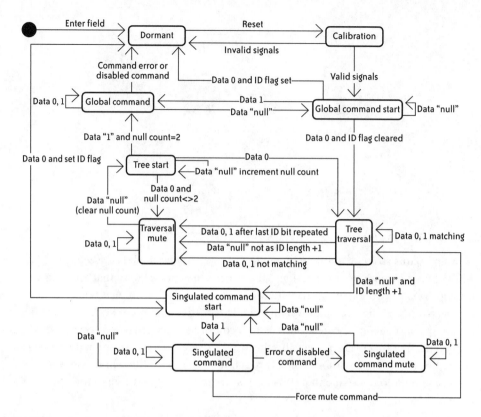

FIGURE 4-10. Adaptive Binary Tree protocol state diagram

Here's a breakdown of the Adaptive Binary Tree protocol states:

Global states

The following are global states, which may be entered at almost any point:

Dormant

The Dormant state is the initial state a tag enters when powered. It is also the state a tag enters after it has been read.

Global Command Start

After a successful calibration, the tag enters the Global Command Start state and waits for a 1 or a 0 from the reader. A 1 sends the tag to the Global Command state, while a 0 sends the tag to the Tree Traversal state (unless the tag has already been read, in which case a 0 causes the tag to proceed to the Dormant state).

Global Command

In this state, the tag is ready to receive and process commands that affect all tags or groups of tags that have not been singulated. Some commands, such as kill, are not available as global commands.

Calibration

Whenever a tag receives a "reset" message from the reader, it enters the Calibration state and expects oscillator and data calibration pulses from the reader. If any of these are invalid, the tag returns to the Dormant state.

Tree walking states

The following states occur while the protocol is traversing the binary tree itself:

Tree Start

In this state, a data null will increment the null counter by 1. A 0 will send the tag to the Tree Traversal state. A 1 will send the tag to the Traversal Mute state unless the null counter is at 2, in which case the tag will go to the Global Command state. This null trick is used to address groups of tags that match (or do not match) a partial singulation string.

Tree Traversal

When the tag enters this state it immediately sends its most significant bit. The reader then responds with a bit. If it matches the bit the tag sent, the tag will send the next bit, and so on. If the bit does not match, the tag goes to the Traversal Mute state and waits for a data null. If the singulation is using a pseudoID, every 10th bit is considered a "boundary bit." If the singulation is using the EPC itself, the boundary bit is the last bit of the EPC plus the CRC. At the boundary bit, the tag sends the bit as usual; if the reader confirms this bit, the tag then sends the same bit again in the case of the EPC or the next bit in the case of a pseudoID. If the reader responds with a 1 or a 0, the tag enters the Traversal Mute state. If the response from the reader is data null, the tag enters the Singulated Command Start state. If the tag receives a data null at any other time, it enters the Traversal Mute state.

Traversal Mute

A tag waits quietly in this state until it receives a data null, at which point it proceeds to the Tree Start state and resets the local null counter.

Singulated states

These states occur when a single tag remains after the binary tree has been walked:

Singulated Command Start

A tag enters this state from the Tree Traversal state after the last bit of its ID has been confirmed and it has received a null from the reader. Any further nulls are ignored, while a 1 will send the tag to the Singulated Command state. A 0 will set an identified flag, and the tag will go to the Dormant state. This identified flag indicates that the tag has been read.

Singulated Command

Here, the tag receives 8-bit commands from the reader. If an error occurs, the tag enters the Singulated Command Mute state.

Singulated Command Mute

In this state, a tag waits quietly until it receives a data null, at which point it proceeds to the Singulated Command Start state.

Slotted Terminal Adaptive Collection (STAC)

The STAC protocol is similar in many ways to Slotted Aloha, but some of the details of this protocol make it more complex and otherwise different enough to warrant separate treatment. STAC is defined as part of the EPC specification for HF tags. Because it defines up to 512 slots of varying lengths, it is especially well suited to singulation of large populations of tags. This protocol also allows for the selection of groups of tags based on matching lengths of EPC code beginning with the MSB. Because the EPC code is organized by Header, Domain Manager Number, Object Class, and Serial Number (in that order) from MSB to LSB, this mechanism can easily select only tags belonging to a particular Domain Manager or Object Class. Since HF tags are often used for individual item identification, this is especially useful if, for example, the application would like to know how many of the items on a mixed pallet are boxes of A4 paper.

Like Slotted Aloha, STAC uses slots. Figure 4-11 illustrates how the slots are used.

FIGURE 4-11. STAC slots

The F or "fixed" slot is always present and is always the same length. Numbered, variable-length slots follow. These slots must begin with a slot named "0," and there must be enough of these numbered slots to equal some power of two. The exact number of slots is selected and continually adjusted by the reader to most effectively balance the need for quick reads and few collisions. Fewer slots make for faster reads, while more slots make for fewer collisions.

STAC defines only a small set of states and commands, but the steps of the protocol require some explanation. Figure 4-12 shows the states and the commands that trigger transitions.

Note that whatever state a tag may be in, it will return to the Unpowered state if it moves out of the reader's field. (The exception to this rule is the Destroyed state, which indicates that the tag has been permanently disabled and may not be read or reused.) A variation on this protocol allows for tags to remember that they were in the Fixed Slot state for a short time even if power is lost. In this variation, a Complete Reset command allows the reader to force tags to the Ready state when necessary, even if the tag remembers having been in the Fixed Slot state previously. This scenario may occur in the case of a tag moving down a conveyor between readers. Having been read by the first reader, the tag believes

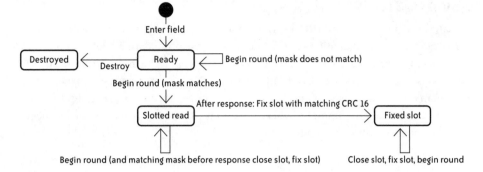

FIGURE 4-12. *STAC protocol state diagram*

its state should be Fixed Slot. However, the new reader has not seen this tag yet and will need it to go to the Ready state when powered, so the new reader issues a Complete Reset.

The list below describes each STAC state associated with singulation, plus the Destroyed state. The Write state, which in current EPC Class 0 HF tags is issued only by the tag manufacturer to set the tag's EPC ID, is not shown. The states are:

Unpowered

When outside the reader's field, a tag is in the Unpowered state. Upon entering a reader's field, the tag enters the Ready state.

Ready

In this state, a tag waits for a Destroy, Write, or Begin Round command. If the tag receives a Begin Round command containing either no selection or a selection of equal length to the tag's EPC, the tag enters the Slotted Read state.

Slotted Read

In this state, the tag picks a slot at random from those presented by the reader. The slot may be any slot except the F slot. If the tag receives a Fix Slot command after sending its information, it proceeds to the Fixed Slot state. If a Fix Slot, Close Slot, or Begin Round command comes along with a matching selection, the tag will remain in the Slotted Read state. If a Begin Round command arrives with a selection that does not match, the tag will return to the Ready state.

Fixed Slot

When a tag enters the Fixed Slot state, it responds on the F slot and will continue to do so for any subsequent responses until loss of power occurs (i.e., exiting the reader field).

Destroyed

If a tag receives a Destroy command and the password contained in the command matches the password contained in the tag, the tag will send its ID one more time and then permanently cease to function. Once destroyed, a tag may not be returned to service.

EPC UHF Class I Gen2

The latest revision of the EPC UHF Class I air interface is called the "Gen2 protocol." Gen2 addresses some of the limitations of the first UHF protocol standard by defining protocol variations that are able to work under European (CEPT) and North American (FCC) RF regulations. It also specifies variations in the protocol for operating environments where more than one reader is within another's receiving range, including a special set of protocol requirements for environments where the number of readers is equal to the number of available communication channels.

The EPC Gen2 protocol supports much faster tag singulation than the previous protocol, with tag reads rates as fast as 1,600 tags per minute in North America and 600 tags per minute under the more constrained power and frequency ranges in Europe. One of the primary concerns it addresses is added security for the protocol. Key to the solution Gen2 offers is the recognition that signals the reader transmits may be received over a far greater distance than signals generated by the tags. The specification considers two readers to be in the same operating environment if they are within one kilometer of each other.

The protocol describes three procedures for communication between readers and tags. A reader may *select* tags by asking tags to compare themselves to a bitmask, or it may *inventory* tags by singulating tags until the reader has recognized each tag within range. A reader may also *access* tags, which includes reading information from a tag, writing information to a tag, killing a tag, or setting the lock status for various sections of tag memory by memory bank number.

Tag memory

The Gen2 protocol recognizes an optional user memory area and a Tag Identifier (TID) in addition to the CRC+EPC, which is called an Object Identifier (OID) in the specification. Each section of tag memory is organized into an addressable bank (see Table 4-5), and read and write commands in the protocol accept a bank address to determine which bank the operation affects.

The new specification also requires that, in addition to the kill code, each tag have an access password. Though the tag is required to support commands that use an access password or kill code, either or both may have a value of zero. Any reader command that selects a bank may operate only on that bank. To switch banks, the reader must issue a new command.

BITMASKS

The Gen2 specification describes several different features in terms of bitmasks. For those of us who haven't written low-level code in a while, a *bitmask* is a series of bits that can be compared to another series of bits using the binary operators "|" (OR), "&" (AND), "~" (NOT), and "^" (XOR). As an example, imagine that you need to find out if a value named thisID (which, for our example, will be equal to 7) has a 1 in the twos position and in the fours position—that is, the second and third least significant bits, or 0110, which equals 6. You could do this easily by evaluating the following expression:

```
6 & thisID = 6
```

If this expression evaluates to true (not zero), those three bits are 1s. Bitwise AND returns a 1 if the corresponding bits are 1 in both operands. So, for the example above, we would do the following test:

```
0110  = 6
0111  = 7
-----
0110  = 6
```

Notice that this test would return true for 6 and for 15, but not for 8 or 14, for instance. So why would we care if thisID has 1s in those bits? For the Gen2 protocol, this issue comes up in two places. First, Gen2 uses bitmasks to compare values in tag memory against a Select command that works very much like the example above. Second, and more complex, is the way Gen2 uses bitmasks as a "cover code" to protect sensitive communications from the reader to the tag. On a Req_RN request from the reader, the tag generates a 16-bit random number and sends it to the reader. Tags transmit at low power, so only a nearby receiver can intercept this communication. The reader then uses this 16-bit number to XOR blocks of data sent back to the tag. For example, if the reader wanted to send a block of data equal to 0xAFAF and the random number from the tag was 0x7E21, the reader would evaluate the expression as follows:

```
0xAFAF ^ 0x7E21 = 0xD18E
```

or:

```
1010 1111 1010 1111 = 0xAFAF
0111 1110 0010 0001 = 0x7E21
-------------------
1101 0001 1000 1110 = 0xD18E
```

The reader would then send 0xD18E to the tag. Next, the tag would repeat and then XOR the same cover code against this value by evaluating the following expression:

```
0xD18E ^ 0x7E21 = 0xAFAF
```

The reader has thus sent the data as ciphertext over its relatively powerful signal, which helps thwart eavesdropping. An observer trying to determine the data sent to the tag would have to know the cover code to retrieve the data 0xAFAF, and to do that, he would have to be near enough to have received the cover code when it was transmitted (one time) via the weak backscatter from the tag.

TABLE 4-5. Tag memory banks

Bank	Contents
00	Reserved (access password and kill code, protocol bits, etc.)
01	OID (CRC+EPC)
10	TID (Tag manufacturer's ISO 15693 serial number)
11	User

Inventory commands

When a reader starts an inventory over a group of tags, this is called a *session*. A tag will participate in only one session (i.e., talk to only one reader) at a time, but it may time-slice up to four sessions, which makes it appear as though the tag is talking to four readers at once. To support this, tags keep four inventoried flags: S0, S1, S2, and S3. Inventoried flags may have one of two values, A or B. While stepping through an inventory with a group of tags, a reader will set the inventory flags for the particular session that "belongs" to that reader until they all share the same value. Think of this as moving all of the singulated tags into a set named "A" or "B" for a particular session.

A reader working on session zero cannot see the values of the inventoried flags for the other three sessions, but if another reader were to alter some other value on the tag—for example, if it were to lock the OID bank—this would affect all sessions.

During the inventory, the reader uses the Slotted Random Anticollision method. This method, as its name implies, uses slots to determine when a tag should respond to the reader, but unlike with Slotted Aloha, the tag actually chooses its own slot by setting a slot counter to a 16-bit random number at the start of an inventory round and then decrementing until it reaches zero. When a tag's slot reaches zero, it sends a new 16-bit random number to the reader. The reader will then use this number to mask blocks when communicating with the tag. This effectively creates a one-time pad encryption for reader-to-tag communications. Tag-to-reader communications are still unencrypted but are transmitted at much lower power. The inventory commands are:

Query

> The reader begins an inventory by issuing a Query command, which specifies the session and the number of slots. Tags generate random numbers and use them to determine which slot to use for responses. Tags that pick slot zero enter the Reply state, while tags that pick another slot remain in the Arbitrate state (tag states are discussed in the later section "Tag states").

Query Adjust

> A Query Adjust changes the number of slots in an inventory round. The Query Adjust command can add one to the number of slots, subtract one from the number of slots, or leave the number unchanged. Tags generate random numbers and select random slots from the new range. Tags that pick slot zero enter the Reply state, while tags that pick other slots remain in the Arbitrate state.

QueryRep

When the reader issues a QueryRep, tags decrement their slot counters. If the counter becomes zero, the tag enters the Reply state; otherwise, the tag remains in the Arbitrate state.

ACK

A reader responds to a tag with an ACK, sending a 16-bit value back to the tag. If the tag is in the Reply or Acknowledged state, the reply is the 16-bit random number just sent by the tag as it transitioned from the Arbitrate state to that state. If the tag is in the Open or Secured state, the 16-bit ACK number is the tag's handle.

NAK

A reader can emit a NAK, which is 8 bits long with a value of 0xC0. When a tag receives a NAK, it returns to the Arbitrate state unless it is in the Killed or Ready state, in which case the tag ignores the NAK.

The Select command

A reader may choose not to inventory all of the tags within range. A Select command asks tags to compare the contents of a particular bank of memory against a bitmask (see the "Bitmasks" sidebar). If the bitmask matches the tag's memory, the tag sets either its selected flag (SL) to true or its inventoried flag (one of S0–S3) to a value specified by the Select command. A single Select command can set the value of either the select flag or a single inventoried flag (one per command).

Access commands

The access commands allow a reader to change the contents of a tag's memory, read from that memory, lock memory banks, kill a tag, or request a 16-bit random number generated by the tag. The reader must identify a single tag in order to use any of the access commands. Access commands that transmit sensitive data such as passwords, IDs, or user memory from a reader to a tag may be sent as ciphertext using a cover code, as discussed in the "Bitmasks" sidebar. The Gen2 standard requires both tags and readers to support the following access commands unless otherwise indicated:

Req_RN

Requests a random (or, more likely pseudorandom) number from the tag. The "randomness" of this number is strictly defined in the Gen2 specification.

Read

Reads data from a particular bank of tag memory.

Write

Writes data to a particular bank of tag memory. Before each write, the reader issues a Req_RN. The tag responds with a new 16-bit random number, which the reader then uses as a cover code to protect the 16 bits of data sent in the Write command. For longer data streams, the Req_RN-Write sequence is repeated as many times as necessary.

Kill

Permanently disables a tag. This command is similar to Write in that the reader first requests a 16-bit random number from the tag, which it uses as a cover code for the first 16 bits of the kill password. The sequence is then repeated for the second 16 bits. Once this command completes, the tag will never respond to another request. However, if a tag's kill password is zero, the tag can't be killed and will ignore this command.

Lock

Sets the read/write privileges for banks of memory or specific passwords. This may be a "permalock," in which case these privileges can never be changed again.

Access (optional)

If a tag has a nonzero password, the reader can use the Access command to put a tag that is in the Open state into the Secured state. If the tag is already Secured, it will remain Secured. Since this command includes the password, it is issued twice with a cover code—that is, the reader issues a Req_RN, gets the cover code, uses it for the first half of the password, and then repeats the sequence for the last half of the password.

BlockWrite (optional)

This command is similar to Write but is able to write multiple 16-bit blocks at once without a cover code. Thus, this command doesn't need to be repeated block by block, nor does it require a previous Req_RN.

BlockErase (optional)

This command allows a reader to erase multiple blocks from a single tag memory bank. The BlockErase command is protected with a CRC-16 and includes the tag's handle (i.e., its 16-bit tag authentication number).

Tag states

We can see the high-level structure of the EPC Gen2 protocol in Figure 4-13.

Notice that this is a slightly simpler state machine than that defined earlier for the Adaptive Binary Tree protocol.* The tag states are:

Ready

This is the state in which a tag waits when it is not part of the current inventory.

Arbitrate

This is the state in which a tag waits when it is part of an inventory, but not yet in slot zero.

---

* For a full diagram of Gen2, see *EPC Radio-Frequency Identity Protocols Class-1 Generation-2 UHF RFID Protocol for Communications at 860 MHz 960 MHz Version 1.0.9*, p. 41, Fig. 6.19 (*http://www.epcglobalinc. org/standards_technology/EPCglobalClass-1Generation-2UHFRFIDProtocolV109.pdf*).

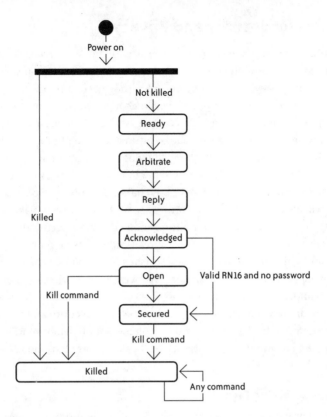

FIGURE 4-13. Gen2 protocol state diagram

Reply

When a tag enters the Reply state, it generates a 16-bit random number and sends it to the reader. If it gets back an ACK, it enters the Acknowledged state; otherwise, it returns to the Arbitrate state.

Acknowledged

A tag may go to any state except Killed from this state.

Open

A tag with a nonzero password enters this state when it is in the Acknowledged state and receives a Req_RN from the reader. A tag in this state can go to any state except Acknowledged.

Secured

A tag with a password of zero enters this state when it receives a Req_RN while in the Acknowledged state, and a tag with a nonzero password enters this state from the Open state when it receives an Access command. A tag in this state can enter any state except Open or Acknowledged.

Killed

When a tag enters the Killed state, it sends a success response to the reader and is then permanently disabled; that tag will never respond to a request from a reader again.

Tag Features for Security and Privacy

There are justifiable privacy and security concerns with any sort of identification technology, and RFID, as much as biometrics, has raised popular concern because of its possible impact on personal privacy. A common concern is that an unauthorized person will be able to obtain information from, or possibly even change information stored on, an RFID tag. There is some legitimacy to these concerns. A tag that does not use a secure protocol might be read by anyone, just as a bar code or printed label might be read by anyone. A writable tag might also be maliciously altered if it does not implement a secure protocol for communication with a reader. This alteration might be less obvious than someone placing a false bar code or printed tag on a piece of merchandise. Unlike printed tags and bar codes, which will always remain at risk, future secure protocols will make RFID tags very difficult to forge or even read without authorization. The more secure the tag, however, the more expensive it is, and an unencrypted, read-only tag is no more risky in the right application than a bar code is now. For these reasons, many supply chain applications currently use less-secure RFID implementations. As overall RFID prices drop due both to wider adoption and standardization, the cost of more secure will also drop, and these in turn will become more widely adopted. Chapter 10 covers security and privacy for the entire RFID system, but because some of the implementation details of RFID security are specifically concerned with the tag protocols, we'll take a closer look at tag destruction and data encryption here.

Destroying and Disabling Tags

A key concern of privacy advocates is the longevity of an identification mechanism such as RFID. Few privacy concerns arise from tracking pallets in a warehouse, or even from tracking individual items from the warehouse to the shelf. The point when an end user or customer first touches an item is the point where most privacy concerns arise. Within the store, expectations of privacy are tempered somewhat by the current precedent of surveillance from cameras and electronic anti-theft devices. But when RFID tags may still be attached and even active when a product leaves the store, there is a real possibility that tracking may continue outside the store, and this raises many concerns.

At the checkout counter, the respective interests of the seller and customer diverge. The seller, as represented by the manufacturer, the distributors, and the store itself, would very much like to know what happens to the item after it leaves the store. For example, sensors in the packaging that identify changes in temperature, acceleration, and shock could help the manufacturer design better packaging; readers in garbage collection systems could recover this information and report it back to the manufacturer. Supermarkets and distributors would like to know how long an item sat in the refrigerator or pantry before the customer used it. They would especially like to know what other products were in the trash in those households. It's the dream of market researchers everywhere to be able to definitively answer the question, "What else are my customers buying?"

The customer, in contrast, would rather not reveal too much information beyond the doors of the store. Discarded packaging for medicines might reveal sensitive information about a person's health. Simply adding up the cost of discarded goods and packages would provide a good estimate of the household's real cash flow and pinpoint items worth stealing or households worth targeting in an easily manageable shopping list for thieves. Although much of this information is already available, it requires physically sorting through a household's weekly garbage. With a little imagination, the possible abuses for automated "dumpster diving" are numerous. Notice that this is still an issue even when the RFID tags are only on a product's packaging, which will likely be discarded. For the sake of privacy, many consumers would like to have any RFID tags disabled before leaving the store.

Privacy is not the only reason to disable a tag. Pharmaceutical manufacturers are interested in authenticating bottles as an anti-counterfeiting measure. Unless tags can be permanently and irreversibly altered or disabled in someway at the point of sale, these bottles could be refilled with counterfeit products and sold again.

So how is an RFID tag disabled? The implementation of the kill command is left to the manufacturer, but many use embedded fuses on a chip that physically disable it. Others set a "killed" value in memory, which disables the protocol state machine. In either case, the death of the chip is triggered by a Destroy command containing the appropriate password, which is set by the manufacturer. Even in the case of chips that are otherwise writable, EPC standards require that this password is unable to be changed or read by any command, including diagnostic commands intended for use only by the tag's manufacturer.

This raises its own set of security questions about how to distribute these kill codes. The password must somehow arrive at the point of sale, yet it cannot be public knowledge since this might allow a prankster to disable tags maliciously. The problem is clearer if we think of the lifecycle of a tag in a supply chain.

At the beginning of its journey to the store, each tag leaves its manufacturer in a box bound for a widget factory. For the sake of simplicity, we will assume that the tags are smart labels and that each tag on this particular roll will accept the same kill code (say, 23532). The kill code may be sent to the widget factory on a slip of paper in the box. The widget factory produces the widgets and places a tag on each of them. These widgets are placed on pallets and picked up by a distributor, who sends them to one of three wholesalers. Fifty different retailers buy these widgets, along with others from earlier and later runs. Some of these retailers are small and don't track IDs at all. Others disable tags at the checkout, while still others allow customers to choose whether the tags should be disabled or not. Which kill codes should be sent to which retailers, and how should it be done? Figure 4-14 illustrates the problem.

Creating a "push" solution in which the manufacturer sends the kill codes to each retailer won't work because the widget manufacturer has no easy way of knowing which retailers have which batches of their products at any given moment. A "pull" makes much more

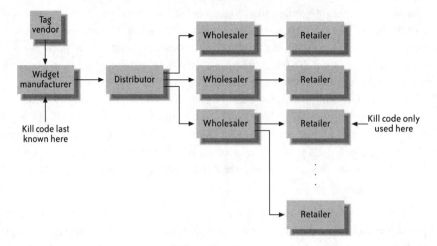

FIGURE 4-14. Life of a tag

sense. This is where the Object Naming Service comes in. We'll discuss the details of how this works in Chapter 8, but for now, it's enough to know that the ONS allows a retailer to look up information concerning tags on its products. This information can include kill codes, which might be stored on a secure web server or on an EPC Information Service (EPCIS) server. Requests for kill codes can be authenticated with unique store identifiers and tracked by the manufacturer to discourage unauthorized access.

This example points out how even seemingly simple cases of use, such as theft prevention using EPC tags, may require a relatively sophisticated information infrastructure. EPCglobal's choice of a password-based method for disabling tags shows that the standards bodies expect that most users of EPC tags will be doing more than simple Electronic Article Surveillance. The build-out for this infrastructure is only now beginning, though, so in the meantime, a retailer or end user might choose to ignore the EPC kill codes altogether and simply destroy tags with a hammer or a sharp knife.

Encrypting Information

Before the Gen2 specification, any EPC Class I reader was able to read any EPC Class I tag. As we described in the earlier section "EPC UHF Class I Gen2," tags using the Gen2 protocol generate 16-bit random numbers, which readers then use to mask similar-sized blocks of data when communicating with the tags. This effectively creates a one-time pad encryption for reader-to-tag communications. Tag-to-reader communications are still unencrypted but are transmitted at much lower power and so are less vulnerable to snooping. This technique makes eavesdropping on RFID communications more difficult. The capability to secure a tag with a password helps to further thwart attempts to read or modify tags using unauthorized readers.

Learn to Troubleshoot Tag Communications

Troubleshooting tag and reader communications is the sort of subject that could (and probably someday will) fill up an entire book, but a few general techniques can solve the most common problems. Not many of us have spectrum analyzers, but RF questions can usually be approached indirectly. First, think of ways to halve the problem. In the usual case, where one reader fails to talk to one tag, we can halve the problem by asking, "Is it the reader or the tag?" Try another tag with the reader. If the new tag works, you have a faulty tag. If the new tag doesn't work, you have a faulty reader (or two faulty tags; in this case, it's best to try a few more tags just to be sure). The reader uses one or more antennas to talk to the tags. Can you swap antennas with another reader that works?

> **WARNING**
> Be careful! Only swap antennas from identical readers and consult the reader manual first for more precautions.

Chances are that instead of being broken, the reader is simply misconfigured. Most readers these days support multiple tag types. Is the reader configured to speak to an ISO 18000-6 Type A tag only? If so, an EPC tag won't work (this week). Is it configured (or built) for HF or UHF? What about the tag? Was it tuned to work on a metal can or a rubber tire? Try it on the appropriate item.

A simple trick for testing packaging is to place a tag—one that you know to work—in different locations on the packaging of an item already in the field of a reader that provides a visible read light. Move the tag around and watch the read light come on and go off. In this way, one can develop a very good idea of the RF profile of an item and its packaging in just a few minutes. To "hide" a tag, place your body between the tag and the reader. Squishy humans are great RF shields.

In a story (possibly apocryphal) often told around the RFID camp, two technicians testing a reader and tag combination found that they could read the tag at a great distance in some cases but only at a short distance in others. To demonstrate, one technician would hold a portable reader near an item bearing the tag and then slowly step back. At roughly a half a meter, the tag would cease to register. This seemed to be the "dead zone." Another technician would then hold the end of a tape measure and the technician with the reader would step back to nearly 10 meters away. All the way from the outside of the dead zone to this limit, the reading was strong. An observer then pointed out that the metal tape measure might make an excellent antenna…

The lesson here is to look for unexpected variables. For example, if you get slow reads while using a filter, it might mean that many tags are responding but most don't fit the filter criteria. This could look as if a single tag is reading slowly, since the time spent turning off the excluded tags is not reflected in the single tag identity that's returned. Try reading a few times with no filters set.

Summary

Understanding tag protocols, including singulation and encodings for identities, prepares the way for our discussion of readers in the next two chapters, as well as for understanding the reader protocols and RFID middleware discussed in Chapters 6 and 7. While these tag protocols have been the area most affected by what David P. Meany of Cisco Systems called the "tornado of obsolescence" that surrounds RFID technology,* the much-anticipated Gen2 specifications from EPC have removed some of the uncertainty. Anyone working with RFID should keep up with at least the high points of the ongoing debate over adoption of this protocol, as well as some of the intellectual property issues currently in the news. The organizations and publications listed in Appendix B are a good place to start.

In this chapter we learned:

- That a protocol is a set of formal rules describing how to transmit data
- The meaning of the terms *singulation*, *anti-collision*, and *identity*
- How to encode identities for storage on an EPC RFID tag
- About singulation and anti-collision protocols, including Slotted Aloha, Adaptive Binary Tree, STAC, and the EPC Gen2 protocol
- About some of the features available in the tag protocols to increase security and privacy through encryption and careful planning
- A few tips on troubleshooting reader/tag communications

---

* David P. Meany, speaking at the 2004 ECPglobalUS conference in Baltimore, MD.

CHAPTER FIVE

Readers and Printers

PASSIVE TAGS MUST HAVE RADIO TRANSMITTERS SOMEWHERE TO POWER THEM, along with receivers to hear those transmissions. Even active tags typically require contact with some sort of transmitter attached to the network. In RFID circles, this transmitter/network endpoint is typically called a *reader*. Readers are located between the tag and the event filter in an RFID system. It's the reader's role to know how to talk to tags, how to create low-level events from reads, and how to send these events to an event filter.

This chapter describes the parts of a reader from two points of view. The first view presents the physical components of a reader: the things you can touch or find on a circuit board. The second view describes the logical parts of a reader, dividing its functions into imaginary "components" that may or may not correspond to separate physical components on a real reader. As an example, the event management logical component may be a particular set of instructions that runs on the same physical controller component as the communications logical component, or it may be hosted on its own physical controller.

We'll then go on to examine the physical and logical components of an RFID printer and applicator, or "print and apply" device. These print and apply devices are, along with tag and ship applications, one of the symbols of the Compliance era. Finally, we will describe some of the ways readers differ, provide an overview of some common physical antenna and reader layouts for different applications, and take a brief look at reader configuration.

Physical Components of an RFID Reader

Since the reader communicates with tags using RF, any RFID reader must have one or more antennas. Because a reader must communicate with some other device or server, the reader must also have a network interface of some sort. Examples of common network interfaces are the serial Universal Asynchronous Receiver/Transmitters (UARTs) for RS 232 or RS 485 communications and the RJ45 jack for 10BaseT or 100BaseT Ethernet cables; some readers even have Bluetooth or wireless Ethernet communications built in. Finally, to implement the communications protocols and control the transmitter, each reader must have either a microcontroller or a microcomputer. Figure 5-1 shows the physical components of an RFID reader.

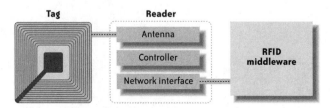

FIGURE 5-1. Physical components of a reader

Antenna Subsystem

Although the antennas themselves are simple in concept, engineers work constantly to get better reception at lower power and to adapt the antennas to special circumstances. Some readers have only one or two antennas, packaged with the readers themselves; other readers may be able to manage many antennas at remote locations. The primary limitation on the number of antennas a reader can control is the signal loss on the cable connecting the transmitter and receiver in the reader to the antennas. Most installations keep the reader within about six feet (two meters) of the most distant antenna, but much longer runs are possible.

Some readers use one antenna to transmit and one to receive. In this sort of configuration, the tag's direction of motion through the reader's fields is particularly important. If the transmitting antenna is "ahead" of the receiving antenna, the receiving antenna will have a longer amount of time to receive signals from the tag. If the antennas are reversed, the tag will spend much less time energized and within range of the receiving antenna. Figure 5-2 shows a conveyor belt with tagged boxes passing first a transmitting (TX) antenna and then a receiving (RX) antenna.

The arrow indicates the conveyor's direction of motion. The tag on each box becomes energized as it passes the TX antenna and begins broadcasting a response. Because it is further down the conveyor, the RX antenna has a longer period in which to receive the response than it would if the two antennas were reversed, which means that there is a better chance that the tag will be read.

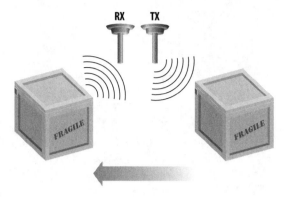

FIGURE 5-2. Preferred placement of receiving and transmitting antennas

Controller

The computing device that controls a reader can vary in complexity from a simple state machine on a chip, which might be used for a tiny embedded reader on a telephone or PDA, to a complete microcomputer system capable of running a server operating system as well as end user applications and accumulating a large amount of data on an internal hard disk. The controller is responsible for controlling the reader side of the tag protocol (described in Chapter 4) as well as determining when information read from a tag constitutes an event to send to the network. The reader controller is also responsible for managing the reader's end of the reader protocol (described in Chapter 6).

Network Interface

Reading tags and recognizing events wouldn't be much use if the reader never told anyone about those events. Readers communicate with the network and other devices through a variety of interfaces. Historically, most RFID readers have had serial interfaces using RS 232 or RS 422 (point to point, twisted pair) or RS 485 (addressable, twisted pair). In recent years, more and more readers have supported Ethernet, and in the last 18 months, some have begun to support built-in wireless Ethernet, Bluetooth, and even ZigBee (for more on ZigBee, see Chapter 11).

Logical Components of an RFID Reader

Within an RFID reader's controller, we can imagine four separate subsystems that handle different responsibilities. These are the same logical subsystems we first saw in Chapter 2, where we discussed how readers fit into the overall RFID architecture. Figure 5-3 shows the logical components of a reader again, for reference.

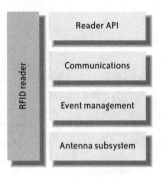

FIGURE 5-3. Logical components of a reader

Reader API

Each reader presents an application programming interface (API) that allows other applications to request tag inventories, monitor the health of the reader, or control configuration settings such as power levels and the current time. This component is mostly concerned with creating messages to send to the RFID middleware and parsing any messages received from the middleware. The API may be synchronous or asynchronous. For a particular implementation of this component, see Chapter 6.

Communications

The communications subsystem handles the details of communicating over whatever transport protocol the reader may use to communicate with the middleware. This is the component that implements Bluetooth, Ethernet, or a proprietary protocol for sending and receiving the messages that make up the API.

Event Management

When a reader "sees" a tag, we call this an "observation." An observation that differs from previous observations is called an "event." Separating out these events is called "event filtering." The event management subsystem defines what kinds of observations are considered events and which events are considered interesting enough to put in a report or send immediately to an external application on the network. As readers become smarter, they will be able to apply more complex processing at this level to reduce network traffic. Essentially, some parts of the event manager component of the middleware will naturally migrate to merge with the event management component of the reader. (More on this in Chapter 7.)

Antenna Subsystem

The antenna subsystem consists of the interfaces and logic that enable the RFID readers to interrogate the RFID tags and control the physical antennas. This component implements the protocols described in Chapter 4, as well as working with the reader's onboard RF electronics to implement the air interface described in Chapter 3.

Parts of an RFID Printer and Applicator

Many of the most commonly used tags for Compliance-era applications are smart labels. As we described previously, these are RFID tags embedded in adhesive paper labels. The primary advantage of this sort of tag is that the user, in addition to encoding the RFID tag with an identity, can print a bar code and/or human-readable text onto the paper label before attaching it to an item.

RFID printers are devices that both encode tags and print to the paper labels that house the tags. Remember that a reader can also "write" to a tag that allows writes, so the primary difference between an RFID reader and an RFID printer has nothing to do with the capability to encode tags; the difference has only to do with the laser or inkjet printer component of the RFID printer.

For low-volume applications, an operator may manually apply smart labels, but high-volume applications require a so-called "print and apply" device. These specialized devices contain an RFID reader, a printer, and an automated system for applying tags to passing items (usually boxes). The applicator may be a pneumatic arm (a tamp pad) that presses printed and encoded adhesive tags onto a box, or a "wipe-style" applicator that works like a manual pricing gun, with the tags peeling off of a roll directly onto the items. Because encoding tags takes time and because some tags fail and must be discarded and replaced while the applicator continues to tag passing items, these devices may be deployed in pairs or gangs. These considerations can make print-and-apply devices somewhat slower than high-speed bar code applicators. At the time of writing, you may reasonably expect to see throughput rates of 30 to 60 tags per minute with these systems. However, there are indications that these speeds may double by the time this book is printed, due in part to the new Gen2 specification discussed in Chapter 4. Figure 5-4 shows the parts of a print and apply device.

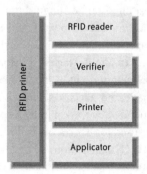

FIGURE 5-4. Parts of a print-and-apply device

Reader

RFID printer vendors, with some exceptions, are not usually reader vendors, so print and apply devices typically incorporate readers from one of the usual vendors. The print and apply device usually wraps the reader API in a print and apply API, but then offers a way to get to the reader API if necessary.

Printer

The printer on an RFID print and apply device is no different than the printer on any other bar code printer, but bar code printers are very different than the office inkjet. These printers typically run a tape or "tag web" through spools so that they can print to one side and then flip the tag into position for application. All of these printers have the ability to print tags according to templates that describe the proper tag layout. For instance, a template may say that a two-inch-wide bar code should go across the bottom of the tag and a specific logo should go at the top. It may also set the position of a human-readable part number, serial number, and company name field. The printer's API receives messages just about the parts of the tag that change, such as the part number and serial number, and prints these in their appropriate locations along with a properly encoded bar code and the static parts of the label (such as the logo and company name). In any system that uses print and apply devices, someone generally has to lay out the templates, convert the logos to the proper image format, and upload them to the printer as part of the development process.

Verifier

Print and apply devices usually include an RFID verification step as well as a bar code verification step. Typically, the RFID verification is performed by the same reader that wrote the tag and the bar code verification is performed by an optical scanner located just past the printer. However, some systems place an optical scanner or a second verification just downstream on the conveyor to guarantee that the tag did not fail after application and that the RFID reader has not somehow encoded a tag that only it can read. (These concerns will become less important as the quality of tags and readers and the stability of the reader protocols increase.)

Applicator

The applicator is one of the most important distinguishing characteristics of print and apply systems. Wipe-style applicators and tamp pad–style applicators have differing strengths and weaknesses. A wipe-style applicator has fewer moving parts and does not require an air compressor, but it can jam if a tag curls incorrectly. Tamp pad–style applicators are more reliable and arguably faster, but as mentioned earlier, many require an air compressor to drive the pneumatic ram. Electric solenoids can also be used to drive tamp pads, but the magnetic field generated by the coil may be a problem in RFID applications. An additional type of applicator used for bar code systems blows the tag onto the item with a puff of compressed air. This is called "non-contact labeling." Non-contact applicators are not currently as common as wipe-style or tamp pad applicators in RFID systems, due in part to concerns about possible electrostatic discharge (ESD). ESD can destroy small electronic components like those in a smart label, but several vendors have recently claimed to have overcome this concern. At the time of writing, we don't know of a controlled study supporting or refuting a relationship between ESD and RFID tag failure in a production environment.

Types of Readers

Readers, like tags, differ in many ways, and no one reader is a perfect fit for all occasions. Readers come in many shapes and sizes, support different protocols, and often must conform to regulatory requirements, which means that a particular reader may be acceptable for an application in one region of the globe but not in another.

Shapes and Sizes

Readers range in size from half an inch (two centimeters) across to the size of an old desktop computer. Readers may be embedded in handheld devices or even cell phones. They may be fixed to the wall in an explosion-proof housing. Readers may even be built into shelving units and doorways along with antennas for smart shelf and portal applications. (Layout will be discussed in the next section, "Layout for Readers and Antennas.")

Standards and Protocols

Readers conform to the same standards and protocols as the tags they read, but some readers can support multiple tag protocols. Some readers are proprietary and support only tags made by a particular vendor. The most important standards for readers include the ISO and EPC tag standards described in Chapters 2, 3, and 4.

Regional Differences

Permissible power levels, frequency variations, and regulatory requirements vary from region to region, even when applied to the same type of tag. For example, EPC UHF readers read the same tags at 915 MHz in the U.S. and at 869 MHz (and lower power) in Europe due to regulatory constraints. EPCglobal, ISO, and other standards organizations are working to come up with standards that will be able to operate globally, but for now, readers must be selected carefully to ensure that they comply with local regulations. For more information, consult the manual for a specific reader. It will list the regions within which the reader is certified to operate.

Layout for Readers and Antennas

A reader and its antennas must be installed to be of any use. Since with RFID we are attempting to sense qualities of the physical world—in this case, the presence or absence of particular items—the physical world dictates the specifics of any installation. For this reason, every sensor installation is different. The possible variations are infinite, but examining a few archetypal applications of RFID can help you to understand the broad categories of installation. These categories include portals, tunnels, handhelds, forklift readers, and smart shelves.

Portals

The word "portal" means doorway or entrance, and an RFID portal is an arrangement of antennas and readers designed to recognize tagged items entering or leaving through a doorway. This is a common setup for warehouses, where items arrive and leave through loading docks. It can also be useful for items moving between sections of a factory, where tagged items might travel through doors (for example, moving from storage to the assembly floor). Portals may also be mobile; in these applications, the reader and antennas are built into a framework on wheels that can be pushed into a truck or down an aisle. This is useful for loading and unloading and for material tracking. Figure 5-5 shows a typical portal.

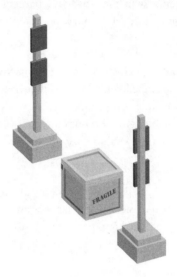

FIGURE 5-5. An RFID portal

Tunnels

A tunnel is an enclosure, usually over a conveyor belt, in which the antennas (and sometimes even the reader) may be housed. A tunnel is like a small portal, with the advantage that a tunnel may also include RF shielding, which absorbs reflected or misdirected RF energy that might interfere with other readers and antennas nearby. This can be useful for assembly lines or packaging conveyors where the reader identifies the station through which an item is currently passing on the conveyor. Figure 5-6 shows a typical tunnel over a conveyor.

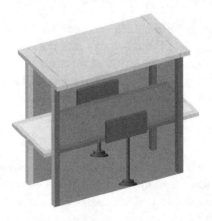

FIGURE 5-6. A tunnel

Handhelds

A handheld reader with integrated antenna, controller, and communications can allow personnel to scan tagged items in situations where it is inconvenient or impossible to move the items to a reader. The use of handheld RFID readers is very similar to that of handheld bar code readers. Not surprisingly, many of these RFID handhelds can also read bar codes and are made by the same manufacturers that make the bar code readers. They may communicate by wireless Ethernet, RF modem, or, for historical reasons, "keyboard wedges" that actually simulate an operator typing on a keyboard when the handheld is connected to the keyboard port or a USB port on a personal computer. Figure 5-7 shows what a typical handheld reader might look like.

FIGURE 5-7. A handheld RFID reader

Forklift Readers

Forklifts, too, may carry RFID readers, for the same reason that a person might carry a hand-held reader. Forklift manufacturers are beginning to offer RFID readers as part of the optional equipment on their products, just as they have offered bar code readers and opera-tor terminals in the past. One pitfall of adding forklift readers in-place is the liability and reg-ulatory concerns of adding equipment to these vehicles. Even prototype implementations must take care to include the manufacturer or even delegate installation of the hardware to the forklift manufacturer. Figure 5-8 shows how a forklift reader might be mounted.

Smart Shelves

One of the most talked about but least common applications of RFID is the smart shelf. Smart shelves are shelving units with antennas incorporated into them in such a way that readers can recognize the arrival and departure of items from the shelves, or read all the items on the shelves on demand. This potentially allows for a real-time inventory of all the items in stock. The system can not only measure the current stock levels of items, but it can also do things like match item IDs against a database of expiration dates and notify personnel about expired items. Prototypes are just now exploring the possibilities for this kind of item-level, real-time monitoring. Figure 5-9 shows one possible smart shelf design.

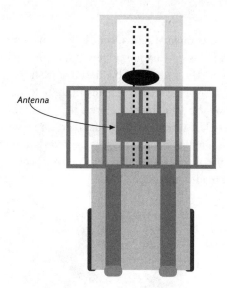

FIGURE 5-8. A forklift with an RFID reader

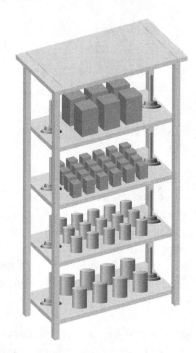

FIGURE 5-9. A smart shelf system

Configuring Readers

Even EPC readers vary greatly by manufacturer in the number and type of options that they offer, but some things are relatively common. Readers usually support ad hoc queries of the type, "What IDs do you see right now?" They also usually support an asynchronous configuration, where a host on the network essentially asks the reader to send it any updates whenever the reader "hears" something. Chapter 6 describes these options in detail.

Readers that support multiple antennas usually support two different ways of using them. One configuration treats all of the antennas as if they are part of one big antenna and treats tag reads that come in from any antenna as having come from one logical "source." This might be the configuration for a portal, as discussed in the previous section, where we care that a tag has passed through but not which antenna it was closest to. Another option is to configure each antenna as if it represents a unique location, a unique source. A good use of this configuration would be for items passing on a conveyor, where one reader might monitor antennas at multiple stations. For instance, each antenna might be in its own tunnel enclosure and represent a different stage in an assembly process. Figure 5-10 shows an example of both configurations.

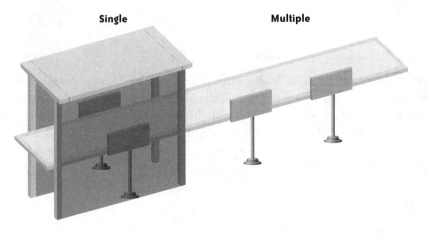

Single **Multiple**

FIGURE 5-10. Single- and multiple-source antenna configurations

Another consideration is environments in which multiple readers may be within reception range of each other. In this case, the readers can interfere with each other. One solution is to "strobe" the readers, forcing them to trade off such that only one reader operates at a time. To support strobing, the readers must be able to sense each other's operation or be connected in such a way that they can share a clock to drive their duty cycles. This connection might be via a cable or a wireless network connection. Figure 5-11 shows how a strobing configuration works when the readers are connected.

The new EPC UHF Gen2 specification requires tags to work in conditions where two readers are active simultaneously. The specification calls this a "Dense Interrogator Environment" and prescribes two different approaches to avoid collisions, depending on the regulatory conditions. This is necessary because under CEPT regulation in Europe, licensing in some cases requires only a single RF channel but in other cases allows multiple channels. Under FCC (U.S.) regulation, licensing always allows multiple channels in the 915-MHz range.

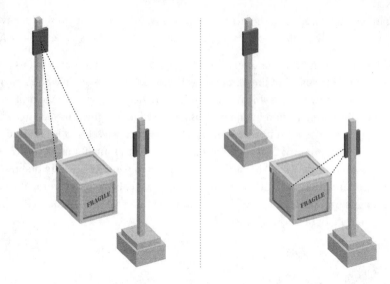

FIGURE 5-11. A strobing reader configuration

Although conceptually simple, readers can be complex devices with many different options and physical configurations. Designing an appropriate placement for antennas and readers in a production environment is a task that requires both skill and expensive RF site survey equipment. RF devices also typically require licensing and even periodic inspection in many countries. Be sure to check with your local authorities to avoid expensive fines.

Summary

From this chapter, you learned that:

- The physical parts of a reader are the antenna, the controller, and the network interface.

- The logical parts of a reader are the reader API, the communications subsystem, the event management subsystem, and the antenna subsystem.

- Print and apply devices for smart labels incorporate a reader, a printer, a verifier, and an applicator and can print bar codes and human-readable information onto the paper tags. Tags are typically applied by either wipe-style or tamp pad applicators.

- Readers may differ in shape and size, adherence to standards, and suitability for various regional regulatory domains.

- Readers and antennas are commonly configured as portals, tunnels, handhelds, forklift readers, or smart shelves.

CHAPTER SIX

Reader Protocols

WE HAVE SEEN HOW A READER COMMUNICATES WITH TAGS, but a reader must also communicate with the network and the applications and middleware hosted on the network. While most of the early standardization work has centered on tags and tag protocols, the next year should see important progress in standardization of reader protocols. This is in keeping with a transition from the Compliance era to the era of the RFID-Enabled Enterprise, where greater demand for standards-based interfaces will drive procurement decisions and so drive reader development. An understanding of these protocols will directly help in configuring middleware and applications as well as in debugging communications between readers and applications or middleware on the network.

In this chapter we will discuss the general structure all modern reader protocols share. We'll also take a look at some specific proprietary protocols that have been developed by vendors in recent years, a new reader protocol standard developed by EPCglobal, and a competing standard introduced by the Internet Engineering Task Force (IETF). We will then discuss what to expect from future reader protocol development.

Parts of a Reader Protocol

Any modern reader protocol must provide certain capabilities to operate in a production environment. These capabilities together imply a general structure that all reader protocols tend to follow. To describe these capabilities and the basic structure of a reader protocol, we will first need to introduce some new terms:

Alert

An alert is a message from a reader to a host indicating a change in reader health or containing a scheduled update of reader health information.

Command

A command is a message from a host to a reader that causes a change in state in the reader or a reaction from the reader.

Host

A host is an application or middleware component that communicates with readers.

Observation

An observation is a record of some value somewhere at some time—for example, the exact temperature inside a refrigeration unit at a particular point in time, or the appearance of ID tag 42 at dock door 5 at 16:22:32 on July 23, 2005.

Reader

A reader is a sensor that communicates with tags to observe identities and then communicates these observations to a host.

Transport

A transport is a communications mechanism used by readers and hosts to communicate with each other.

Trigger

A trigger is some criterion, such as time of day, that will cause some activity to occur. An example might be a timed read trigger that causes a reader to attempt to read any tags present every 12 minutes.

With these terms described, we can define a reader protocol as a set of formal rules defining how one or more hosts and one or more readers may communicate commands, observations, and alerts over a transport.

Any reader protocol must deal with three major types of communication: commands passing from the host to the reader, observations passing from the reader to the host, and alerts passing from the reader to the host. Figure 6-1 shows how the information flows.

FIGURE 6-1. *Flow of information in an RFID system*

Although this diagram shows only one reader and one host, any number of readers could theoretically communicate with any number of hosts. Existing and proposed reader protocols tend to limit the number of hosts a reader may communicate with, for the sake of network efficiency and simplicity in implementations of the protocol. The host, however, typically may communicate with any number of readers in these protocols.

Let's take a closer look at the kinds of information passed between readers and hosts.

Commands

A host sends commands to a reader to cause some reaction from the reader or to change the state of the reader in some way. We can broadly divide the commands a host sends to a reader into three categories:

Configuration commands
  These commands are for the setup and configuration of the reader.

Observation commands
  These commands cause the reader to read, write, or modify tag information immediately.

Trigger commands
  These commands set triggers for events such as reads or notifications to occur.

Notifications

Once a reader makes an observation or generates an alert, it must communicate notifications concerning those observations or alerts to the host. The communications can be initiated either by the reader (asynchronous communication) or via polling requests from the host (synchronous communication).

Asynchronous

Using an asynchronous approach, the reader notifies the host of an observation or alert either immediately or when a trigger occurs to cause the reader to send any pending notifications. Figure 6-2 shows the simplicity of this approach.

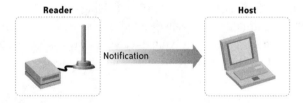

FIGURE 6-2. An asynchronous notification

This can be a very efficient and scalable method for sending notifications from a large number of readers to a host. One complex aspect of this approach is determining how to handle failover should a host fail. Depending on the transport, this can be resolved by typical load-balancing techniques.

Synchronous (polling)

For synchronous communications, the host sends a command to the reader and requests either an immediate observation or a report of any pending observations and alerts. The reader responds with a list of the requested information. The process of making repeated requests from the host, each followed by a single response from the reader, is called "polling" the reader. Figure 6-3 shows the steps.

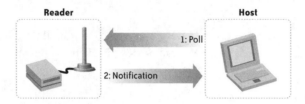

FIGURE 6-3. Acquiring notifications by polling

Polling is easily implemented and allows for hosts to fail over gracefully, but this approach imposes overhead in the form of additional CPU cycles on the host and reader and requires more usage of the transport; requests for notifications will often return an empty list, whereas with the asynchronous approach, communications generally occur only when new information is available.

> **NOTE**
>
> Some asynchronous approaches do include a "keepalive" feature, in which an otherwise empty notification goes out from reader to host at set intervals to indicate that the reader is still operating even though no notable observations or alerts have occurred. However, this is usually scheduled much less frequently than a reader poll would be in the synchronous approach.

Vendor Protocols

Different RFID reader vendors have created significantly different reader protocols, but all of them perform the same basic functions. In the following sections, we examine a simple "hello world" RFID application using reader protocols from two of the leading reader manufacturers, Alien and Symbol. The Symbol reader we discuss is the Matrics AR-400 (Symbol acquired another leading reader vendor, Matrics, in 2004).

Alien

Alien Technology prefers to use the terms Interactive mode and Autonomous mode for these two types of communication rather than synchronous and asynchronous, but the respective steps performed by the reader and host are the same. The Alien reader accepts commands over a serial port or through a telnet session via the Transmission Control Protocol (TCP). Some configuration commands may also be supplied through a web interface using HTTP GET and POST commands (implemented as a web GUI). Alien supports notifications of observations or alerts by email (via the Simple Mail Transfer Protocol), over a TCP socket, or over the serial port, using several configurable formats for the information. In the following example, we use an XML format to show a TCP socket notification. The host listens on a configurable socket. The reader connects to this socket, sends a notification like the following (give or take a few lines) to that port as XML text, and then closes the socket:

```
<Alien-RFID-Reader-Auto-Notification>
  <ReaderName>Dock Reader</ReaderName>
  <ReaderType>Alien RFID Tag Reader (Class 1 / 915Mhz) </ReaderType>
  <IPAddress>192.168.0.3</IPAddress>
  <CommandPort>23</CommandPort>
  <Time>2005/01/03 01:48:00</Time>
  <Reason>EXAMPLE MESSAGE FOR CHAPTER SIX</Reason>
  <Alien-RFID-Tag-List>
    <Alien-RFID-Tag>
      <TagID>0102 0304 0506 0709</TagID>
      <CRC>87B4</CRC>
      <DiscoveryTime>2005/01/02 23:40:03</DiscoveryTime>
      <Antenna>0</Antenna>
      <ReadCount>837</ReadCount>
    </Alien-RFID-Tag>
    <Alien-RFID-Tag>
      <TagID>2283 1668 ADC3 E804</TagID>
      <CRC>9FD0</CRC>
      <DiscoveryTime>2003/01/03 01:48:00</DiscoveryTime>
      <Antenna>0</Antenna>
      <ReadCount>1</ReadCount>
    </Alien-RFID-Tag>
  </Alien-RFID-Tag-List>
</Alien-RFID-Reader-Auto-Notification>
```

Writing a client to receive these notifications is as simple as attaching a daemon to the socket the reader is configured to connect to and streaming the incoming XML into a parser that updates a persistent store of some sort.

However, writing a complete middleware implementation becomes much more challenging when we consider the need to monitor and manage the reader, configure replacement readers, and push software upgrades to the reader as updates come out. Alien provides a management console for its readers, but it cannot manage readers from other vendors or other types of sensors. (Chapter 9 discusses reader management, along with management of other edge systems, in more detail.)

Symbol

The AR-400 from Symbol Technologies accepts commands as XML over HTTP or as XML over a TCP socket or a serial port; it also supports a vendor-specific byte stream protocol over a TCP or serial connection. Notifications may be configured as synchronous, which Symbol calls "Query mode," or asynchronous, called "Publish/Subscribe mode" in the documentation. The AR-400 supports the Simple Network Management Protocol (SNMP) for alerts and configuration and can also accept configuration as XML or byte stream commands. It supports Ethernet and serial transports.

The AR-400 has an embedded HTTP server, which provides the Reader Administration Console. To enable notifications, we first set the Host Notification link in the Event Notification Preferences page of the console to the following URL:

```
http://host.localdomain/cgi-bin/listener.cgi
```

The reader expects the servlet or CGI script at this URL to accept an oper argument, which may be test or notify. Our host is running its own web server and supports CGI scripts, so when the reader makes the following HTTP GET request:

```
http://host.localdomain/cgi-bin/listener.cgi?oper=test
```

the protocol requires the host script to respond with a properly formed HTTP response containing only the following as content:

```
<Matrics>
<HostAck/>
</Matrics>
```

To indicate that an event has occurred, the reader makes a request like the following:

```
http://host.localdomain/cgi-bin/listener.cgi?oper=notify
```

In this case, the host should again respond with:

```
<Matrics>
<HostAck/>
</Matrics>
```

and then make a request for an event list at:

```
http://dockdoor.localdomain/cgi-bin/dataproxy?oper=queryEvents
```

The list returned will contain all of the observations that have been generated by the reader since the last event query from the host. The list will be in the form:

```
<Matrics>
<EventList>
<Tag event="0" id="305000181CB50C8000001070" type="10000303900D432" uid="CCC"
time="41D8E1BE" RPL="1,2"/>
</EventList>
</Matrics>
```

Notice that although the host does request a list of observations, just as in a synchronous approach, this is still an asynchronous notification, because rather than polling the host waits for the reader to announce that observations are ready.

Looking at the information returned by the reader, we see a single XML tag named <Tag>. Table 6-1 breaks down the various attributes of <Tag>.

TABLE 6-1. <Tag> attribute values

Attribute	Values
event	0 = New tag 1 = Tag not visible 2 = Tag visibility changed 3 = Threshold event
id	A hex tag value
type	A hex value representing the EPC or Matrics type (in this case, EPC type 1 with four bytes for the General Manager and three bytes for the Object Class)
uid	A user-assignable ID for a particular tag or set of tags (think human-readable product names for SKUs)
time	The number of seconds since the Unix Epoch (0:00, Jan 1, 1970 GMT), in hex
RPL	A comma-delimited "Read Point List" indicating the read points at which the tag was observed (e.g., 1, 2)

EPCglobal Protocol Overview

The various vendor protocols are similar in intent, but different enough that no single client can communicate with all readers without a custom adapter to translate each vendor's protocol. EPCglobal is close to releasing a new standard for reader protocols to accompany its newest tag standards. This new standard will provide a minimal subset of the protocol for all vendors to implement (ensuring basic cross-compatibility) and a way of extending the protocol for vendor-specific features.

At the time of this writing, EPCglobal has not yet published the Reader Protocol Version 1.0 specification, but that document has moved into a last-call working draft. Because the protocol is not yet ready, no example implementation exists for us to compare with our vendor examples, but we can look at the parts of the protocol as currently described and see how EPC has defined the same procedures that we have seen before. (See Appendix B for information on where to obtain EPCglobal specifications for the EPCglobal Reader Protocol.) EPCglobal defines its Reader Protocol in terms of three layers, as shown in Figure 6-4.

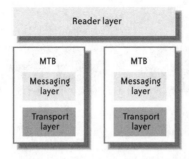

FIGURE 6-4. Layers of the EPCglobal Reader Protocol

Message Transport Bindings (MTBs) encapsulate the Messaging and Transport layers and present a standard interface to the Reader layer. The three layers may be defined as follows.

Reader layer

The Reader layer defines the allowable content and format of messages sent between the reader and host. This layer comprises the Open System Interconnection (OSI) Presentation and Application layers. The protocol specifically allows this layer to make use of multiple MTBs, although a particular instance will use only one MTB at a time. Also, regardless of the MTB, the reader can hold a conversation with only one host at a time.

Messaging layer

This layer lives on top of the Transport layer and is responsible for managing connections and security and for packaging the host commands and reader responses and notifications so they can pass back and forth on the Transport layer. Any encryption, authentication, or session management occurs in this layer. This layer describes how a conversation between the reader and host starts and stops and defines the shape of the *frame*, or the envelope in which messages pass back and forth. This layer is logically identical to the OSI Session layer.

Transport layer

This is the lowest layer, and it describes either the services provided by an OS or the hardware needed to support networking. It corresponds roughly to the OSI Physical, Data Link, and Network layers. The Transport layer is the physical connection and the networking connection between the reader and host—for instance, TCP over Ethernet using Cat 5 cables, an RS485 network over twisted pair, or a wireless Bluetooth implementation.

The following sections explore what goes on in each of these layers.

The Reader Layer

The Reader layer is made up of four subsystems: the Read subsystem, which is responsible for acquiring data; the Event subsystem, which smooths the incoming data and generates events; the Output subsystem, which collects and buffers events as well as determining which events to report to the host; and the Communication subsystem, which manages the conversation with the host. Figure 6-5 shows the subsystems.

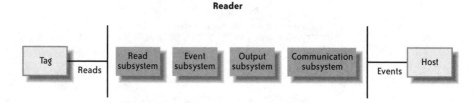

FIGURE 6-5. The four Reader subsystems

Read subsystem

The Read subsystem is responsible for reading tags and supplying tag information to the Event subsystem. Figure 6-6 shows the three stages in the Read subsystem.

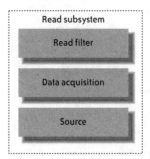

FIGURE 6-6. The Read subsystem stages

The three stages are each explained in more detail in the list below:

Source

> The Source stage reads a tag ID out of the ether. A source might be a single antenna or a logical grouping of antennas, or a checkout scanner reading optical bar codes. By keeping track of the source of a read and passing this information along to later stages, the protocol allows the Event subsystem, the Output subsystem, and eventually the host to make decisions based on the source of a read.

Data Acquisition

> This stage determines the timing of reads. Three parameters govern this timing: the duty cycle, the number of read cycles per trigger, and the read timeout. The duty cycle determines how often the reader will attempt to start a reading. Once started, the number of read cycles determines how many times the reader will attempt to read. The timeout determines how long the reader will wait before determining that no tag is present.

Read Filtering

> The Read Filtering stage drops or "filters out" tag reads that don't match a pattern set by the host. For instance, a pattern might say something like, "Show me every tag with a filter type of 2."

Data passes sequentially up the stack, with the Source stage feeding the Data Acquisition stage, which in turn feeds the Read Filtering stage. At the end of the process, the Read Filtering stage then feeds the Event subsystem. The Read subsystem is stateless, so every time it reads a tag, it's as if it were reading it for the first time. This subsystem doesn't know the difference between a newly arrived tag and a tag that has been detected in previous cycles; this discrimination must be made further up the chain by the Event subsystem.

Event subsystem

The Event subsystem is responsible for turning tag reads into meaningful events. Figure 6-7 shows the Event subsystem's single stage.

This stage is responsible for applying a smoothing filter over the data to help recognize the difference between a tag that has simply been missed in a few reads and one that is no longer present. The Read subsystem is stateless and so will report a tag's presence each

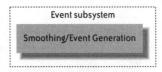

FIGURE 6-7. The single Event subsystem stage

time it is read. The Smoothing/Event Generation stage maintains state over time, so it can compare reads and pass on only meaningful events, such as the arrival of a new tag or the absence of a tag that was read previously. In other words, it winnows down the data generated by the Read subsystem to a more manageable volume. This stage also tracks the relationship between sources and tag IDs in order to distinguish between a tag that has remained near source A and one that has moved to source B (which may be a different antenna attached to the same reader). This state information is available for the host to query, but this is a rarely done in most cases. Events generated by this stage are sent to the Output subsystem to be filtered and put into reports that will be sent to the host.

Output subsystem

The Output subsystem decides what data the reader will report, buffers the data, and then sends the report either in response to a trigger set by the host or at the direct request of the host. Figure 6-8 shows the stages of the Output subsystem.

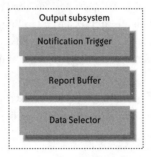

FIGURE 6-8. The Output subsystem stages

The three stages of the Output subsystem are outlined in the following list:

Data Selector

This stage applies the filters set previously by the host and rejects any data that doesn't fit those filters. This stage can also determine what fields are reported. To use a database analogy, the filter patterns do the work of a WHERE clause, while other commands issued by the host can set the fields, similar to the work a SELECT does in an SQL query. (For more about the fields available, see the next subsection, "Reports.")

Report Buffer

This stage is a holding place for events that have not yet been delivered to the host. The events are gathered into a list known as a report. The host may request these reports by polling the reader, or they may be delivered to the host via the notification channel when some trigger occurs. Events are always cleared from the Report Buffer as soon as they are delivered to the host. The protocol does not specify what should happen if the reader is power-cycled or the buffer's capacity is filled, but in most implementations, the buffer will lose its contents when power is lost and the buffer itself will be a simple FIFO or ring buffer that discards the oldest events in favor of the newest whenever it overflows.

Notification Trigger

This stage determines when to send reports to the host, according to triggers set previously by the host. For example, the host may ask to receive notifications every 2,000 milliseconds, or whenever the operator presses a button (at which point a digital input built into the reader transitions from 0 to 1).

Reports. The reports themselves are lists of events, with a set of host-configured fields for each event. The protocol describes a long list of fields that may appear in the report but requires reader vendors to implement only a small subset. This is one of the details that is likely to change in the future as more fields become mandatory and new optional fields are added. For now, Table 6-2 is a good baseline of mandatory fields that are likely to reappear in future protocol specifications.

TABLE 6-2. Report fields that readers must support

Name	Example	Description
ReaderID	urn:epc:id:giai:007654321.12345	A unique ID set by the manufacturer. The format is not specified, but here we assume a GIAI, as described in Chapter 4.
ReaderName	Dock Door Three	A name set by the host.
ReaderRole	Receiving	A role description set by the host.
TagID	315461CE90773593FE000000	The ID of the tag in binary format (shown here in hex), without the CRC.
AllSupported	ReaderID,ReaderName,ReaderRole,TagID, AllSupported	All of the fields supported by a reader. This is all the reader will return if no data selector is set.

Some of the most useful optional fields a reader might support are shown in Table 6-3.

TABLE 6-3. Important optional fields

Name	Example	Description
EventTimeUTC	0006:12:15:20:05:00.007	The time the event occurred in UTC, with millisecond precision. (The format is dependent on the MTB.)
TagIDasPureURI	urn:epc:id:sgtin:00012345.054322.4208	A pure identity in URI notation (see Chapter 4).
TagIDasTagURI	urn:epc:tag:sgtin-96:2.00012345.054322.4208	A tag identity in URI notation (see Chapter 4).

Triggers. The Reader Protocol defines one implicit trigger and two explicit triggers to drive activity through the processing stages:

Implicit trigger

The implicit trigger for activity is a request for information by the host over the command channel (channels are discussed in the next section, "The Messaging Layer"). This implies that the Data Acquisition stage will perform a read cycle over the sources and then pass the data through the stages, all the way up to the Report Buffer stage, for delivery to the host in a response on the command channel.

Explicit triggers

Two types of explicit triggers are:

Read trigger

This trigger fires the Data Acquisition stage in the same way as does a host READ command, but the data is buffered in the Report Buffer without the host being notified.

Notify trigger

This trigger causes reports in the Report Buffer to be delivered to the host, but does not cause any new reads to occur.

A host can also trigger a read directly using an IssueReadTrigger command. Again, this causes a read but doesn't trigger notification. Table 6-4 describes the types of triggers defined in the protocol. These triggers may be used as Read or Notify triggers. Reader vendors are not required by the protocol to implement these triggers, but many already do.

TABLE 6-4. Triggers

Trigger	Description	Parameters
Timer	This trigger fires every so-many milliseconds.	Milliseconds between triggers
IO Edge	This trigger fires when an "IO Pin" on a digital "IO Port" changes state from 1 to 0 or from 0 to 1. This doesn't have to be an actual I/O device and may instead represent flags set by the reader firmware.	Transition to: [0 | 1] IO Port IO Pin
IO Value	This trigger fires when the value of "IO Port" represents some arbitrary integer value. This may be some scaled analog input, or it may be a logical input generated by the reader firmware.	IO Port Integer trigger value (not a range)
Continuous	This trigger fires in a tight loop.	None
None	This trigger fires only if the host specifically fires it. (Read and Notify also happen when the host makes a synchronous READ.)	None
Vendor Extension	The reader vendor may add additional types of triggers.	Vendor-specific

Communication subsystem

The Communication subsystem is responsible for implementing the MTB on the reader side. Reports stored in the Report Buffer stage are sent to the Communication subsystem when the Notification Trigger stage fires. The MTB stage packages and translates the data in the report fields to comply with the particular Transport layer requirements. Figure 6-9 shows the single stage contained in the Communication subsystem.

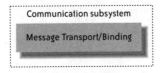

FIGURE 6-9. *The single Communication subsystem stage*

As described earlier, the MTB encapsulates the Messaging and Transport layers, which is equivalent to encapsulating the OSI Physical, Data Link, Network, and Session layers. This abstraction provides a simpler communication interface for the reader that may be implemented on a variety of transports, like Bluetooth or TCP/IP over 802.11b wireless Ethernet.

The Messaging Layer

The Messaging layer provides three message channels: a command channel, a notification channel, and an alarm channel for alerts. The word "channel" in this case indicates a discrete, logical conduit along which messages from the Reader layer can flow. Each channel has its own set of rules and a distinct purpose, as shown in Figure 6-10.

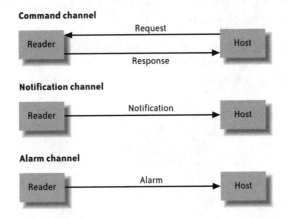

FIGURE 6-10. *The Messaging layer channels*

The following list further explicates those purposes:

Control channel

This channel is for synchronous messages in the form of requests initiated by the host. Both the requests from the host to the reader and the responses to those requests, from the reader to the host, travel on this channel. The reader never initiates communications over this channel.

Notification channel

This channel is for the reader to send asynchronous messages to the host. The host never initiates communications over this channel. A reader might send observations or alerts to a host in this way.

Alarm channel

> This channel is for the reader to send asynchronous alarm messages to the host. The host never initiates communications over this channel. A reader might send health monitoring information to the host in this way, such as an alarm indicating loss of connection to an antenna.

The Transport Layer

The various MTBs for the Reader Protocol are not completely defined yet. Also, vendors are allowed to support MTBs that are not defined in the protocol but that conform to the same channels and messages. The following sections describe two very different MTBs to help clarify how all of this comes together in practice.

The TCP MTB

The "Simple TCP" MTB is a minimal MTB that uses TCP as the transport. The most interesting thing about this MTB is some of the detail concerning connection handling. This MTB specifies that a reader will listen by default on port 8080 until a host makes a connection. Once a host establishes a connection, the reader should refuse all connections from other hosts. For developers used to working with other TCP-based applications, this behavior may seem odd, but it is a deliberate consequence of the Reader Protocol's limitation of one host for reader communication.

This MTB frames Reader layer messages with a header indicating the channel to which the message belongs and a 4-byte length, in octets, for the message, which includes both the header and the payload. Figure 6-11 illustrates the structure of the frame.

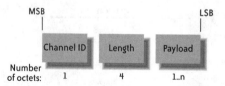

FIGURE 6-11. *Reader layer message frame*

The Reader layer message frame elements are explained further in the following list:

Channel ID

> This field can be either 2, for the control channel, or 3, for the notification channel. The ID for the alarm channel is currently undefined.

Length

> This field is an unassigned value from 5 to 2,147,483,648. (How's that for headroom?)

Payload

> This is the Reader layer message itself.

This frame is used for messages from the reader to the host and from the host to the reader. The host creates a connection and sends a HostGreeting message to the reader. The reader, on detecting the connection and without waiting for the HostGreeting message, sends a ReaderGreeting message. When the two parties receive the greetings, they begin processing Reader layer messages. The ReaderGreeting and HostGreeting are each five octets long, with the least significant octet set to a value of 5. The most significant octet of the ReaderGreeting is set to 1, while the most significant octet of the HostGreeting is set to 2. The other octets are set to 0. Figure 6-12 shows the structure of the greetings.

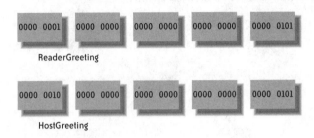

FIGURE 6-12. Host and reader greetings

The HTTP MTB

The HTTP MTB creates one HTTP 1.1 connection between the host and the reader for the command channel and a separate connection between host and reader for the notification channel. Note that this does not violate the protocol requirements because each of these connections is between the reader and a single host.

The reader listens by default on port 80. Just as in the TCP MTB, the reader accepts a connection from one host and then denies any subsequent connection attempts by other hosts. Since HTTP doesn't require a constant connection, the host may terminate the TCP connection and the reader will still consider itself "connected" to this single host, retaining any state and denying connections by other hosts. Once the connection is established, the host begins to send Reader layer messages. There is no equivalent to the TCP MTB's greetings. Messages are framed as HTTP GET, PUT, or POST commands with the actual Reader layer message encoded in the Request-Uri field of the HTTP request. The reader responds using an HTTP response with the Status-Code field set to indicate whether the message is a response to a command or an error. One proposed change is to use only POST and place the commands and responses into an XML document.

The notification channel is formed when the reader connects back to the host. This is accomplished using an HTTP URL supplied in the CONTACT argument of a command (on the command channel) from the host requesting notification.

Simple Lightweight RFID Reader Protocol

The Simple Lightweight RFID Reader Protocol (SLRRP) is an Internet-Draft from the Internet Engineering Task Force (IETF). This protocol has a stated goal of interoperating with both ISO 18000 and EPC readers. SLRRP differs significantly from the EPCglobal

Reader Protocol, but it is considered a "work in progress," so we may see some reconciliation between the two standards.

The host in SLRRP is always an RFID Reader Network Controller (RNC), which implements the host portion of the protocol and provides a client interface to connect to client applications and middleware. Figure 6-13 shows how the RNC sits between the readers and RFID middleware clients or application clients.

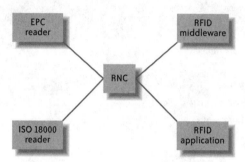

FIGURE 6-13. *The RNC sits between readers and RFID middleware*

The RNC implements the SLRRP protocol, so middleware clients and application clients may delegate the host role to the RNC and implement only one protocol—that required to communicate with the RNC itself. The current draft of SLRRP does not define this protocol for communication between the RNC and the clients. The reader-to-RNC protocol for SLRRP supports only a TCP transport and defines only a synchronous polling approach for notifications. The current Internet-Draft for SLRRP will have expired by the time this book hits the shelves, so it's possible that a more complete specification is already available, or will be soon. Please see Appendix B for where to get news and links to the SLRRP standard itself.

Future Protocols

Current efforts provide a standard reader protocol that addresses the basics of reading and writing tags, configuring readers, and monitoring reader health. Future protocols will deal with more advanced concerns, such as how to cover an area by extending the range of available readers when one reader fails, and how to integrate other edge devices (including other types of sensors) in order to capture more complex observations. A critical feature for any future protocol will be the capability for a reader to "announce itself" to the network and for middleware to be able to discover new readers and configure them without having to know beforehand which model of readers or even which vendor's readers will join the network. We will talk more about management of readers and other edge devices in Chapter 9.

Summary

In this chapter, we learned that:

- All reader protocols must describe how hosts and readers exchange commands, observations, and alerts.
- A reader may provide notification of observations and alerts to the host via responses to synchronous polling requests or via asynchronous messaging.

In addition:

- We saw examples of actual reader protocols from Alien, Symbol, EPCglobal, and the IETF.
- We talked about how future reader protocol standards will address more of the management and operation concerns arising from large deployments of RFID readers.

CHAPTER SEVEN

RFID Middleware

AS WE SAW IN **C**HAPTER 2, **SELECTING THE RIGHT TAGS AND READERS** and determining where to place the antennas is only the first step in building a working RFID system. Chapters 3 through 6 explained how some of the physical RFID components work. Now let's see how the information collected by this physical infrastructure can be exposed to and digested by your enterprise applications, and why RFID middleware is necessary.

Motivations

There are three primary motivations behind using RFID middleware: to encapsulate the applications from device interfaces; to process the raw observations captured by the readers and sensors so that applications see only meaningful, high-level events, thereby lowering the volume of information that they need to process; and to provide an application-level interface for managing readers and querying RFID observations. Most RFID middleware available today provides these features. Figure 7-1 shows the principal components of RFID middleware.

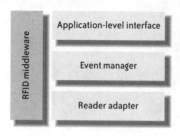

FIGURE 7-1. Components of RFID middleware

Chapter 2 provides the motivations for each of these components. Let's look at them individually.

Providing a Reader Interface

Consider how applications will interface with readers and other sensors in your physical infrastructure. One option is to have each application write to the APIs provided by each of the reader types, but this will not work for anything but trivial scenarios, as a typical enterprise is bound to use at least half a dozen different types of readers from one or more providers. Most companies would benefit by letting specialist software providers keep up with the reader APIs and write custom device drivers or reader interfaces. A reader adapter provides the means to eliminate the vagaries of the differing readers and APIs and expose a single abstract interface to your applications.

Filtering Events

A typical RFID-enabled distributor or retailer with several hundred or more stores will have hundreds, if not thousands, of readers. Each of these readers will be chirping away several times a second in order to read the RFID tags around them. As we discussed in Chapter 2, this can result in millions of RFID read observations per second. Exposing raw observations from the readers and sensors to enterprise applications would be akin to trying to drink water through a fire hose. In addition to the sheer volume of data, the raw observations need further processing to be meaningful to enterprise applications. Owing to the physics of radio frequency communications, the present technologies produce read rates that could be anywhere from 80 to 99 percent accurate in commercial environments. This means that if there were 100 tags near a reader, it would probably register anywhere between 80 and 99 tags for every read cycle. Because read rates are not 100 percent accurate, an item that is picked up in one read cycle could be missed during the next one. Say you have a smart shelf application that integrates with your inventory control system. Would you want to pass each of the raw observations from the smart shelf system to the inventory system? If you did so, the inventory control system, in addition to being bogged down by the sheer volume of incoming data, would have to continuously adjust to the fluctuating observations coming from the smart shelf readers.

As shown in Figure 7-2, the raw observations from RFID readers and sensors lack application-level context. More processing needs to be done to map these raw observations to coarser events that are meaningful to applications. For instance, an order management application would want to know when the in-store inventory for a particular item drops below its threshold. As you can imagine, an order management system wouldn't be the least bit interested in knowing whether RFID readers are employed in tracking the items in the stores, let alone how many readers there are per store and in what configuration. Exposing an order management system to every scan of an RFID reader without any application-level filtering would be unnecessary and counterproductive. Consequently, there's a need for middleware that can not only consolidate, aggregate, and filter raw observations coming from readers and sensors, but also provide application-level context. As you can see, this requires some processing of the raw RFID observations before they are sent to your applications. The process of smoothing out the raw RFID observations coming from readers and sensors or otherwise making them more meaningful for enterprise applications is called *event filtering*. The component that provides the event filtering functions is called the *event manager*.

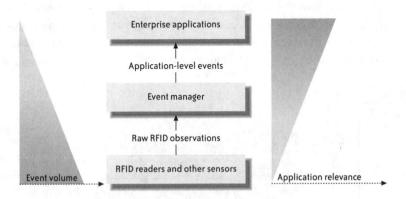

FIGURE 7-2. *Event volume and relevance through different layers of an RFID system*

Providing a Standards-Based Service Interface

One of the primary benefits of using RFID middleware is that it provides a standardized way of dealing with the flood of information created by the tiny RFID tags. What is needed is a service-oriented interface—we'll call this the application-level interface—that provides application-level semantics to the collection of RFID data. Following the principles of service-oriented architecture, we would want this interface to be loosely coupled and asynchronous and to follow the present-day web services standards.

Logical Architecture

RFID and other remote sensing technologies provide a level of automation that was not previously possible with labeling technologies such as bar codes that needed human intervention. However, this level of automation requires that the readers and sensors be monitored and managed remotely. A middleware solution that operates at the edges is best suited to monitoring and managing edge devices. Thus, in addition to the three functions described above, an RFID middleware solution should also provide, or at least integrate with, a management and monitoring interface.

More data and more transactions mean a greater load on your network, server, and storage infrastructure. Enterprise applications are generally deployed in data centers, so exposing them directly to the RFID reader observations will not only strain your applications but also introduce a lag in processing and tax your WAN infrastructure. Therefore, except for in trivial applications or proofs of concept, you should plan on using RFID middleware between your applications and your edge devices. This middleware should, at a minimum, encapsulate the peculiarities of the available reader types from your applications and allow them to focus on meaningful, application-level events without being bombarded by raw observations piped in from readers. As mentioned previously, you should also look for remote monitoring and management capabilities in such middleware.

Figure 7-3 shows a conceptual model of the RFID middleware. The RFID middleware receives raw observations from one or more data sources. A data source can be any sensor that collects data about the physical world, like an RFID reader or temperature sensor. After receiving observations from the readers, the event manager component of the middleware aggregates, transforms, or filters them to prepare them for consumption by applications. In addition to making the RFID observations more relevant to applications, the event manager helps reduce the sheer volume of data that the applications must process.

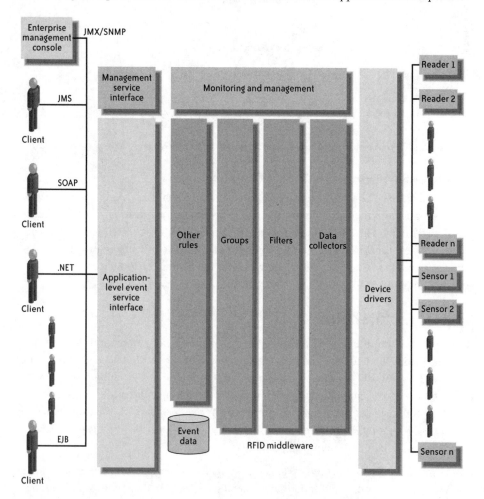

FIGURE 7-3. Conceptual architecture for an RFID middleware product

As shown in Figure 7-3, RFID middleware can support reader discovery, provisioning, monitoring, and management; provide data collection, translation, aggregation, filtering, and grouping mechanisms; support service-oriented interfaces using standards such as Java, J2EE, .NET, and web services; and offer remote provisioning, monitoring, and management capabilities.

While there are many possible implementations of this logical architecture, we're going to examine the one you are most likely to encounter: EPCglobal's Application Level Events (ALE) specification. The ALE specification defines a reader-neutral interface for receiving events from RFID readers and filtering and grouping them. The remainder of this chapter provides an overview of the ALE 1.0 specification as published by EPCglobal. We'll describe this specification in considerable detail so that you can familiarize yourself with its key concepts and API, but you should be aware that several vendors' implementations of the ALE specification are available in the market, each providing its own extensions and benefits. We'll cover a few of these implementations toward the end of this chapter. You can reference the Application Level Events specification in its entirety at *http://epcglobalinc.org*.

Application Level Events Specification

The ALE specification is the application-level interface standard developed by EPCglobal to allow clients to obtain filtered and consolidated EPC observations from a variety of sources. The ALE interface allows clients to set up event processing methods and request filtered events in the form of reports. Like its predecessor Savant (discussed in the sidebar "ALE and Savant"), the ALE specification provides a means to push EPC data processing nearer to the source of that data. It does so by defining a service interface and an interaction model between ALE clients and ALE servers. However, unlike the Savant specification, the ALE specification does not dictate how the service interface must be implemented or where it can be deployed. For example, an ALE service can be deployed on its own, on a reader, or on an application server cluster. In addition, the ALE specification provides vendors with the ability choose on the implementation technology. As long as the ALE interface specification requirements are met, the service will be considered EPCglobal ALE specification–compliant (although EPCglobal does plan to provide a means of testing to certify software as ALE-compliant). The principal benefits of the ALE specification include:

Standards for event management
: At its core, the ALE specification provides a reader-neutral interface for receiving, filtering, and grouping events from RFID readers. Applications using ALE-compliant middleware don't have to have device drivers for individual readers and don't have to use their proprietary programming interfaces.

Extensibility
: The ALE specification is highly extensible. For instance, although the ALE specification targets EPC event sources, you can create extensions to connect to non-EPC tags or interface with devices other than RFID readers.

Separation of interface from implementation

The ALE specification provides an interface between clients and RFID middleware, while leaving the implementation details to the vendors. This approach allows vendors choices in terms of technology platforms, deployment options, add-on features, and so on. For example, the software providing an ALE service could be deployed as a standalone module at the edge or inside of an application container, or it could reside on an RFID reader. Each deployment option has its own benefits and drawbacks. The implementation details are left to you.

The Application Level Events specification provides a WS-*-compliant web services bindings interface for accessing application-level events services. Implementations have the flexibility to expose the ALE interface using either a wire protocol (such as SOAP/HTTP) or a language API.

ALE AND SAVANT

Before ALE came about, the Auto-ID Center had proposed a component called a "Savant." The term "Savant" generally meant any piece of software situated between a group of data sources (readers) and enterprise applications with the specific aim of filtering data. The Savant specification was the original attempt at providing a standard for RFID event processing, but it focused more on how the event managers were implemented than on the services they provided. The Savant specification has been deprecated in favor of EPCglobal's specification for RFID event management, the ALE specification.

Before diving into the ALE service interface, let's first familiarize ourselves with some important concepts and terms.

Key Concepts and Terminology

To understand how the ALE specification works, we need to describe some key concepts and terms. We will begin by describing event originators. We will then look at read cycles and event cycles. Once we understand the concepts behind event originators and event cycles, we will look at the primary interaction models supported between applications and RFID middleware that implements the ALE specification.

Event originators

An *event originator* is any device that captures the presence of an RFID tag or any other observation from the physical world. RFID readers and sensors are examples of event originators. The ALE specification distinguishes a physical device from a Reader (we will capitalize the term "Reader" when it is referred to in the context of the ALE specification).

Within the context of the ALE specification, a physical device can be an RFID reader with one or more antennas, an EPC-compatible bar code scanner, or any similar device. The ALE specification defines a Reader as an abstract concept. Essentially, a *Reader* is a data source that provides raw EPC events (or observations). A Reader can be manifested in a variety of ways:

A Reader mapping to a single physical device
> A Reader may be implemented as a single physical device, e.g., a single-antenna RFID reader, an EPC-compatible bar code scanner, or a reader with multiple antennas where the observations from all the antennas are aggregated.

Several Readers mapping to the same physical device
> A Reader can manifest as multiple devices, such as in the case of a reader that has multiple antennas that are treated as distinct sources.

A Reader mapping to multiple physical devices
> Multiple readers can be configured to work together to derive synthesized observations. For instance, two or more readers could be used to triangulate location information.

The ALE specification also supports the concept of *logical readers*, which is a label (or a name) used to refer to one or more Readers. Essentially, this is a grouping mechanism provided by the ALE specification for cases in which you want to have a set of Readers capturing observations from a particular area. As an example, if you had a warehouse with 10 loading docks, each of which had a couple of Readers, you could group them under one or more logical readers. This way the application could query a small number of logical readers for incoming product information rather than having to aggregate events from each of the individual Readers.

The concept of logical readers enables applications to be encapsulated from the deployment configurations of readers. For instance, you could have a logical reader called "loadingdock 1" that maps to multiple physical readers and sensors in your loading dock(s). Over time, as your physical reader configurations change, you can just change the mapping between physical and logical readers—you won't have to reprogram your application.

Read cycles

To understand event management, it is important to understand how events are originated and passed from the Readers to the ALE server and then on to the clients of the ALE server. A Reader can scan for RFID tags or other physical observations at a set frequency or on demand. When scanning is done at a set frequency, each scan is called a *read cycle*.

A read cycle is a unit of interaction with a Reader. Each read cycle results in a Reader returning a set of RFID observations. In the context of the ALE specification, each observation is an Electronic Product Code (EPC). The ALE specification does not restrict how Readers support read cycle timing. Read cycles can be based on time duration, data volume, other sensor inputs, and so on. Figure 7-4 depicts read cycles coming from a single reader.

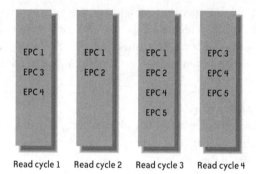

Read cycle 1   Read cycle 2   Read cycle 3   Read cycle 4

FIGURE 7-4. Example read cycles

The set of EPCs read in a read cycle is denoted by an *S*. Four read cycles are depicted in Figure 7-4:

    S1 = {EPC1, EPC3, EPC4}
    S2 = {EPC1, EPC2}
    S3 = {EPC1, EPC2, EPC4, EPC5}
    S4 = {EPC3, EPC4, EPC5}

This means that, for example, Read Cycle 1 (S1) returns the following observations: EPC1, EPC3, and EPC4.

Event cycles

Sometimes, an application may want information collected over several read cycles. For example, an inventory management system may want to get updates every hour on what inventory items should be ordered. This suggests that we need a higher-level abstraction that can group a series of read cycles. Here is where the concept of the event cycle comes in.

An *event cycle* is a unit of interaction that a client uses with an ALE service. There is considerable flexibility in how event cycles map to read cycles. For instance, an event cycle can span multiple read cycles, and multiple event cycles can span a given set of read cycles. An event cycle can also span read cycles from multiple readers. Given this flexibility, it is important to note that a client sees an event cycle as a unit and does not see the individual read cycles that make up a given event cycle.

Continuing with the example of read cycles depicted in Figure 7-3, let's say that Event Cycle 1 from Client 1 spans the first three read cycles: Read Cycle 1, Read Cycle 2, and Read Cycle 3 (see Figure 7-5). Since the event cycle is a unit of interaction between a client and an ALE service, the client will not see the individual sets of EPCs collected by the read cycles. It is possible in this case that all the client wants to know is the union of all the EPC observations collected within the event cycle. Thus, our event cycle (E1) would return S1 U S2 U S3 and would report the following observations:

    E1 = S1 U S2 U S3 = {EPC1, EPC2, EPC3, EPC4}

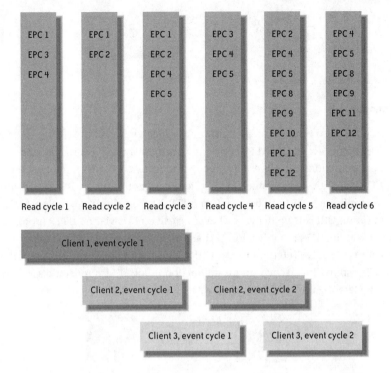

EPC 1	EPC 1	EPC 1	EPC 3	EPC 2	EPC 4
EPC 3	EPC 2	EPC 2	EPC 4	EPC 4	EPC 5
EPC 4		EPC 4	EPC 5	EPC 5	EPC 8
		EPC 5		EPC 8	EPC 9
				EPC 9	EPC 11
				EPC 10	EPC 12
				EPC 11	
				EPC 12	
Read cycle 1	Read cycle 2	Read cycle 3	Read cycle 4	Read cycle 5	Read cycle 6

Client 1, event cycle 1

Client 2, event cycle 1   Client 2, event cycle 2

Client 3, event cycle 1   Client 3, event cycle 2

FIGURE 7-5. Mapping event cycles to read cycles

More than one event cycle can be active at a time, and different event cycles can begin and end on different read cycles. Multiple event cycles can arise from a single client, as that client can initiate multiple simultaneous requests. Similarly, multiple event cycles can arise as a result of multiple clients making simultaneous requests.

Event cycles and read cycles are important concepts that allow applications to specify the time intervals or event windows for capturing events. Because event cycles can span multiple read cycles, they enable applications to set up logical, more meaningful observation windows.

Interaction Models

Now that we appreciate the flexibility that the ALE specification affords by distinguishing between read cycles and event cycles, let's look at the interaction models available between a client and an ALE service. The interaction models supported by the ALE specification should come as no surprise to application developers: a client can either request services on demand (synchronous mode) or register for information to be sent to it when certain conditions are met (asynchronous mode).

Synchronous mode

The primary interaction model is a request/response models, wherein all the method calls into the ALE service are executed synchronously. Figure 7-6 shows the synchronous interaction model. The ALE specification supports two modes of interaction in the synchronous model: immediate and polling. We will cover both of these modes in depth a little later in this chapter, under "Usage Scenarios."

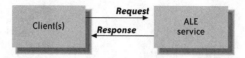

FIGURE 7-6. Synchronous interaction model

Asynchronous mode

The ALE interface also provides an asynchronous model, wherein the clients can subscribe to events. As events occur, the ALE service asynchronously delivers the data back to the clients. Implementations can choose between various messaging technologies, including JMS, TIBCO, MQ-Series, email, and SOAP. Clients use notification URIs to subscribe to events. The notification URI can be based on HTTP, TCP, or simple file types. An HTTP-based notification URI sets up delivery of event cycle reports via the HTTP protocol, using the POST operation. A TCP notification URI allows delivery of event cycle reports using raw TCP connections. A FILE notification URI allows writing of event cycle reports to a file. Figure 7-7 shows the asynchronous interaction model. This model is also discussed further in the later section "Usage Scenarios."

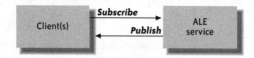

FIGURE 7-7. Asynchronous interaction model

Data elements

Now that we've covered the primary interaction models, let's look at the principal data elements exchanged between the components.

At its core, a client's main purpose is to request EPC data. It does so by providing an event cycle specification (ECSpec) to the ALE service. An ECSpec describes an event cycle and provides specifications for the reports that should be generated. The ECSpec is one of the two primary data types associated with the ALE API (the other one is the event cycle report, or ECReport). An ECSpec specifies rules for determining the start and end of event cycles and the reports to be generated from them. It also contains a list of logical readers, as an event cycle draws data from the read cycles of one or more Readers. A sample ECSpec looks like this:

```
ECSpec

readers : List
// An ECSpec contains a list of logical readers, as an event cycle
// draws data from the read cycles of one or more Readers.

Boundaries : ECBoundarySpec
// Specifies how the beginning and the end of event cycles are
// to be determined.
```

```
reportSpecs : List
// Specifies a list of reports to be returned after an event cycle
// is executed.

includeSpecInReports : boolean
// If set to true, the ALE implementation includes the complete
// ECSpec in the reports that are generated.

<<extension point>>
```

A *report* in ALE-speak is the output from an event cycle, which is returned as an ECReport instance. A report specification, represented as ECReportSpec, provides filtering, grouping, and other data processing instructions. Figure 7-8 shows the primary data elements. We'll discuss these further in the ""Data Model" section.

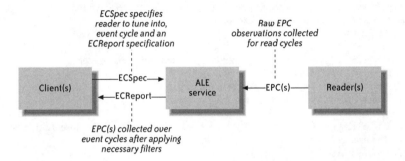

FIGURE 7-8. Primary data elements

ALE Service Interface

Now that we understand the principal concepts and terms underlying the ALE specification, let's look at the primary ALE service interface. The EPCglobal ALE specification provides an abstract definition for the primary ALE API. The specification also provides a WS-I-compliant SOAP binding for the ALE API. All that the ALE specification requires is that the vendor implementations are compliant with the WS-I specification for its interface schema and SOAP bindings. Figure 7-9 shows the main ALE interface.

```
                       <<interface>>
                        ALE service
  +define(String: specName, ECSpec: spec): void
  +undefine(String: specName): void
  +getECSpec(String: specName): ECSpec
  +getECSpecNames(): String[]
  +subscribe(String: specName, String: notificationURI, String: notificationURI): void
  +unsubscribe(String: specName, String: notificationURI, String: notificationURI): void
  +poll(String: specName): ECReports
  +immediate(ECSpec: spec): ECReports
  +getSubscribers(String: specName, String: notificationURI): notificationURI[]
  +getStandardVersion(): String
  +getVendorVersion(): String
```

FIGURE 7-9. Main ALE service interface

The primary interface for the ALE service is represented below in Java syntax (vendor implementations will differ somewhat):

```
public interface ALE {
    public void define(String specName, ECSpec spec) throws
DuplicateNameExpcetion,ECSpecValidationException, SecurityException,
ImplementationException;
    // Defines an ECSpec
    // An ECSpecValidationException is raised if:
    // - the readers parameter is not defined or
    // contains unknown logical reader names; or
    // - if the reportSpecs parameter is not
    // defined, is null, or contains
    // duplicate ECReport names

    public void undefine(String specName) throws NoSuchNameException,
SecurityException, ImplementationException;
    // Releases the specName

    public ECSpec getECSpec(String specName) throws NoSuchNameException,
SecurityException, ImplementationException;
    // Releases the event cycle specification
    // mapped to the specified specification name

    public String[] getECSpecNames() throws SecurityException, ImplementationException;
    // Returns all the event cycle specifications
    // defined with the ALE service

    public void subscribe(String specName, String notificationURI) throws
NoSuchNameException,invalidURIException, DuplicateSubscriptionException,
SecurityException, ImplementationException;
    // Subscribes an ALE client to receive reports
    // for events returned per the specified
    // event cycle

    public void unsubscribe(String specName, String notificationURI) throws
NoSuchNameException,invalidURIException, DuplicateSubscriptionException,
SecurityException, ImplementationException;
    // Unsubscribes the ALE client for the
    // specified event cycle specifications

    public ECReports poll(String specName) throws
NoSuchNameException,SecurityException, ImplementationException;

    public ECReports immediate(ECSpec spec) throws ECSpecValidationException,
SecurityException, ImplementationException;
    // An ECSpecValidationException is raised if:
    // - the readers parameter is not defined or
    // contains unknown logical reader names; or
    // - if the reportSpecs parameter is not
    // defined, is null, or contains duplicate
    // ECReport names

    public notificationURI[] getSubscribers(String specName) throws
NoSuchNameExpcetion, SecurityException, ImplementationException;
    // Returns a list of subscriber URIs
```

```
public String getStandardVersion() throws SecurityException;
// Returns the version number of the ALE Specification

public String getVendorVersion() throws SecurityException;
// Returns the version number relevant to the vendor
```

}

Usage Scenarios

As discussed earlier, the ALE specification supports both synchronous and asynchronous models of interaction between the clients and the ALE service. Now that we have seen the ALE interface API, let's look at how these interaction models are intended to be used. We'll also develop a deeper understanding of some of the key components of the ALE schema.

Synchronous mode

Let's start by looking at how a client would make a one-time request for events coming from a set of Readers and, along the way, specifying how the raw EPC observations should be filtered and grouped. The ALE specification calls this mode of interaction "immediate."

Immediate mode. Immediate mode is one of the two synchronous methods available to access an ALE service. The client first creates and configures an ECSpec, and then invokes the "immediate" service of the ALE server. The ALESpec looks at the ECSpec that is passed as a parameter of the immediate service. As shown in the previous section, "Data elements," the ECSpec specifies a list of Readers from which the client wants to receive events. It also specifies the event cycle boundaries (in the boundary object) and the filtering and grouping mechanisms for the raw EPC observations collected from the Readers in the report specifications, or ECReportSpecs. An ECSpec can contain many report specifications, which gives the client multiple ways to filter and group data coming from the same raw observation set. For instance, if you wanted to group all the EPCs for razors separately from the EPCs for shaving cream, you could ask the ALE service to do it for you. We will look into filtering and grouping capabilities in more depth in the later section "Filtering and Grouping."

Figure 7-10 is a sequence diagram depicting what happens when a client invokes the immediate service. This request is supported by the ALE service, which registers with the necessary set of Readers for the appropriate read cycles and gets the event data back from the Readers. The ALE service digests the data and returns the results after processing the request.

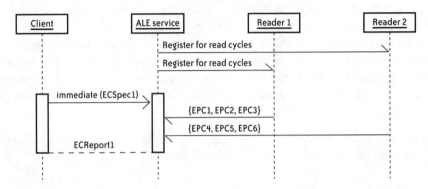

FIGURE 7-10. Sequence diagram for immediate mode

We just saw how the ECSpec provides rules for getting raw EPC observations from Readers, processing them through filters, grouping them in data sets, and finally packaging them as reports. Now let's take a look at the state transitions for the ECSpec as a client submits it for processing in the immediate mode. As shown in Figure 7-11, the ECSpec has three states:

Defined but Unrequested

An ECSpec enters this state when, using the defined method of the ALE service, it is created and associated with an ECSpecName (a string). The immediate mode is intended for one-time requests of data. Thus, in this mode there is no need to assign a logical label (ECSpecName) to the ECSpec for later reuse. Polling and asynchronous modes (discussed later in this section) use the Defined but Unrequested state.

Requested

When an ECSpec is in the Requested state, it is awaiting processing by the ALE service.

Active

When an ECSpec is in the Active state, the ALE server accumulates raw EPC observations from Readers according to the specified event cycle.

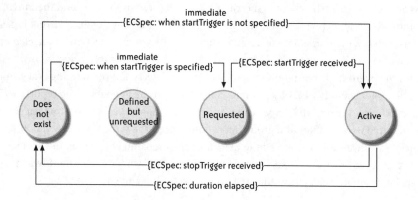

FIGURE 7-11. ECSpec state model—immediate mode

When the client invokes the immediate method, the ECSpec sent as a parameter is considered to be in the Requested state if its boundary specification (ECBoundarySpec)contains a valid start trigger (ECSpec.ECBoundarySpec.startTrigger). What this means is that the start trigger has to go off for the ALE server to start collecting data based on the ECSpec. This trigger could be an input received by another sensor—for example, an electronic eye on a conveyor belt for a palletizing application. Upon receiving a corresponding stop trigger (specified in the ECSpec.ECBoundarySpec.stopTrigger attribute), the ALE server stops collecting data from Readers targeted by this ECSpec and returns the filtered and grouped data to the client.

If a start trigger is not specified, the ECSpec is considered to be in the Active state. In this case, upon the expiration of the specified duration for collecting events (ECSpec.

ECBoundarySpec.duration), the ALE server stops collecting data from the Readers corresponding to the current ECSpec and returns the filtered and grouped data to the client.

Polling mode. A client that wants to get regularly scheduled updates rather than one-tme reports, on EPC event data would use the ALE server's polling interface. Polling is executed synchronously. To some extent, it is similar to subscribing and then unsubscribing after an event cycle is generated. As shown in Figure 7-12, the client first creates an ECSpec and then assigns it a logical name by invoking the define method of the ALE service. Once an ECSpec is defined, the client can invoke the poll method. To process the poll method, the ALE service looks through the ECSpec and determines the event boundaries, logical readers, and so on (similar to the process explained for the immediate mode). Upon the completion of an event cycle, the ALE service returns the reports containing the requested EPC data.

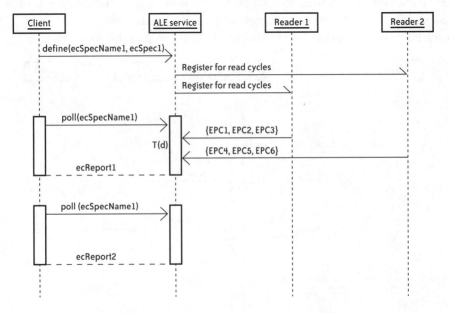

FIGURE 7-12. Sequence diagram for polling mode

Let's look at how the ECSpec state transitions work for polling clients. The ECSpec reaches the Defined but Unrequested state when the client invokes the "define" service. When the ALE service is asked to poll on a defined event cycle specification, it awaits a start trigger to begin recording the Reader observations and processing them according to the filtering and grouping mechanisms requested by the client (again, these are defined as part of the event cycle specification). During this period, the ECSpec is in the Active mode. When the polling period expires, the ECSpec goes back to the Defined but Unrequested state. If the client wants to collect more data based on this specification, it needs to invoke the poll method again, as shown in Figure 7-13.

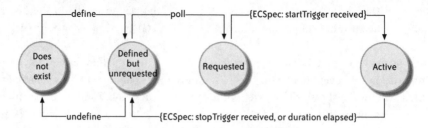

FIGURE 7-13. *ECSpec state model—polling mode*

Asynchronous mode

The asynchronous ALE service interaction mode uses the classic publish/subscribe mechanism used in other asynchronous messaging architectures. As shown in Figure 7-14, after defining an event specification, the client subscribes to get regular updates on it. Once subscribed, the client will get regular filtered and grouped EPC data from the ALE service. When it no longer wishes to receive updates, the client can unsubscribe.

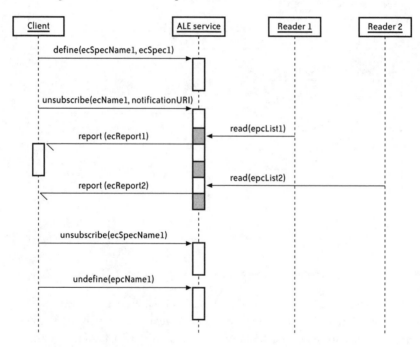

FIGURE 7-14. *Asynchronous interaction model*

In the asynchronous interaction mode, the ALE specification allows the reports to be published in three ways: over HTTP, over TCP, and written directly to files. This is accomplished by clients registering three types of URIs as subscribers. Here is a brief description of each of the notification URIs:

HTTP notification URI

The HTTP notification URI allows ECReports to be published over the HTTP protocol. The reports are sent in the XML format using the HTTP POST operation. The HTTP URI takes one of the following familiar forms:

```
http://hostname:port/remainder_of_URL
http://hostname/remainder_of_URL
```

The hostname is the DNS name or IP address of the subscriber, and the port is the TCP port on which the subscriber is listening. If the port number is not provided, it defaults to 80. The remainder_of_url portion provides a URL to a resource running on the hostname:port server that will be able to process the HTTP POST operation.

TCP notification URI

The TCP notification URI allows clients to subscribe to ALE servers using TCP connections. The ECReports are again delivered in XML format. The TCP notification URI uses the following format:

```
tcp://hostname:port
```

FILE notification URI

If a client subscribes using a FILE notification URI, the ALE server will publish the ECReports in the XML format in a file. The ALE service will append the output of the event cycles to the target file. The FILE notification URI uses one of the following formats:

```
file://hostname/path//hostname/path/
file://path
```

As before, the hostname is the DNS name or IP address of the machine on whose filesystem the reports should be published. The path is the path to the file within the host's filesystem.

Figure 7-15 depicts the state model for the ECSpec in the asynchronous mode. As shown, when a client subscribes to a valid ECSpec, the event specification enters the Requested state. Once the ECSpec is in the Requested state, the ALE service will begin collecting and processing EPC data either when it receives a start trigger (ECSpec.ECBoundarySpec.startTrigger) or when the repeat period elapses after the previous event cycle. Upon receiving a stop trigger (ECSpec.ECBoundarySpec.stopTrigger) or when the event cycle (ECSpec.ECBoundarySpec.duration) expires, the ECSpec goes back to the Requested state.

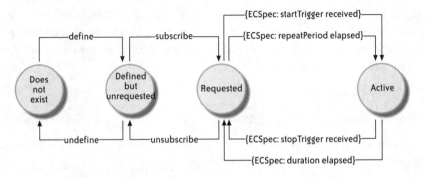

FIGURE 7-15. ECSpec state model—asynchronous mode

Filtering and Grouping

A client can specify how the raw EPC observations should be processed before they are included in the report. The ALE specification provides two distinct mechanisms for event processing: filtering and grouping. *Filtering* provides capabilities to tune into specific patterns in the event data. *Grouping* provides means to group data collected from different Readers and over multiple event cycles. The ECFilterSpec and ECGroupSpec are provided for filter patterns and grouping patterns, respectively. An ECSpec can contain multiple report specifications, and a client can specify a filter specification (ECFilterSpec) and a group specification (ECGroupSpec) as a part of every report specification (ECReportSpec):

```
ECReportSpec

reportName : string
reportSet : ECReportSetSpec
filter : ECFilterSpec
group : ECGroupSpec
output : ECReportOutputSpec
reportIfEmpty : boolean
reportOnlyOnChange : boolean
<<extension point>>
```

Filters provided by the ECFilterSpec should be applied to the raw EPC observations coming from Readers before grouping patterns are applied:

```
ECFilterSpec

includePatterns : List
excludePatterns : List
<<extension point>>
```

The ECGroupSpec specifies how filtered EPCs should be grouped for reporting:

```
ECGroupSpec

patternList : List

<<extension point>>
```

Filtering

Clients can specify filtering schemes with the help of two pattern lists: includePatterns and excludePatterns. An EPC is included in the final report if it matches *at least* one pattern in the includePatterns list *and* does not match *any* pattern in the excludePatterns list. The expression below provides a formal definition:

```
F(R) = { epc | epc ∈ R &
(epc ∈ includePattern1 | epc ∈ includePattern2 |  ...  | epc ∈ includePatternN) &
(epc ∉ excludePattern1 & epc ∉ excludePattern2 &  ...  & epc ∉ excludePatternN)}
```

A filtering pattern denotes a single EPC or a set of EPCs and is formatted as a URI string. A filtering pattern uses the following general format:

```
urn:epc:pat:TagFormat:<data fields>
```

TagFormat denotes a tag format, as defined by EPCglobal's Tag Data Specification (tag formats are also discussed in Chapter 4). The general representation for the data fields is given below, but these fields will differ based on the specific tag format used:

`urn:epc:pat:TagFormat:FilterValue.CompanyPrefix.ItemReference.SerialNumber`

The FilterValue.CompanyPrefix.ItemReference.SerialNumber fields map to the data fields of the EPC. The TagFormat used determines the number of fields used to specify the EPC and their meaning. For example, the GID-96 format lacks the FilterValue data field and represents an EPC as follows:

`urn:epc:pat:GID-96:CompanyPrefix.ItemReference.SerialNumber`

Each of the data fields (FilterValue.CompanyPrefix.ItemReference.SerialNumber) can be a decimal, an asterisk/wildcard (*), or a decimal range (denoted as [low-high]). Table 7-1 provides some example filters.

TABLE 7-1. Example filters for the GID-96 tag format

Filter	Types used	Description
`urn:epc:pat:gid-96:18.200.3000`	Decimal	Returns the EPC that has Company Prefix 18, Item Reference 200, and Serial Number 3000.
`urn:epc:pat:gid-96:18.200.*`	Wildcard, decimal	Returns EPCs for all the Serial Numbers that are matched for the Company Prefix 18 and Item Reference 200.
`urn:epc:pat:gid-96:18.[190-200].*`	Range, wildcard	Returns EPCs for all the Serial Numbers that are matched for the Company Prefix 18 and Item References in the range of 190–200.
`urn:epc:pat:gid-96:*.*.*`	Wildcard	Returns all the EPCs for the GID-96 tag format.

We have taken a conceptual approach to filtering in this section, as most programmers probably won't have to worry about the nitty-gritty of all the tag formats and filtering options available to them. Please see Chapter 4 for further details on filters. For readers who need more familiarity with the various tag formats and filters available to them (or for those who are just gluttons for punishment), EPCglobal's Tag Data Specification is the authoritative source.

Grouping

Grouping patterns use mechanisms similar to the ones described above for filtering, but in addition to decimal, wildcard (*), and range specifiers, X is used as a special value in the URI fields. Table 7-2 lists all the parameters available for specifying grouping patterns.

TABLE 7-2. URI field values for grouping patterns

Pattern URI field	Description
*	Group together all the values in this field.
X	Create a different group for each distinct value of this field.
Number	Only EPCs having the specified number in this field will belong to this group.
Range [Low-high]	All the EPCs whose value for this field falls within the specified range will belong to this group.

Table 7-3 lists some examples of grouping patterns.

TABLE 7-3. Examples of grouping patterns

Pattern URI	Description
urn:epc:pat:sgtin-64:*.*.*.*	Group together all the EPCs.
urn:epc:pat:sgtin-64:X.*.*.*	Group by Filter Value.
urn:epc:pat:sgtin-64:*.*.X.*	Group by Item Type.
urn:epc:pat:sgtin-64:X.X.*.*	Group by Filter Value and Company Prefix.
urn:epc:pat:sgtin-64:3.*.*.[0-100]	Group together everything that has 3 as the Filter Value and a Serial Number in the 0–100 range.
urn:epc:pat:sgtin-64:3.X.*.[0-100]	Create a separate group for every company and include all the EPCs that have 3 as the Filter Value and Serial Numbers in the 0–100 range.

The ALE specification requires that every filtered EPC that is part of an event cycle be part of exactly one group. To ensure that each EPC will belong to only one group, the specification requires that the patterns used for grouping must not all include the same results (i.e., must be disjoint).

Data Model

In this section, we'll take a look at important data elements of the ALE specification. If you are not going to be programming using ALE-compliant middleware, you can safely skip this section.

Figure 7-16 shows a class diagram for the important data types in the ALE specification. As shown, an ECSpec provides a means to specify the data that a client is interested in receiving; the client specifies the names of Readers from which it wants to receive data, and how the event cycles map to the Readers' read cycles. The ECBoundarySpec data type is used for specifying the event boundaries. Instructions for filtering (ECFilterSpec) and grouping (ECGroupSpec) the Reader observations are provided in the ECReportSpec. The ECReportSpec also provides specifications for what data should be reported back and how.

The ECReport defines what kind of reports the ALE servers will produce. An ECReport provides a single report produced within an event cycle. Data within an ECReport is grouped using ECReportGroup instances. Each instance of ECReportGroup represents one grouping of EPCs within an ECReport. The EPCs can be reported in hexadecimal or decimal format. ECReportGroupListMember type provides the template for how the EPCs are reported back.

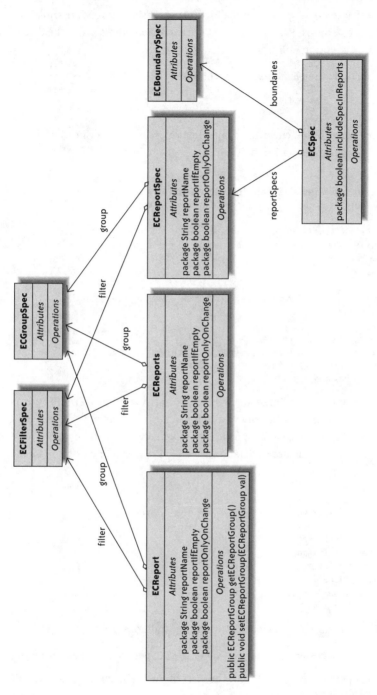

FIGURE 7-16. ALE schema

Please note that the ALE specification allows for extension by vendors and also by EPCglobal in its future versions. We have marked the extension points inside the data type definitions using <<extension point>>.

Let's take a look at the elements of the ALE schema.

ECSpec

One or more reports are generated from an event cycle. The specifications for the reports that are generated are described by ECSpecs.

```
readers : List
// An ECSpec contains a list of logical readers, as an event cycle
// draws data from the read cycles of one or more Readers.

Boundaries : ECBoundarySpec
// Specifies how the beginning and the end of event cycles are
// to be determined.

reportSpecs : List
// Specifies a list of reports to be returned after an event cycle
// is executed.

includeSpecInReports : boolean
// If set to true, the ALE implementation includes the complete
// ECSpec in the reports that are generated.
<<extension point>>
```

ECSpec is one of the two primary data types associated with the ALE API (the other one is ECReport). An ECSpec specifies rules for determining the start and end of event cycles and the reports that are to be generated from those event cycles. It also contains a list of logical readers, as an event cycle draws data from the read cycles of one or more Readers.

ECBoundarySpec

The ECBoundarySpec specifies the start and end of event cycles.

```
startTrigger : ECTrigger
stopTrigger : ECTrigger
repeatPeriod : ECTime
duration : ECTime
stableSetInterval : ECTime
<<extension point>>
```

An event cycle is started if one of the following conditions occurs:

- The specified start trigger is received while an ECSpec is in the Requested state.

- The repeat period has elapsed from the start of the last event cycle and the ECSpec is still in the Requested state.

An event cycle ends when one of the following conditions is met:

- The time interval specified in the duration field expires.
- The stop trigger is received.
- The ECSpec transitions to the Defined but Unrequested state.

ECTime

The ECTime defines a span of time measured in units of physical time.

```
duration : long
unit : ECTimeUnit
```

ECTimeUnit

ECTimeUnit is an enumerated type that denotes different units of physical time to be used in an ECBoundarySpec.

```
<< Enumerated Type>>

MS  // Milliseconds
```

ECTrigger

A URI denoted by ECTrigger shows a start or stop trigger for an event cycle. The interpretation of this URI is left to the ALE implementations.

```
triggerValue: URI
```

ECReportSpec

An ECReportSpec describes a report returned from the execution of an event cycle and provides rules for what set of EPCs should be considered for reporting. It provides these rules by specifying whether all the currently read EPCs should be reported and, likewise, whether the additions or deletions from the previous event cycle should be reported.

```
reportName : string
// Provides the name for the ECReport to be generated. This string is
// copied to the ECReport instance created at the end of
// an event cycle.

reportSet : ECReportSetSpec
// Specifies what set of EPCs should be input for filtering.
// ECReportSpec is an enumerated type with values:
// {CURRENT, ADDITIONS, DELETIONS}

filter : ECFilterSpec
// Specifies how the Reader observations should be filtered.

group : ECGroupSpec
// Specifies how filtered EPCs should be grouped together.
```

```
output : ECReportOutputSpec
// Specifies how the EPCs should be reported after filtering and
// grouping is done.

reportIfEmpty : boolean
// Should a report be produced even if it has no values?

reportOnlyOnChange : boolean
// Should a report be produced if the values have not
// changed from the last time it was generated?

<<extension point>>
```

ECTerminationCondition

ECTerminationCondition is an enumerated type specifying how an event cycle should
end.

```
<<Enumerated Type>>

TRIGGER
// Event cycle should end when an explicit stop trigger is received.

DURATION
// Event cycle should end when the duration expires.

STABLE_SET
// Event cycle should end when the observered EPCs have been stable
// for a duration.

UNREQUEST
// Event cycle should end when there are no requesting/subscribed
// clients.
```

ECReport

An ECReport specifies a single report within an event cycle. Data within an ECReport is
grouped using ECReportGroup instances.

```
reportName : string
// Report name is a copy of the reportName field from the ECReportSpec.

group : List
// Specifies a list of ECReportGroup instances.

<<extension point>>
```

ECReports

Output from an event log is described in ECReports.

```
specName : string
date : dateTime
```

```
ALEID : string
group : ECGroupSpec
totalMilliseconds : long
terminationCondition : ECTerminationCondition
spec : ECSpec
reports : List
<<extension point>>
```

ECReportSetSpec

ECReportSetSpec is an enumerated type that shows the set of EPCs to be used for filtering and output.

```
<<Enumerated Type>>
CURRENT
ADDITIONS
DELETIONS
```

ECReportOutputSpec

ECReportOutputSpec provides the layout of the event cycle report.

```
includeEPC : boolean
includeTag : boolean
includeRawHex : boolean
includeRawDecimal : boolean
includeCount : boolean

<<extension point>>
```

ECReportGroup

A single group within an ECReport is presented by an ECReportGroup.

```
groupName : string
groupList : ECReportGroupList
groupCount : ECReportGroupCount

<<extension point>>
```

ECReportGroupList

An ECReportGroup shows an ECReportGroupList when any of the includeEPC, includeTag, includeRawHex, or includeRawDecimal parameters of the corresponding ECReportOutputSpec are true.

```
members : List  // List of ECReportGroupListMember instances.

<<extension point>>
```

ECReportGroupListMember

An ECReportGroupListMember allows multiple EPC formats to be included in the reports. The URIs in the ECReportGroupListMember must correspond to the Boolean values in the ECReportOutputSpec. For instance, if the value for the includeEPC attribute of the ECReportOutputSpec is true, the URI value for epc must be non-null.

```
epc : URI
tag : URI
rawHex : URI
rawDecimal : URI

<<extension point>>
```

ECReportGroupCount

An ECReportGroupCount is part of an ECReportGroup. The includeCount of the corresponding ECReportOutputSpec must be true to get an ECReportGroup.

```
count : int

<<extension point>>
```

ECFilterSpec

An ECFilterSpec describes which EPCs are to be included in the final list of EPC patterns.

```
includePatterns : List
excludePatterns : List

<<extension point>>
```

EPCGroupSpec

An ECGroupSpec defines filtered EPCs and how they are grouped together for reporting.

```
patternList : List
```

Commercial RFID Middleware

Many flavors of event management middleware are currently available. Some are based on the ALE specification proposed by EPCglobal, while some predate ALE but provide similar event management capabilities. This section provides an overview of some of the RFID event managers out there. What we have included here is a representative sample, not a comprehensive list, of available products. Our decisions about which productes to include were based primarily on the availability of information and our ability to get permission from the companies to include their short descriptions. Forrester and other analysts periodically evaluate RFID middleware, so you should refer to them and other sources for guidance on purchasing decisions. Our goal is simply to increase your awareness of some of the available implementations and their capabilities.

The four middleware products included in our discussion each provide the core functions of encapsulating reader interactions, managing events, and providing a high-level service-oriented interface for applications. In addition to these core functions, these products provide varying degrees of management and monitoring capabilities, service-oriented architecture integration capabilities, and built-in adapters to various ERP packages.

Sun Microsystems

Sun Microsystems was one of the early entrants into the RFID market. Sun provides a Java-based RFID middleware platform called the Sun Java System RFID Software. Sun's RFID software is designed specifically to provide high levels of reliability and scalability for your EPC network, while also simplifying the task of integrating with multiple existing backend enterprise systems. Sun's RFID middleware is part of the Java Enterprise System (JES) and supports standards-based integration with leading enterprise integration servers, including the Sun Java Enterprise Integration Server (formerly SeeBeyond).

The four components of the project are the RFID Event Manager, the RFID Management Console, the RFID Information Server, and a software development kit (SDK) for creating adapters and standalone applications:

RFID Event Manager

The RFID Event Manager is a Jini-based event management system that facilitates the capture, filtering, and eventual storage of EPC events generated by RFID readers connected to the network. Its main goals are to interface with RFID readers, gather EPC events, filter redundant information, and feed relevant events to the RFID Information Server or other ERP software for further processing. The RFID Event Manager Jini Services are managed through Rio, an open source container of Jini Service Beans.

RFID Management Console

The RFID Management Console (MC) is a browser-based graphical interface used to manage and monitor the RFID Event Manager. It allows the user to view and modify the RFID reader attributes and components of the Event Manager, such as filters and connectors. The RFID MC is a Struts application that provides the same look and feel as the Sun Control Station 2.2. It provides the user with a table-based display of RFID readers and RFID Event Manager components. The attributes of these readers and components can be modified to alter the behavior of a running system. The RFID MC allows the user to group readers and display the status of a group for easy viewing. It also implements an alarm table of readers and their attributes. Each reader is displayed by group and is selectable. Once selected, the reader's attributes are displayed. The Management tool implements an alarm display framework to display reader and RFID Event Manager system health status. The user is able to receive email notifications when alarms are triggered. The RFID MC uses a JDBC-compliant relational database to persist reader grouping information, alarms, and system settings such as access rights and email configuration. It is qualified with Oracle 8i, Oracle 9i, Oracle 10g, and PostgreSQL 8.0.3.

RFID Information Server

The RFID Information Server (IS) is a J2EE application that serves as an interface for the capture and query of EPC-related data. EPC-related data can include tag observation data from Event Managers as well as information that maps EPCs to higher-level business data. The RFID IS is typically used to translate a set of low-level observations into higher-level business functions. It has been qualified on the Sun Java System Application Server Version 8.1 and on BEA Weblogic 9.0. Other applications interface with the IS through XML message exchange. The IS provides an XML message interface over HTTP and JMS message transports and persists all data in a JDBC-compliant relational database. The IS has been qualified with Oracle 8i, Oracle 9i, Oracle 10g, and PostgreSQL 8.0.3.

SDK

The well-documented SDK allows developers to extend the product if they choose to create a custom application rather than using the components as they are shipped.

Version 3.0 of this product adds support for the latest readers and printers. The product is built on top of Jini 2.0.1, Rio 3.1, the Java Web Services Developer Pack 1.5, and the Sun Java System Application Server 8.1, but it is designed for maximum portability and supports a wide variety of platforms, including Solaris, Linux, Windows XP, and an ALE implementation for J2ME CDC (embedded devices).

Figure 7-17 shows the important logical elements of Sun's Java System RFID Software.

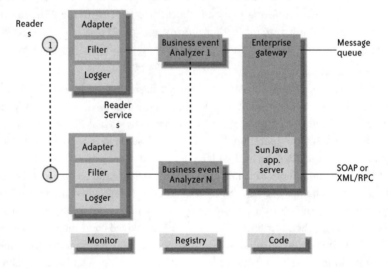

FIGURE 7-17. *Sun's Java System RFID middleware*

ConnecTerra/BEA

ConnecTerra's primary product, RFTagAware, is a software infrastructure platform for the development of device applications and RFID solutions. ConnecTerra was one of the first companies to implement a middleware solution based on the Application Level Events (ALE) standard. ConnecTerra is very active in the EPCglobal standards groups, and its founder and CTO Dr. Ken Traub was the lead author for the Application Level Events specification.

With RFTagAware, devices such as RFID readers are abstracted, similar to how a database is abstracted by SQL. Users simply describe the events they are interested in, much like a database query, and subscribe to the results that are produced based on the RFID activity. The RFTagAware Edge Server, a piece of software deployed on or near a device, processes the raw tag information and, based on any number of outstanding queries (known as Event Cycle Specifications), delivers qualifying results to any number of subscribing applications. Queries can be added, changed, or removed independently in real time without affecting the queries or results used by other applications. The Edge Server takes care of optimizing the use of the hardware, ensuring device utilization is optimized for the collection of outstanding queries.

RFTagAware provides the following capabilities:

Data filtering and aggregation
RFID readers generate a continuous stream of low-level raw data every second. RFTagAware lets you define the information you want, then controls, filters, and aggregates incoming RFID data.

Monitoring and managing an RFID infrastructure
RFTagAware provides an Administration Console that lets you centrally monitor and manage a reader. In contrast to standard information technology products, RFID devices present unique management challenges for the enterprise. While there are architectural similarities between readers and PCs, there are vast differences in how they are configured, in how their operational state is verified, and in the ways they fail. ConnecTerra's RFTagAware provides tools for monitoring the unique attributes of these devices and identifying problems, or potential problems, before they impact business operations.

Integrating data with enterprise applications
RFTagAware provides an ALE-compliant application programming interface to enable integration with existing enterprise tools and applications, including warehouse management systems, supply chain management systems, and ERP applications. RFTagAware provides adapters to the ALE interface that allow developers to use existing .NET and Java tools to create and deploy local workflows. The Edge Server makes use of an ever-growing suite of notification drivers to provide applications with the option of using a variety of industry standard, de facto standard, or propriety messaging mechanisms. Standard mechanisms such as HTTP, SOAP/XML, and JMS, as well as proprietary variations for Enterprise Application Integration platforms such as TIBCO, SeeBeyond, and SAP, are provided as part of the current offering.

Rapid application development

In addition to the application integration capabilities listed above, ConnecTerra offers a range of pre-built local workflows covering areas such as EPC tagging of pallets, complex portals, and various mobile reader scenarios. Adapters for SAP AII, enterprise message queuing products, and popular enterprise applications are also provided, and simplify the integration of RFID data with existing systems. Figure 7-18 shows the RFTagAware middleware platform.

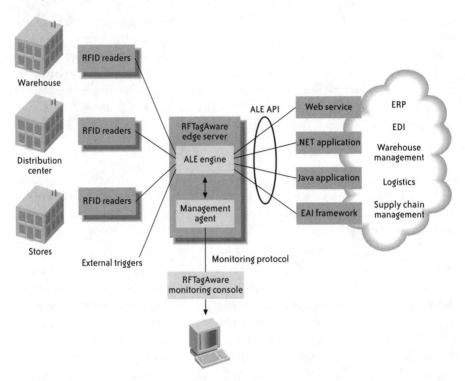

FIGURE 7-18. ConnecTerra's RFTagAware RFID middleware platform

The main components of this Edge Server offering include the Filtering and Collection Engine (also known as the ALE Engine) and the device management agent. The RFTagAware Edge Server interfaces to a wide variety of popular readers and printers, as well as various sensor inputs that are used as triggers to the reader control. The Edge Server implements the EPCglobal ALE API and includes extensions for tag writing and other capabilities not yet covered by the standard. It also includes APIs for managing and monitoring the Edge Server and devices, as well as an Administration Console that provides remote visibility into Edge Server Operations.

The ConnecTerra technical architecture mirrors the architecture framework that is being used by EPCglobal in its standards-creation efforts. The stack uses a number of layers with defined APIs. These APIs are then mapped into a number of implementation-specific protocols. In addition to the standards, ConnecTerra has added architectural interfaces in the areas of real-time reader monitoring, tag writing, tag provisioning, as well as key local workflow components.

GlobeRanger

GlobeRanger is one of the early pure-play RFID middleware companies focused on providing an edgeware platform for RFID, sensors, and other edge devices. GlobeRanger offers its iMotion software platform through partners OEMs and VARs who then build solution offerings for their clients across multiple industries.

The iMotion software platform incorporates visual tools to simplify solution development, deployment, and management.

The iMotion platform is built on Microsoft's .NET framework and takes advantage of several emerging standards, including the ALE and EPCIS specifications. The iMotion platform consists of four major system components:

Edge Device Management
    The Edge Device Management component provides comprehensive, out-of-the-box functionality for managing RFID, mobile, and sensor devices. Data management delivered through ALE provides flexible interoperability with any ALE-conforming applications.

Edge Process Management
    The Edge Process Management component delivers visual event workflow capabilities, giving process designers the ability to visually craft RFID data and business process flows.

Enterprise Management Console
    The Enterprise Management Console provides a centralized mechanism for monitoring the performance and health of edge devices and networks.

Visual Device Emulator
    The Visual Device Emulator provides a deployment emulation environment for testing and integration, a first in this industry.

Figures 7-19 through 7-21 show snapshots from the Visual Device Emulator, Edge Management Console, and Event Workflow Editor tools provided by GlobeRanger.

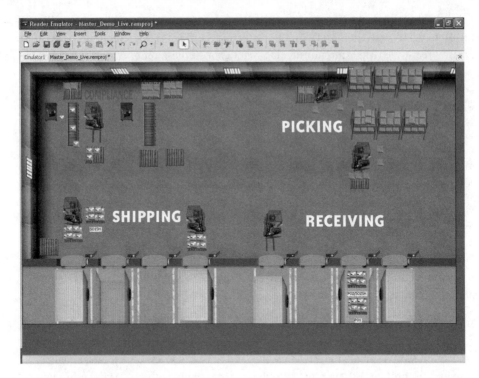

FIGURE 7-19. GlobeRanger's Visual Device Emulator

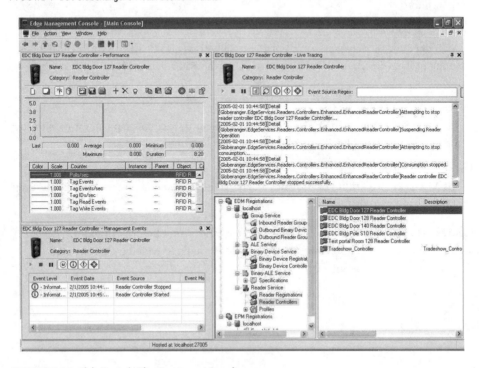

FIGURE 7-20. GlobeRanger's Edge Management Console

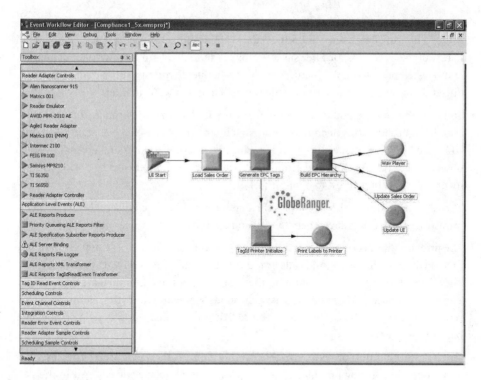

FIGURE 7-21. *GlobeRanger's Event Workflow Editor*

Summary

To recap the main points of this chapter:

- RFID middleware is an important element of your RFID solutions.

- There are three primary motivations behind using RFID middleware: to provide connectivity with readers while encapsulating the applications from the device interface and interconnections; to lower the volume of information that applications need to process by filtering and grouping raw RFID observations coming from readers; and to provide an application-level interface for managing readers and querying RFID observations.

- Many implementations are possible for RFID middleware. EPCglobal's Application Level Events (ALE) specification provides a standard interface for clients to obtain filtered, consolidated EPC data from a variety of sources, such as RFID readers and other sensors.

- The Savant specification is no longer a part of the EPCglobal architecture. All functionality of Savant has been subsumed in the ALE standard.

- Basically, the ALE specification allows applications to describe what information they are interested in and how they wish to receive it, without worrying about the physical RFID infrastructure.

- Prior to ALE, application developers had to write custom code for communicating with devices, filtering data, and presenting data to applications for consumption. Changes in hardware, applications, or filter specifications required code to be rewritten, debugged, and retested prior to deployment. Even in smaller deployments, this paradigm introduced significant risk and cost into the rapidly changing RFID market.

- To lower the volume and improve the relevance of data that applications have to process, RFID observations need to be processed before they are sent to applications. The ALE specification provides simple yet flexible mechanisms to filter and group raw RFID observations. This filtering and grouping capability provides a means to isolate and focus on events of interest to applications.

- The ALE specification also decouples the applications from the physical layers of the infrastructure, freeing developers to focus on application-level semantics.

- The primary interaction model supported by the ALE specification is a request/response model wherein all the method calls into the ALE service are executed synchronously. There are two modes of interaction in the synchronous model: immediate and polling. The ALE interface also provides an asynchronous model in which the clients can subscribe to events. As the events occur, the ALE service asynchronously delivers the data back to the clients.

- The ALE specification provides two distinct mechanisms for event processing: filtering and grouping. Filtering provides capabilities for tuning into specific patterns in the event data. Grouping provides means to group data collected from different readers and over multiple event cycles.

- A number of ALE-compliant middleware products are already available in the marketplace. In addition to providing basic event management capabilities and supporting the ALE specification, these products provide varying levels of breadth and sophistication in the areas of reader and sensor monitoring and management and workflow capabilities.

CHAPTER EIGHT

RFID Information Service

SO FAR WE HAVE DISCUSSED HOW **RFID** TAGS AND READERS WORK, how applications interface with the RFID infrastructure at the edge of the network, and why you should consider using RFID middleware. We have spent little time describing the nature of RFID data and how it might be shared between applications or even enterprises as RFID-tagged items move through supply chains. (Although in this chapter we use the retail-oriented example of items moving through a supply chain, the principles and tools we discuss are also applicable to other applications, such as asset tracking.)

One of the promises of RFID is that business partners will be able to automatically collect and share up-to-the-minute tracking information about items in their supply chains. To realize this benefit, businesses need to agree on what information will be collected (and its semantics), when and how this information will be collected, where and how it will be stored, and, finally, where and how to access it. Of course, the infrastructure used for sharing RFID information must also provide the normal security features we have come to expect in service-oriented architectures, such as authentication and authorization. Do these issues sound familiar? They should, as B2B information networks are nothing new. Standards such as RosettaNet and UCCNet target similar problem domains. We're not in uncharted waters from a technology perspective either, as service-oriented architectures backed by web services standards and platforms such as Java/J2EE and .NET provide adequate means for integrating applications by divulging information or business processes as services.

Even though custom approaches are always available for RFID information sharing, standardization with respect to the structure and meaning of RFID data, and the implementation of mechanisms that collect and share information of mutual interest, the participants in a supply chain can reduce the time to market and the cost of information sharing. This chapter examines the need behind and mechanisms available for sharing RFID information. We will begin by looking at the characteristics of RFID data, and then move on to discuss the concepts underlying B2B RFID information networks. Finally, we will look at the vision for EPC information sharing proposed by EPCglobal as the EPCglobal Network.

RFID Data

RFID data can be classified under two broad categories: event data and master data. As the term suggests, event data relates to dynamic tracking information about RFID-tagged assets. In comparison, master data provides supporting contextual information about the event data.

Event Data

Event data is tied to a specific moment in time and communicates the whereabouts of an RFID-tagged asset as it moves through a supply chain. An example of event data is: "At 2:01 p.m. on 9 October 2005, EPC X was observed at Location L."

In essence, RFID event data is made up of observations of the existence of some thing at some place at some time. The following list covers these elements in more detail.

Identity

Any RFID observation must communicate some identity. We discussed identities at length in Chapter 4. Those were the same kinds of identities we expect here—for example, an SGTIN, a GRAI, or an SSCC.

Location

Location also ties into some of our earlier discussions. A particular location can be recorded as a GLN (see Chapter 4), but it probably corresponds physically to a specific source antenna (see Chapter 5).

Time

Time is one of those recurring problems in designing any system. How many times have you written a new "days between dates" for a new language or platform? It never seems to be part of the standard library. For sensor observations, time raises some specific problems. Will the time be set to local time or Coordinated Universal Time (UTC); clock ticks since power on, or ticks since last communication? If it's UTC or local, how often will the time be set on individual sensors to avoid drift? How precise should the timestamp be? The standards seem to be moving toward using UTC, possibly with a Network Time Protocol (NTP) server to set time. Timestamps in milliseconds are probably precise enough for almost all applications.

As RFID moves into common use, applications will increasingly require additional sensor observations besides identity, location, and time. We have used temperature as an example, but almost any measurable quality is a possible candidate for monitoring. Some material-handling applications may need to monitor exposure to light or air. Other systems may need to integrate Real Time Location Systems (RTLSs) to provide pinpoint location information.

Some of the information provided by these sensors fits easily into the observation format we described above—for instance, we could substitute temperature readings for location readings, such that one observation might indicate that ID 123 was observed at location y at 15:00:00 while another observation might indicate that ID 123 was observed at 20 degrees Celsius at 15:00:00. In this case, the item ID and time tie the two observations together. The difficulty arises if the observation of temperature occurred at, say, 15:00:01. Do we consider this to be the same time as the location reading? If we say that any reading within 15 seconds is related, what do we do with two different location readings and a single temperature reading that occurred during this time? As we build more experience with multi-sensor applications, the answers to these questions may become more obvious, or we may all settle on a "good enough" abstraction. For now, this is a rich area for debate for those inclined to join the standards bodies and offer their opinions.

And what about information that doesn't fit so easily into the same ID, quality, time triplet? What is the single quality that can place an item in three-dimensional space? If we say it's some concatenation of x-, y-, and z-axis measurements, aren't we really just stuffing three fields into one? That's poor design. We can expect, then, that whichever data representation is ratified as a standard will not be a simple triplet of fields, but a more complex data structure capable of nesting other complex data structures. After all, what if what we need to record is the location of an item and the *retinal scan* of the person checking it out?

As we saw in Chapters 2 and 7, RFID events come in varying levels of granularity, ranging from a single reader observation to filtered and aggregated application-level events. As an example, an application-level event could communicate that "stock level is low for SKU 1234567 at location 123456789012." These high-level events are much more coarse-grained than the individual observations, and it is upon these high-level events that we will build our applications.

It should be noted that event data is transactional in nature and that the quantity of event data will grow over time as more business is transacted (as this could mean you have more trackable assets). Special consideration should be paid to the need for archiving event data.

Master Data

In addition to these core attributes, which are collected as event data, you may have a host of other reference or contextual information about the item being tracked that is meaningful in your business context. Master data provides supporting contextual or reference information about the event data. This could include a description of the product referenced by the EPC, information about its manufacturer, or other kinds of information such as details about the physical location where the event was captured.

Generally, your RFID master data will not grow at the same pace as the event data.

Data Volume

The impact of RFID data on your supply chain and other asset tracking systems will depend on what data you collect using your RFID infrastructure, how often you collect it, how much of it you collect, and what you plan to do with it. Depending on the size of your RFID infrastructure and the granularity at which you need to track your assets, RFID data volume can potentially overwhelm your networks and storage. Just how much data are we talking about? The amount of data is a function of the number of observations made by the system and the size of the observations themselves. To get an idea of the amount of data that will be generated and of the data storage requirements, let's go back to our Nirvana Electronics example from Chapter 2. Obviously, this is just an example, but it should give you an idea of how to estimate your own data volume and storage requirements.

As you might remember, Nirvana sells consumer electronics and tracks these items using smart shelves. Table 8-1 presents some numbers on the volume of data Nirvana can expect to amass.

TABLE 8-1. Data volume factors

Attribute	Magnitude
Items on a shelf (average)	25
Shelves per rack	4
Aisles	20
Racks per isle	20
Stores	10
Total items tracked in real time	400,000

With what we know now about reader configuration, we'll assume that the readers are configured to perform a read cycle twice every second. During normal operation, the event filters are configured to pass on information only when an item that was previously identified no longer appears or when an item appears that was not previously present. This is called a *delta filter*. If we assume that in each of Nirvana's 10 stores, 5 items on average and 50 items at peak times are added or removed from the shelves at any given moment, we can calculate the number of events we can expect at any given moment as ranging from 50 on average to 500 at peak times.

If we assume each event contains a 1-byte header, a 2-byte event type, a 96-bit (12-byte) ID, a 12-byte location, and a 6-byte timestamp followed by a 16-bit (2-byte) checksum, we can make a rough estimate of the data size as $1 + 2 + 12 + 12 + 6 + 2$ bytes, or 35 bytes. Assuming that someone will decide it's a good idea to report these observations in XML form, we will double the size to 70 bytes for tags and delimiters. This means that across all of Nirvana's stores, we might expect at any given instant to have somewhere between

3,500 bytes to 35,000 bytes of observations traveling from the event manager to the EPCIS server and on to the enterprise bus as events. Even if we were to double the size of the observation messages, the number of reads, or both, this would be a very manageable amount of data. This is primarily because the event filtering mechanism has done its job.

Now let's look at what might happen if a manufacturer were to recall one of the goods for sale at Nirvana. The inventory application would ask the ALE server to query every single reader, asking for an immediate report on any items matching a particular Company Prefix and Item Reference with a Serial Number between, say, 5000 and 7000. What happens then? Let's say there are 1,000 of these items in each of the 10 stores. That's 10,000 observations each at 70 bytes, or 70,000 bytes per store and 700,000 bytes overall. This is much larger than the typical traffic load, but still not unmanageable. Also notice that this would happen in one, quick burst, not as 700,000 bytes every second for an extended period.

This sort of spike in reads is a fundamental property of RFID data. It tends to come in a steady stream for some period, and then suddenly in a large cluster of observations. Any RFID system must be scaled to manage these bursts. There's one more burst to consider, though. What if we had some reason to query the readers as to what is on every shelf at every store right now? This might happen for a quarterly physical inventory, or to correct some error in the inventory system, for instance. With 400,000 items per store and 70 bytes per observation, the bandwidth required would be 28,000,000 bytes per store. A megabyte equals 1,048,576 bytes, so that is a little less than 27 MB per store (270 MB total). With just a little ingenuity, this also can be manageable, even with a small pipe to the stores. We might scan only one aisle at a time, for instance, which would mean 140,000 bytes per aisle. On a DSL line, assuming a 128-KBps uplink speed, each store would then take about 9 x 20 minutes (3 hours) to perform a complete, automated inventory.

Data Storage

What about storage? The database back at headquarters will be accumulating the observations and storing them for some period of time. How much data will collect for observations in a day? A week? A year? If we look at the preceding numbers and assume that we have about 6 recalls a year, perhaps 4 inventories a year, and about 30 minutes per day of peak inventory activity (sales and stocking) with the rest of the hours of operation being closer to the average, we can estimate our storage requirements for one store to reflect those presented in Table 8-2.

TABLE 8-2. Storage requirements for one store

Event type	Number of observations	Daily	Weekly	Freq	Yearly
Sales/stocking (avg)	X	180,000	1,260,000	365	65,700,000
Sales/stocking (peak)	X	90,000	630,000	365	32,850,000
Recalls	10,000	X	X	6	60,000
Inventory	400,000	X	X	4	1,600,000
Total	X	X	X	X	100,210,000

This table assumes seven 10-hour days per week and 30 minutes of peak sales and stocking activity per day. This does not take into account activity at the registers or other inventory changes, such as returns. The total yearly raw observations come to 100,210,000, or about 669 MB. For real-time tracking of 400,000 items, this seems like a reasonable amount of data to manage; even for all of the stores together it only amounts to about 6690 MB of data, which will fit on two DVDs.

The EPCglobal Network

EPCglobal envisions a network of EPC-enabled data services that is used by trading partners to enable near-real-time tracking information on items in their supply chains. This vision is termed the EPCglobal Network. (As you can see, this is a CPG-oriented vision, but even today, adoption of RFID technology is expanding well beyond the CPG industry and supply chains.) The EPCglobal Network introduces a few dedicated components, such as the Object Naming Service (ONS) and the EPC Information Services (EPCIS), that you may or may not need for your applications. However, chances are that you will end up using or developing similar components to meet your requirements. Understanding what these components have to offer will help you make the right architectural choices regarding distributed recording and querying of EPC (or any RFID event) data.

The EPCglobal Network aims to provide real-time data about individual items as they move through a global supply chain. Centered around the EPC and RFID technologies, and building on the existing Internet infrastructure, the EPCglobal Network offers the potential for increased efficiency and accuracy in tracking products between trading partners. The EPCglobal Network is made up of five principal services:

Assigning unique identities
> Tracking items is not possible without the capability to uniquely identify them. This is where the Electronic Product Code comes in. Like the Universal Product Code (UPC) or bar code, the EPC is an identification system for products. However, unlike the UPC, the EPC enables item-level tracking by identifying not only the manufacturer and product type, but also a unique serial number.

Detecting and identifying items
> The identification system consists of EPC tags and readers. An EPC tag contains a microchip attached to an antenna. The EPC is stored on this microchip. At the most basic level, the EPC provides a coding scheme for RFID tags to help identify an item's manufacturer, product category, and unique serial number. The tag is applied to an item either during the manufacturing process or somewhere down the supply chain. The EPC readers use radio frequency waves to interrogate the EPC tags, which communicate their EPCs back to the readers. EPC readers then deliver this information to local business information systems via EPC middleware.

Collecting and filtering events
> EPC middleware provides specifications for services that enable data exchange between EPC readers and business information systems. Many of the raw EPC observations coming from the readers would be noise to the enterprise applications, so event

management middleware is needed to facilitate the collection of observations from the readers and filter and group them for consumption by the applications. We looked at EPC middleware in detail in Chapter 7.

Storing and querying events

The EPC Information Service enables users to exchange EPC data with trading partners. The EPCIS specification (not available at the time of writing) aims to provide standards for capturing and querying EPC data that is between trading partners.

Locating EPC information

To enable trading partners to share EPC observations, it is necessary to provide lookup services that can locate repositories for the required EPC data. The EPCglobal Network envisions two types of repositories: static data repositories from a manufacturer (for data such as expiration dates, manufacturing timestamps, and so on) and dynamic repositories from other supply chain participants (including information such as track-and-trace observation data, temperature readings, and other observations made as a product moves through the supply chain). The ONS, as currently specified, is essentially an EPC lookup service that provides the address of the authoritative manufacturer information services. For dynamic data, EPCglobal envisions a "discovery service" based on simple event registries* that supply chain participants can "notify" (note that this complex concept has yet to be specifically outlined by the EPCglobal Architectural Review Committee). More details on the ONS and discovery are included later in this chapter.

Figure 8-1 depicts the EPCglobal Network. As shown, RFID readers pick up observations on RFID-tagged items as they move through the supply chain. Readers pass these observations to RFID middleware after some rudimentary filtering. The RFID middleware (also known as the event manager) gets the data from readers and filters and groups it as needed for downstream applications. The event manager also adds location information to the filtered observations. According to the EPCglobal Network view, the filtered observations (or events) from the event managers are then passed to a local EPCIS server. The EPCIS server records the EPC observations for later use; they may be retrieved by your enterprise applications or shared with your trading partners. The object naming servers maintain a mapping between EPCs and the EPCIS servers that maintain information on them. Just like DNS does for IP addresses, the ONS works in a hierarchical fashion to provide a global lookup service.

Similarly, other trading partners in a supply chain store EPC observations on their local EPCIS servers. Remember, however, that an EPC only identifies an entity. Further information about a product type (say, a user's guide for an electronics item), the manufacturer (a company profile), and so on is not part of the EPC. When an application needs to know the whereabouts of a particular EPC or needs further information about an EPC, it will query a local ONS server. If a local EPCIS server can provide the necessary information, the ONS will return with its location information (IP address and port). Otherwise, it will utilize the global hierarchy of ONS servers to locate an EPCIS server that can provide it.

---

* Graham Gillen, "RE: RFID Essentials," 22 June 2005, personal email.

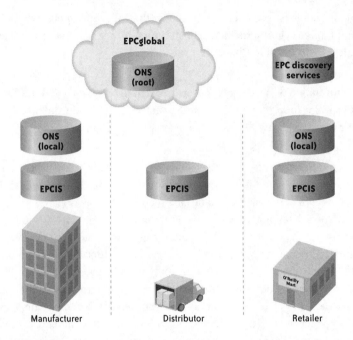

FIGURE 8-1. *Essentials of the EPCglobal Network*

Bear in mind that at the time of writing, the EPCglobal Network is a vision. Developing secure, federated, scalable, and robust data services is not trivial. Putting a business agreement in place, having the necessary security components, developing the means to authenticate trading partners, and restricting a requester's access to just the information that is authorized is a complicated process. Stay tuned—by the end of 2005, EPCglobal is expected to have come up with specifications for some of the vital components of the EPCglobal Network.

The main components of the EPCglobal Network are the ONS and the EPCIS. We'll take a look at them next.

The Object Naming Service

The ONS is the authoritative source for locating EPC Information Services instances. For example, a retailer can locate a manufacturer's EPCIS instance by querying an ONS server. Consider a typical product as it goes through its life cycle, from being manufactured, packaged, shipped to a distributor, shipped to a retailer, and finally purchased by a customer. As the product goes through the supply chain, a lot of valuable information can be captured: where it has been, how it should be used (e.g., links to product manuals), safety recall information, and so on. As products change hands in the supply chain, their ownership often changes as well, and in the process the information stored about those products may become fragmented. Suppose we are talking about medicines, and there is a safety recall on a particular lot. At present, the manufacturer would pass this information to its distributors and also distribute awareness bulletins to the industry publications and all of the pharmacies to which it has access. The distributors maintain information on which pharmacies received which lots, so they can contact pharmacies that receive the recalled lot (via fax, email, EDI, and so on). The pharmacists, in addition to safety recalls, also have to worry about expired lots in their inventories and dispose of them before someone's oversight puts the medicine into a consumer's hands. At present, this process involves a lot of manual steps, and its successful execution depends on many intermediaries. Imagine if a global, networked database existed that—using their EPC codes—mapped the products to relevant manufacturer- and distributor-supplied information. An RFID-enabled pharmacy that is already capable of automatically recording all of its inventory would simply be able to query this database periodically to find out about any medicine recalls and check expiration information.

In addition to tagging medicines with RFID tags and installing readers to record the inventory, two things are needed to make this vision a reality: a service that maps EPC codes to the relevant product information, and a service that can provide the address of a particular EPC code's information lookup service. EPCglobal calls these services the EPC Information Services and the Object Naming Service, respectively. The ONS is essentially an EPC resolution service that provides the means to look up a service resource that provides further information about the item identified by a particular EPC.

The EPCIS is the glue that binds the data collected from the EPC event managers to the enterprise information systems. When in need of further information on an EPC, the RFID integration server goes to a designated object naming server and queries for an EPC information service that might have the necessary data. The ONS in its pure form is simply a mapping service, and it can map an EPC to services other than an EPC information service. For instance, it can map EPCs to web services that provide information on particular product categories.

As mentioned earlier, the ONS was envisioned to be a global and hierarchical service. One of the overarching principles behind the design of the ONS was that it should leverage the existing Internet standards and infrastructure wherever possible. Following this principle, the ONS uses the Domain Name System (DNS) for resolving EPCs. The EPC query and response formats follow the DNS standards. As a result, the EPC being queried is converted to a domain name and the result is returned as a valid DNS resource record. To better understand how the ONS works, let's take a quick look at the workings of DNS.

DNS

The Internet is a mesh of computers and other devices in which any one computer can get information from or talk to any other connected computer using the TCP/IP protocols. The Directory Naming Service (DNS) forms the backbone of the Internet and represents one of the largest and most successful implementations of a distributed database anywhere. This service maps a human-friendly identifier for a web resource (let's say a web site) to its IP address. Network components understand this address and can thus assist in routing web requests. For example, the server that you refer to as "www.cnn.com" has the IP address 64.236.24.4. Every time you use a domain name, you use the Internet's domain name servers to translate a human-readable domain name into a machine-readable IP address. The ability to translate a logical address to an IP address is trivial. What makes the DNS backbone fascinating is its flexibility, manageability, and scalability. Consider for a moment that millions of IP addresses and billions of web requests are made every day. Domain names and IP addresses are hardly static; new ones are added and existing ones are modified every day. To provide the necessary performance, scaling, and availability while maintaining the loose coupling between the various domain administration authorities, the DNS is implemented as a hierarchical, distributed database.

When you type a URL—say, *http://www.oreilly.com*—into your browser's location bar, the browser seeks to convert the domain name into an IP address. To do so, the browser locates a name server (typically provided by your ISP) and requests the IP address corresponding to the domain name. Upon receiving this request, the ISP's name server can either respond with an IP address itself or, if it does not have this information, contact one of the root name servers. The root name server in turn locates a set of the authoritative name servers for the requested top-level domain (.com in this case) and returns their addresses. Next, your ISP's name server contacts one of the authoritative DNS servers referred by the root name server. The authoritative DNS server will either have the information needed or refer you to yet another name server. Eventually, you hit a name server that has the IP address for the requested domain name, and it returns it to your ISP. The ISP's name server caches the domain name/IP address mapping to speed up future queries and returns the IP address to your browser. Finally, armed with this information, the browser submits the web resource request to the corresponding server.

Understanding the ONS

The DNS is the core building block for implementing the ONS. The ONS architecture leverages the standards employed by the DNS. In the previous section, we saw how a DNS query works. In order to work on the same implementation fabric, the ONS query and response formats must adhere to the DNS standards. The steps involved would thus go something like this:

1. An EPC event manager receives a tag reader event and in turn sends the sequence of bits containing the EPC from the tag to an RFID integration server. For example:

   ```
   Bit Format: [10 00000000000000101100 00000000000001111 00000000000000001000001]
   Decimal Format: 2.44.15.65
   ```

2. The RFID integration server converts this bit sequence into the Universal Resource Identifier format and sends it to a local ONS resolver. The ONS, as specified in EPCglobal's Version 1.0 specification (dated August 2003), assumes that the EPC is in its URI form. Here is an example of the URI form of the EPC listed above:

   ```
   urn:epc:2.44.15.65
   ```

3. The ONS resolver converts the URI into a domain name and issues a DNS query for NAPTR (naming authority pointer) records for that domain:

   ```
   15.44.2.onsroot.org
   ```

TYPES OF NAME SERVERS

Authoritative name servers are the ones that hold information on all the servers within a domain. They are sometimes referred to as *master name servers*. Any query for a host within a particular top-level domain will end up at one of the master name servers associated with that domain if none of the servers the request passes through on the way can supply the necessary information. As you might expect, the master name servers are kept fairly well synchronized. The domain's administrator typically sets them up in a master/slave configuration, with one as the *primary* server and the others as *secondary* servers. The master, or primary, name server gets all the updates to the namespace and keeps the secondary servers in sync. This setup serves to distribute the workload and provide redundancy.

The root of the domain name tree is denoted by a single dot and is called the root domain. The root domain encompasses all other domains. The authoritative name servers for the root domain are called *root name servers*. There are many root name servers scattered all over the world. In turn, every name server maintains a list of all of the known root servers.

Caching-only name servers are local name servers and are not authoritative for any domain. As the name suggests, these name servers provide the ability to conduct DNS queries for the applications running on the local network and to cache the information. Caching-only name servers are implemented to improve the performance of DNS lookup. Most ISPs implement caching-only name servers.

NOTE

NAPTR is a type of DNS resource record that uses a regular expression for specifying a delegation point within some other namespace. NAPTR records are used for rules used by Dynamic Delegation Discovery System (DDDS) applications. The DDDS maps unique strings to data stored within a DDDS database by iteratively applying string transformation rules.

Please note that the ONS 1.0 specification does not query for the full EPC, but stops at the product level. For now, the specification guides the users to query the service returned by the ONS query regarding the information about the serial number (65, in this case).

The URI form of the EPC is converted into DNS form using the following process:

a. Remove the `urn:epc:` header. In our example, the URI is `urn:epc:2.44.15.65`. Removing the header gives us `2.44.15.65`.

b. Remove the serial number field from the EPC, giving us `2.44.15`.

c. Invert the order of the remaining fields, giving us `15.44.2`.

d. Append ".onsroot.org," giving us `15.44.2.onsroot.org`.

4. The DNS infrastructure returns a list of URLs for one or more EPCIS servers mapped to the EPC.

5. The local ONS resolver presents the URL of the service to the RFID integration server.

6. The integration server requests relevant product information from the EPCIS server.

Understanding ONS Query Result Formats

The result of an ONS query will be one or more NAPTR records. The DNS resource record consists of the following fields: Order, Pref, Flags, Service, Regexp, and Replacement. Table 8-3 describes the meaning of each of these fields; see the ONS 1.0 specification for more details.

TABLE 8-3. NAPTR fields defined for the ONS

Field name	Description
Order	The Order field describes the equivalence of NAPTR rows returned from a load-balancing perspective.
Pref	The Pref field is also used to designate priority with regard to interpreting the rows in the result set. Records with lower Pref numbers should be processed before those with higher numbers.
Flags	If the Flags field is set to "u," it means the Regexp field contains a URI. The corresponding value in the Service field provides an indication of the type of service.
Service	The Service field is used to designate different types of services. The format of this field is EPC+service_name. The legal values for service_name include pml, html, xmlrpc, and ws. The EPC portion is used to differentiate it from other types of NAPTR records, while the +service_name portion is used to describe the service class.
Regexp	The Regexp field specifies a URI for the service being described. The service types presently envisioned by EPCglobal only need the hostname and additional path information for description, but the regular expression type is used because DNS uses NAPTR records to conditionally rewrite URIs. The POSIX Extended Regular Expression format is used to describe this field.
Replacement	This field specifies the replacement portion of the rewrite expression.

Let's look at the result of an ONS query. As shown in Table 8-4, the result set contains four NAPTR records.

TABLE 8-4. Example ONS result set

Orders	Pref	Flags	Service	Regexp	Replacement
0	0	u	EPC+pml	!^.*$!http://acmewatches.com/sports/cgi-bin/epcpml.php!	.
0	0	u	EPC+html	!^.*$!http://acmewatches.com/sports/epcpml.jsp!	.
0	0	.	u	EPC+xmlrpc	!^.*$!http://acmewatches.com/servlet/sports.acmewatches.com!	.
0	0	u	EPC+ws	!^.*$!http://acmewatches.com/sports/ws/epc.wsdl!	.

The service codes are as follows:

PML

This method is used to obtain Physical Markup Language (PML) documents about a product.

HTML

This service returns a URI that will resolve to static web content. This method can be used to access a web site that contains existing product information. An application would get this information from the RFID integration server and would typically display the contents of this page using a web browser.

XMLRPC

The URI returned by this service will resolve to a server capable of responding to XML-RPC requests. An application would call methods on this server by POSTs containing XML similar to the example below:

```
<methodCall>
  <methodName>someservice.somemethod</methodName>
  <params>
    <param><value><string>some parameter</string></value></param>
  </params>
</methodCall>
```

WS

This method is used to connect to a web service that can get detailed product tracking information by calling public interfaces made available by manufacturers or distributors. The RFID integration server in this case will receive a Web Service Definition Language (WSDL) file that describes the aforementioned web service.

The EPC Information Services

The EPCIS is an upcoming EPCglobal standard whose goal is to enable disparate applications to leverage EPC data via EPC-related data sharing, both within and across enterprises.

The EPCIS defines a standard interface for capturing and sharing EPC-related data. It should be noted that the EPCIS focuses only on the service interface and semantics of EPC-related data, such as location information that gets registered as products move through the supply chain. Vendors are provided the flexibility to compete on implementations and add-on functionality.

EPC observations are captured using the EPC Capture interface, and they are queried using the EPC Query interface. Additionally, the EPCIS provides a common model for location information and other important data. The EPCIS standards were envisioned for use with events within an organization, where they may be subscribed to or stored and queried, or between companies, where the same operations will be able to take place. This provides a common set of semantics that will allow organizations to share EPCIS data and mix data from multiple organizations in a meaningful way. Just as EPCglobal's Reader Protocol interface insulates the higher layers from knowing what RF protocols and reader makes and models are in use, the EPCIS insulates enterprise systems from having to know the details of how individual steps in a business process are carried out. The EPCIS-level data differs from lower layers in the EPC Network Architecture because it incorporates semantic information about the business process in which EPC data is collected and provides historical observations.

Figure 8-2 depicts the key elements of the EPCIS.

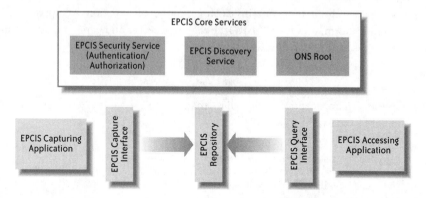

FIGURE 8-2. EPCIS components

We already know about tags, tag protocols, readers, reader protocols, RFID middleware, and the role of the ALE specification, so let's focus on the new components introduced by the EPCIS.

An *EPCIS capturing application* is any program that understands the business context in which the EPCIS information capture takes place. What this means is that an EPCIS capturing application is able to provide a higher-level business context to the RFID data that is captured (remember that according to EPCglobal all RFID identification is based on an EPC). As shown in Figure 8-2, the EPCIS capturing application gets information from an RFID middleware system implementing the ALE specification. The EPCIS interface provides a specification for how EPC data is exchanged between EPCIS capturing applications, EPCIS accessing applications, and EPCIS-enabled repositories. Events at this interface would look something like the following: "At dock 1, at time T, the following cases were verified as being aggregated to (becoming part of) the following pallet..."

The *EPCIS accessing application* is any application that accesses the EPCIS. Generally, this is an application responsible for carrying out some business process, such as an inventory collection, order management, or point of sale system. The accessing application might not reside within your enterprise boundaries. The partner application shown in Figure 8-2 is a type of EPCIS accessing application.

An *EPCIS-enabled repository* records events generated by one or more EPCIS capturing applications and makes them available for later query using EPCIS accessing applications.

Finally, the EPCIS defines a set of core services, such as Security and Discovery. The Security service is intended to provide mechanisms for authentication and authorization for storing and accessing EPC information, whereas the Discovery service provides the means for discovering the presence of EPCIS servers and mapping them to a range of EPCs.

VERISIGN

VeriSign[a] (*http://www.verisign.com/epc*) runs the root ONS server for EPCglobal as well as the root DNS servers for *.com* and *.net* names on the Internet. We appreciate the assistance provided by Graham Gillen, Sr. Product Manager, and others from VeriSign with respect to some of the material used in this chapter. VeriSign's EPC Services is a product suite that enables customers to securely share EPC-related data both within their enterprises and with their partners. It includes four components, as shown in Figure 8-3.

The Discovery components include the ONS and the EPC Discovery Service. These services enable applications to search for and discover EPC-related data. The ONS is the authoritative directory service for the EPC Network. It is the first place that an application will look to find information on a particular EPC. As discussed earlier in this chapter, the ONS is built on the Internet's DNS and can be accessed using existing DNS libraries and tools. Architecturally, the ONS has two layers. The first layer, called the *root ONS*, is a directory of manufacturers. VeriSign runs this layer on behalf of EPCglobal, and manufacturers are added when they purchase Manager Numbers from EPCglobal. Root ONS entries point to *local ONS* instances, which contain product directories for the manufacturers.

The EPC Discovery Service enables efficient track-and-trace capabilities on the EPC Network. It contains pointers to EPCIS servers that have information about a given EPC. For instance, if a tagged product were to move from Manufacturer A to Distributor B and then to Retailer C, the Discovery Service would have pointers to each party's EPCIS server. An interested party could get that information, and then query each EPCIS server to get a rich set of track-and-trace information. VeriSign also offers a separate EPC Track & Trace Service, which eliminates the need to individually query multiple EPCIS servers in order to perform a track-and-trace request. Once queried, the Track & Trace Service will query the EPC Discovery Service, then recursively query each of the EPCIS servers. It will return a full listing of the history for the specified EPC.

The EPCIS provides persistent data storage for the EPC Network as well as security and access to EPC-related data. VeriSign offers the EPCIS as a hosted service. In its second version, the EPCIS is built using available EPC standards.

a. Ibid.

Discovery	Object naming service	Directs general requests for authoritative product manufacturer information in the EPC network.
	EPC discovery service	Directs requests for trading partner-specific data about EPCs, thereby enabling track and trace
Storage	EPC information service	Stores and retrieves serial number-specific information about products as they move through the supply chain
Secure access	EPC trust service	Authenticates user's identity on the EPC network, thereby controlling access to various information services

FIGURE 8-3. Components of VeriSign's EPC Service

Summary

Here are the main points we covered in this chapter:

- RFID data comes in two general flavors: event data and master data. Event data represents tracking information about your assets, whereas master data provides additional contextual or reference information for the event data.

- The volume of event data generated in an RFID system can become very large over time. Special consideration should be given up front to the impact storing, communicating, and sharing this information will have on your infrastructure.

- EPCglobal is an important standards body that is furthering the adoption of RFID by providing standards for various hardware and software components. As one might expect with standards bodies that cater to a wide spectrum of constituents, EPCglobal has to balance its priorities. EPCglobal standards are firmer and have found a wider market adoption the lower down the stack you go. Standards such as the EPCIS are still emerging, and the jury is still out on whether, or to what extent, the market will adopt them.

- Principal application areas that will end up adopting RFID technologies (such as the supply chain, material handling, point of sales systems, and so on) tend to have very well entrenched software and hardware providers and to use mostly proprietary solutions. It is very likely that you will come across vendor extensions to existing solutions, such as bar code scanners, that will fit your needs. Answers to the questions of whether and where EPCglobal standards apply to your industry and whether you should adopt them depend on many factors, not the least of which is the overall adoption of EPC standards by your industry.

- EPCglobal envisions a network of EPC-enabled data services used by trading partners to enable near-real-time information retrieval for items in their supply chains. This vision is termed the EPCglobal Network.

- The EPCIS defines a standard interface for capturing and sharing EPC-related data.

- The ONS maintains mappings between EPCs and the EPCIS servers maintaining information.

CHAPTER NINE

Manageability

MANAGEABILITY REFERS TO HOW WELL A SYSTEM ALLOWS AN OPERATOR TO CONTROL and monitor that system in order to meet other requirements, such as availability or throughput. Different systems may have very different manageability requirements. Managing a server farm in a power-conditioned and climate-controlled data center is very different than managing readers in a smart shelf configuration or in a portal at the door of a coliseum—and readers are just the first of many new sensors and devices that we will connect to our networks in the near future.

The part of the network closest to the physical operations and end users is called "the edge." In the past, we've mostly talked about the edge in terms of moving "smart" routers to the edge and using "dumb" switches on the backbone, but we now refer to devices other than routers as edge devices. Figure 9-1 shows some of the types of devices that might be deployed on the edge of a network.

The middleware and information service servers shown in the diagram emphasize that one of the primary reasons for placing computing devices at the edge of the network is to reduce network load by making decisions as close to the physical processes as possible. For example, the decision to turn on a light when a reader observes a tag should not require an exchange of messages with global headquarters. A local computing device—possibly the reader itself—should make that decision, reducing unnecessary load on the network.

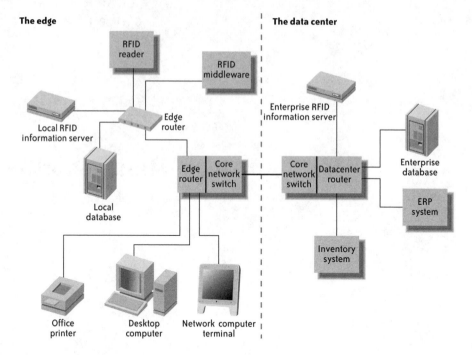

The edge

The data center

FIGURE 9-1. Edge devices

More complex decisions requiring input from several sensors can be handled at the level of the middleware deployed in an edge server.

How edge devices should be monitored and controlled is a less obvious but equally important consideration. If that same reader constantly reports its health to a monitoring application at global headquarters, the traffic it creates is nearly as wasteful as asking headquarters if the light should be on. Still, most organizations prefer to manage their network operations with a central staff rather than having local administrators at each location. For this reason, just as sensors on the edge require middleware to filter observations and manage complex local decisions, middleware plays an important roll in filtering and aggregating monitoring information and managing edge devices through automatic responses to common problems. In the following sections, we will explore three aspects of edge device management:

- Edge deployment options
- Capabilities needed for edge management
- Standards and technologies for edge management

By focusing on managing edge devices rather than simply on managing readers, we hope to inspire you to think about how the rapid adoption of edge computing—not just for RFID, but for many technologies—will affect your organization. Ad hoc manual solutions and management solutions designed around a single brand of reader may require significant reworking in a year or two, as readers and other edge devices take on more and more responsibilities and become increasingly complex. By taking a broader view, organizations can instead use this opportunity to lay a durable foundation for managing more complex, and more numerous, devices on the edge.

Edge Deployment Options

Understanding the manageability of an RFID system requires knowing how the individual components are deployed, either in the data center or at the edge. In this section, we will introduce several approaches for deployment of the components we have discussed in previous chapters and consider some of the strengths and weaknesses of each approach. The primary options we will discuss are centralized deployment, distributed deployment, and self-organizing deployment.

Centralized Deployment

In the centralized approach, every component that can function in the data center remains in the data center, as shown in Figure 9-2.

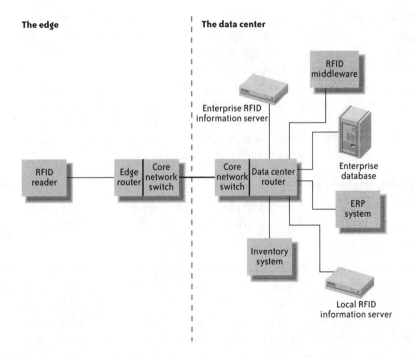

FIGURE 9-2. The centralized approach

In the 1980s and 1990s, microcomputers exploded out of the data centers and onto desktops and into "server closets," enabling end users in new ways and at the same time bringing new challenges to IT operations staff. Over the past few years, most organizations have worked steadily toward a return to more centralized management of computing devices by moving servers out of makeshift server closets and into climate-controlled, secure data centers. The advantages of this configuration include more efficient physical access to systems by IT operations staff and increased reliability due to the protection data centers offer from power and temperature fluctuations, dust, and vibration. Improved physical security is an additional benefit of moving all of these servers to a central location with restricted access.

However, moving all of your servers to a central location also means that information must travel farther to reach the edge, and vice versa. If the data from the edge is no more dense than the typing of a user on a keyboard or an occasional document sent to an office printer, this may be an acceptable cost, but heavy printing loads or devices such as RFID readers registering numerous observations may require larger, more expensive network equipment and greater bandwidth. Also, the longer the distance is from the edge to the server, the more likely it is that the infrastructure in between will be shared with other applications and users. If an operation requires predictable response times, unexpected loads on the network from other applications and users might create unacceptable delays and lead to errors. Opening a door to a moving vehicle and changing lanes on a conveyor belt are examples of operations that must complete in a predictable amount of time to succeed.

While management of centralized servers may be easier, moving all servers into a central location leaves edge devices such as office printers and readers with no localized control or management support. A global enterprise would not design a system where office printers reported paper outages to the IT staff at the corporate headquarters. Printers notify a local user when the paper runs out (usually the next user who tries to print), and this local user either replaces the paper or notifies the right person to do so. Similarly, other edge devices such as RFID readers must be managed according to their locations. A centralized deployment may not provide the necessary infrastructure to support edge devices, which (unlike printers) have no desktop users to notify in the event of a fault.

Distributed Deployment

The distributed approach moves computing devices closer to the edge but keeps some devices in the data center. Figure 9-3 shows how some of the components have moved to the edge.

Edge servers can aggregate management information closer to the edge of the network, sending only summary information and notifications of exceptions to the central management systems. For example, if Reader A registered a fault, it would send a notification to the RFID middleware server, as shown in our diagram. Because this middleware server is close to the problem and knows the details of the local installation, it is able to perform a predetermined remedial action, such as increasing RF power on Reader B and turning off the electricity to Reader A, perhaps by triggering a watchdog device (not shown). The middleware could then notify a local operator of the problem by triggering a pager or activating a light. Only then would the middleware notify the central office of the problem and its partial resolution. A centralized system could do all of these things as well, but because the decisions in the distributed system happen close to the physical location of the edge devices, operations are not interrupted and the system is able to continue to meet availability requirements. The failure of Reader A and the increase in the responsibility of

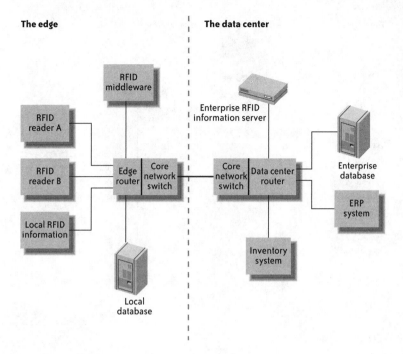

The edge | The data center

RFID middleware

RFID reader A

RFID reader B

Local RFID information

Edge router

Core network switch

Local database

Enterprise RFID information server

Core network switch

Data center router

Inventory system

Enterprise database

ERP system

FIGURE 9-3. The distributed approach

Reader B could all happen quickly enough for Reader B to step in and read the next item on the conveyor belt.

Even a distributed system has its weaknesses, though. A distributed system, like a centralized system, works best in a static environment where the same edge devices report virtually the same things day after day. Adding a new sensor may be fairly simple, requiring only the physical installation and a call to IT operations to update configuration settings, but adding a reader from a different vendor or even a new model from the same vendor may be just as complex in a distributed system as in a centralized system, requiring days or weeks of customization. Adding a completely new type of sensor, such as a Real Time Location System (RTLS), could require a dedicated software development project.

Self-Organizing Deployment

The self-organizing approach is a radical departure from traditional deployments. In this configuration, almost all of the computing power moves to the edge, with the data center no longer central to the system but merely another participant in a mesh network. (For more about mesh networks, see Chapter 11.) Figure 9-4 is an example of a self-organizing configuration.

Unlike in centralized or distributed deployments, new devices added to a self-organizing deployment are themselves responsible for announcing their capabilities and providing software components that allow other devices to interoperate with them. A new reader might announce itself to the network as having the capability to produce ALE events and

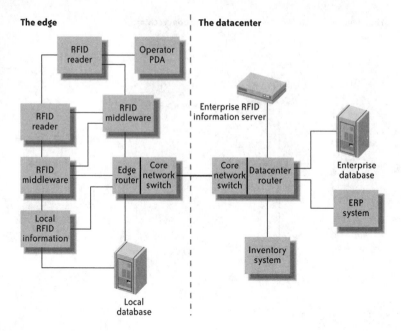

The edge | The datacenter

FIGURE 9-4. *The self-organizing approach*

to read and write EPC Class 0, EPC Class I, and ISO 8000 tags. It might also announce that it has the capability to display an indicator as one of the values Red, Yellow, Green, or Off. The reader offers to the middleware and other authorized clients software components that can monitor and manage it. The middleware, for its part, informs this new reader that it will be "Smart Shelf 25/B" and that it should assume a particular signal power configuration and duty cycle determined to be best for that role.

Likewise, a new middleware edge server added to the network could announce that it has, among other capabilities, the capability to provision readers and monitor reader health, and as an operator walks through the sales floor, her authenticated PDA could announce that it has the capability to "display 640x480x256 colors," to play sounds, and to provide user text and touch input. The end result is a display on the reader's screen of two middleware servers sharing management of several readers, including the new one the operator just plugged in.

Self-organizing systems with most of these capabilities already exist. Readers are quickly becoming smarter, and models capable of participation in a self-organizing network will probably be available by the time you read this page. At present, the main drawbacks of this type of system are cost and complexity. Individual devices in a self-organizing system must have enough processing power to participate as partners in some relatively demanding management tasks.

Organizations currently designing RFID implementations should consider the respective advantages of distributed and self-organizing deployments. While price may rule out self-organizing systems for many applications in the near term, planning ahead can create deployment designs that are able to take advantage of this approach when it becomes cost-effective. The first step to supporting future architectures is to understand the options, so in the next two sections, we will discuss the capabilities required in middleware and the devices for implementing these options.

Capabilities Needed for Edge Management

Managing edge computing devices requires a particular set of capabilities, regardless of which tool or standard is actually used. It might be possible to deploy a fully functional RFID system without these capabilities, but doing so would limit the manageability of the system and increase the system's total cost of ownership (TCO) over the long term. The required capabilities are:

Discovery

New edge devices added to the network must be able to discover resources, such as middleware, network gateways, and other edge devices, that they need for their roles; otherwise, each device will require manual configuration. Conversely, middleware must be able to discover new devices as they are added to the network, or each installation and replacement will require error-prone manual intervention.

Provisioning

Once a new device joins the system, it must be able to receive configuration information from the controlling middleware. Otherwise, devices may be misconfigured due to human error.

Reconfiguration

Devices should be able to accept remote reconfiguration in order to facilitate failover and recovery (discussed later in this list).

Management by group

An organization may have hundreds or even thousands of edge devices. Management software should be able to simultaneously group multiple devices according to multiple criteria at the same time, such as device type, location, and role. As an example, an interface should allow an operator to turn off all dock-door readers in the system, turn off all of the readers in the Allentown warehouse, or turn off all ACME Mark II readers. However, this same system should also allow an operator to turn off only the ACME Mark II dock-door readers in the Allentown warehouse. Despite the obvious value of this capability, many management tools do not support attaching devices to multiple groups.

Patching and upgrades

As much as possible, device behavior and protocols should be implemented as upgradeable software so that owners can get maximum longevity from what is typically an expensive investment. This software should be upgradeable entirely over the network. To support these upgrades, middleware should provide support for recognizing the current version or patch level of a device's software. It should also provide a way to push updates to groups of devices rather than requiring a tedious series of clicks on a user interface for each individual device.

Health monitoring

Devices should be able to report error conditions or changes in status to the middleware. The middleware should provide some way for an operator to view the current status of all devices in "dashboard" summary. It should also have the capability to drill down in order to view the detailed histories and current statuses of individual devices when analyzing problems.

Notification

Almost any management tool provides visual, audible, email, pager, interactive voice, and other sorts of notification to an operator in the event of an error, but for edge devices, the management tool must not only be able to notify operators of problems, but also to determine which operator to notify based on the location and type of the problem. The group management feature mentioned previously can help greatly in managing alarm groups.

Failover and recovery

Middleware should be able to coordinate failover and recovery, taking into account some predetermined failure strategies, and it should also be able to make some limited decisions concerning self-healing. As an example, if one of two readers at a portal fails, the middleware should be able to reconfigure the remaining reader to cover the entire door as completely as possible until a replacement arrives.

Asset management

With so many devices located outside of controlled-access data centers, any but the smallest deployments will require significant time to be spent on manual inventories if the middleware does not have some mechanism for maintaining at least a simple inventory of known devices and their last confirmed whereabouts.

We've discussed our deployment options and the capabilities required to manage edge devices. This should give us the context to understand what the existing and developing standards and technologies for device and server management have to offer.

Standards and Technologies

Current network management systems handle the data center well, but properly managing edge devices will require additional capabilities, as described in the previous section. The following standards and technologies are competing, and sometimes cooperating, to add these capabilities to the tools we will use to manage a growing number of edge devices:

SNMP

The Simple Network Management Protocol (SNMP) was developed to manage nodes on an Internet Protocol (IP) network, but it may be used to manage almost any kind of device with a network connection. SNMP allows an operator to either read accumulated management information from a device or set configuration values. The device can generate "traps," which are alerts sent to the middleware when something of interest happens. The data structure that holds the accumulated information and the configuration settings on the managed device is called a Management Information Base (MIB). Many reader vendors have defined and implemented MIBs for their readers.

EPCglobal Reader Management Protocol

We discussed EPCglobal's Reader Protocol in Chapter 6. The EPC Reader Management Protocol is an extension of this protocol that adds management commands for the command channel and a set of one or more alarm channels for management events of interest. The Reader Management Protocol standard (which is a work in progress) defines an SNMP MIB as well.

JMX

Java Management Extensions (JMX) provides an interface for managing Java applications and containers such as middleware servers, application servers, and information servers. JMX allows an operator to start and stop Java software components in a managed system, to change configuration files, or to trigger predefined behaviors in those components (such as retrieving new configurations from a web server).

Jini/Rio

Sun describes Jini as an "architecture [that] specifies a way for clients and services to find each other on the network and to work together to get a task accomplished."* Jini is a Java-based technology that enables discovery and provisioning of devices. The Rio framework runs on top of Jini to provide reconfiguration as well as failover and recovery. Middleware built on top of this framework can provide additional management features such as health monitoring, notifications, and asset management.

SLRRP

As discussed in Chapter 6, The Internet Engineering Task Force (IETF) is currently working on an RFID reader protocol called the Simple Lightweight RFID Reader Protocol (SLRRP). While still only an Internet-Draft, this standard would include reader management features if adopted. It does not currently define methods for discovery, but it does mention that these might be provided through existing mechanisms. One possibility for discovery is another IETF standard, the Dynamic Host Configuration Protocol (DHCP).

ZigBee

ZigBee is a recently published standard based on the Institute of Electrical and Electronics Engineers (IEEE) standard 802.15.4. It is an always-on, physical and media access control protocol designed specifically for low-power, low-latency communication with sensors and control devices. The simple protocols can be implemented on inexpensive hardware and require very little power. ZigBee can support a large number of sensors

---

* Sun Microsystems, "Jini Network Technology—Overview," February 2005, *http://www.sun.com/ software/jini/overview*.

and controllers with very little latency. ZigBee also defines an application-layer protocol for discovery and for matching services to clients, similar to features offered by Jini.

Because so many tools from so many different vendors implement one or more of these standards, it would be difficult to present a comprehensive list here. For more information on network management, products, and standards, see Appendix B.

Summary

In this chapter, we learned that:

- Distributed deployment is the best choice for now, but it is important to pay attention to the capabilities and standards of your system and to design toward self-organizing sensor networks in the future.

- Edge devices and edge-aware middleware must support discovery, provisioning, reconfiguration, management by group, patching and upgrades, health monitoring, notification, failover and recovery, and asset management.

- SNMP, the EPC Reader Management Protocol, JMX, Jini/Rio, SLRRP, and ZigBee are competing and sometimes cooperating to bring us the capabilities we need to manage edge devices.

CHAPTER TEN

Privacy and Security

I**N THIS CHAPTER, WE BEGIN WITH A LOOK AT THE PRIVACY AND SECURITY ISSUES** inherent in the use of RFID systems and at consumer concerns about this technology. In the rest of the chapter, we cover various security- and privacy-related aspects of an RFID system, from the physical layer to the application layer. We explore some of the measures that are being taken to protect consumers' and citizens' privacy, and we identify potential RFID security vulnerabilities and discuss possible countermeasures.

Privacy and Security Issues

News stories on RFID often lead in with bleak and sometimes inaccurate descriptions of the possibilities for abusing this technology. They paint a picture of a world where every possession you have has a unique identification tag: the wallet you got for Christmas last year, the bank notes in your money clip, medicines in your cabinet, electronic items, toys, media, groceries in your kitchen, your automobile. You are warned that someone might drive past your house and be able to inventory all of your possessions and find out about your tastes, your health, and your lifestyle, all without you knowing about it. You are told that this technology may allow "Big Brother" to locate you automatically in public places, tracking your every movement as you go in and out of stores, churches, and night clubs. What if governments and private sector entities could track every minute detail of your life and use the information they gleaned to decide whether you could access civic services, get life insurance, or get a loan for your next car? While privacy and safety advocates have raised legitimate alarms over the possibilities of abuse in a world where RFID tags seem destined to become more and more pervasive, we must not allow misinformation and hysteria to cloud our consideration of this technology.

It should be noted that even before the advent of RFID systems, companies and governments have had the means to collect, store, transfer, and analyze vast amounts of data about consumers and citizens. Even without RFID, there are many ways in which we willingly surrender our privacy: we routinely buy things with credit cards, use store affinity cards to get discounts, give out our names and addresses when returning merchandise, allow web sites to set cookies on our computers while we're surfing the Web... All of these things allow others to track our buying patterns and lifestyles. Why is it, then, that RFID systems have the privacy advocates so concerned?

The objections seem to fall into two broad categories. One is the expectation that RFID will lead to unique identities for individual items, which can then be associated with individuals in ways that were previously impossible. For example, police might track a uniquely identified glove left behind at the scene of a crime to a particular credit card purchase. While we might agree that this is a reasonable use of the technology, what if this same technique were used to associate someone with an underground newspaper or a protest poster? The other new concern RFID brings to the table has to do with the fact that RFID tags can often be read at some distance. While the "drive-by inventory" is not likely to be a threat with current technology, a passive UHF tag might be read three meters away. Even if the tag only uniquely identifies a glove or a laptop computer, it might be used as evidence that a particular person was in a particular place at some particular time. In wartime, enemies might abuse RFID technologies' various security loopholes to target supply shipments and personnel.

> **NOTE**
>
> One often hears objections to RFID that really seem to be objections to combinations of the Global Positioning System (GPS) and cell phone technology. For instance, you may have heard someone express concerns that RFID will enable people to be "tracked by satellite." This seems to be a confusion of RFID with cell phones (which can be tracked by triangulation while active) and the GPS, which uses satellites. RFID, especially passive UHF, has a very limited read range and would offer no help in tracking someone from orbit.

Although the consumer privacy issues surrounding RFID systems seem to get the most press, there are other aspects of RFID security that are equally important. While RFID privacy concerns mainly have to do with what, when, where, and how much consumer data is tracked without our permission or even our knowledge, RFID security focuses on securing RFID systems from pranksters, spies, thieves, and other unauthorized entities.

Some of the same vulnerabilities identified in this chapter can serve as a threat to an individual's privacy or a corporation's security. As with any other mission-critical system, it is important to consider, and plan to mitigate, potential threats to the availability, integrity, and confidentiality of an RFID system. Security needs differ for different systems. Not all systems need to have five 9's availability (this means that the system is available 99.999% of the time, which translates to a maximum downtime of 5 minutes and 15 seconds a year), or require their operators or users to authenticate themselves via retinal scans. A system's availability, integrity, and confidentiality requirements vary depending on many factors, including its criticality to the mission, the sensitivity of the data it handles, and the loss potential from incidents. Figure 10-1 illustrates the balancing act among these three factors.

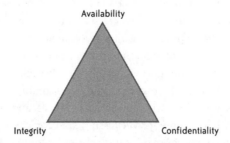

FIGURE 10-1. The three pillars of security: the AIC triad

The three factors are explained further in the following list:

Availability

Availability addresses a system's uptime at the required performance and scalability level. Apart from poorly thought-out architectures, a common threat agent for availability is denial-of-service (DoS) attacks. RFID systems have certain vulnerabilities that can jeopardize their availability. For example, someone could jam the radio waves between the readers and the tags or use a blocker tag (explained later in this chapter in the section "Privacy-enhancing technologies") to cloak all the tags in its vicinity.

Integrity

The primary objective of integrity measures is to assure the accuracy and authenticity of information transmitted by the system by preventing its accidental or malicious modification. Spoofing tags would be an example of an attack against the integrity of an RFID system. Apart from ensuring the integrity of the information concerning products in their supply chains, companies must take extra precautions to maintain the integrity of customer data.

Confidentiality

Confidentiality measures aim at limiting information access to authorized personnel. Consumer privacy issues discussed in this chapter fit into the confidentiality dimension. For companies, confidentiality issues are of utmost importance. Apart from consumer privacy issues, information such as the inventory in a retail outlet or the movement of material in the supply chain must be protected, as this is valuable data that competitors would love to get their hands on. Companies that track some form of consumer data must also take careful precautions to ensure that customer identities do not get into the wrong hands.

There are many ways to strengthen each of these three dimensions. Companies should carefully measure loss potential against the cost of countermeasures necessary to lower or eliminate potential threats.

Of course, privacy and security are not all about technologies and tools. People and processes play an important role in ensuring that the technologies are used effectively. For example, consider the repercussions of an RFID station going down as opposed to a bar code reader failing. In the event of a bar code reader failure, an operator can manually enter the codes into a terminal and business can go on functioning relatively smoothly. However, when a reader that is processing a high volume of items or items that are moving at high speed goes down, its potential impact can be very different. As with any new technology, businesses implementing RFID systems should build in manual contingency plans for various points of failure. Companies should also conduct periodic comprehensive security audits that look at their security policies, procedures, and IT infrastructures. With the prevailing sensitivity to consumer privacy issues, and considering that RFID technologies essentially move large volumes of data and processing to the edge of a company's IT infrastructure, security needs should be carefully thought through up front.

Public Perception Matters

Consumer brands and retailers obviously have a lot to gain by understanding customer behavior and movement in a store and by trying to personalize their marketing messages and coupons to further their sales. Discovering how people shop helps retailers design stores that are both more customer-friendly and more profitable. There are limits, however, to the type, timing, and amount of information about consumers that can or should be tracked. The deciding factors are laws, consumer awareness, industry guidelines, and prevailing notions about privacy.

One of the more recent experiments with RFID technologies also served as a test of public response to privacy issues. The German retail giant Metro Group tested RFID technologies at its concept store in Rheinberg, Extra Future, for nearly a year. As part of the RFID pilot, the store carried RFID-tagged inventory, outfitted its shopping carts with RFID readers, and set up RFID tag deactivation terminals in the store. The store also embedded RFID chips in their customers' loyalty cards. In addition, the store had RFID readers scattered throughout the building that could track the movement of carts, products, and possibly customers throughout the store. Consumer advocacy and privacy groups criticized the store's use of RFID technology.

The aspects of the technology that the groups called into question included tracking of customer movement within the store without their explicit knowledge. Also, the deactivation terminals did not work 100 percent of the time and did not erase all of the information on the tags. The groups felt that the RFID trial failed to notify consumers about what information was being collected about them and exposed them to external snoops as well. In response to the public outcry, the store promised to replace the RFID-enhanced loyalty cards with cards without RFID tags.

RFID Privacy

It is important to examine the reality and practicality of the threats to our privacy and safety resulting from the use of RFID technologies. Every technology brings with it the possibility, but not the guarantee, of abuse. Consider RFID-tagged medications—say, an anti-depressant, or AIDS medication. People might be very concerned that someone could find out they were taking these medications simply by reading an RFID tag from a distance. For this reason, caution is warranted. However, those same RFID tags may help prevent expired or counterfeit medications from being sold, or may be used at the time of sale to inform pharmacists and consumers of possible negative drug interactions. Privacy concerns should be balanced against the benefits offered to consumers. Ironically, sensationalism and paranoia may actually distract us from the real issues.

Privacy means many things to many people. Some have defined privacy as the right to be left alone. The definition we like the most in the current context is: "freedom from unauthorized intrusion: state of being let alone and able to keep certain esp. personal matters to oneself."*

Even before the advent of RFID systems, companies and governments have had the means to collect, store, transfer, and analyze vast amounts of data from and about consumers and citizens. As noted earlier in this chapter, even without RFID, there are many ways in which we willingly surrender our privacy. So why are the privacy advocates so worried about RFID? Some of the reasons are based on today's realities, some on expected technological advances, and some on hype. In this section, we survey the underpinnings of the prevalent views on RFID privacy and security issues and then look at the measures being proposed by governments, consumer advocacy groups, industries, and vendors to address these issues.

Table 10-1 provides an overview of some RFID system characteristics and the privacy and security concerns they engender, as well as the actual capabilities of the technology at the present time.

---

* *Merriam-Webster's Dictionary of Law* (Springfield, MA: Merriam-Webster, 1996), *http://www. dictionaryreference.com/search?q=privacy.*

TABLE 10-1. Understanding RFID security concerns

RFID system distinguishing characteristic	Privacy/security concern	Present capabilities
Line of sight: Because RFID tags do not require line-of-sight reads, a reader can pick up an RFID tag just by being in its vicinity.	The primary benefit of RFID technology also makes it vulnerable to uses that constitute an invasion of privacy. For example, if you are wearing or carrying RFID-tagged items, someone can, possibly from a safe distance, find out what those items are. You might even be completely oblivious to the existence of the tags or the fact that the items are being tracked. In the case of pharmaceuticals, for instance, this could be a serious privacy concern.	Current read ranges for passive tags are around three meters and thus these tags are rather limited within the current standards. Active tags, which have much longer read ranges (around 100 meters), would be more susceptible to stealth reads. However, because active tags are larger and are significantly more expensive, their use will most likely continue to be limited to high-value items and transactions.
Item-level tracking: EPC tags have higher information storage capacities than most bar codes and can include a serial number. This allows manufacturers and retailers, for instance, to track items at an instance level. Used wisely, this provides companies with a valuable tool for tracking and managing inventories, product recalls, and so on.	Item-level tracking can potentially be used to uniquely associate individuals with the objects they purchase. Suppose you purchase a pair of shoes (which incidentally have RFID tags embedded in them) at your local mall and pay for them with your credit card. The store you purchased them from now has sufficient information to associate your identity with that of the pair of shoes you bought. From that point on, you can be identified using the EPC code of the pair of shoes you purchased. It is this very capability to track goods at item level, associate them with individuals, and then be able to automatically locate people in public places by tracking those goods that causes the greatest concern among privacy advocates.	The ability and desire of companies to track most merchandise at the item level remains to be seen. We anticipate that for a few years to come, apart from pharmaceuticals, electronics, and other higher-value items, item-level tracking will find limited usage. Also, existing guidelines require companies to embed the RFID tags in the products' packaging as opposed to inside the products themselves. Doing so lowers the privacy risks considerably.

ANOTHER STEP TOWARD AN ORWELLIAN SOCIETY?

The potential implications of RFID technologies on privacy and the safety of individuals have become an issue in national government. "RFIDs could be secretly read right through a wallet, pocket, backpack, or purse by anyone with the appropriate reader device, including marketers, identity thieves, pickpockets, oppressive governments, and others…. The privacy issues raised by RFID tags are vitally important because they are representative of a larger trend in the United States—the seemingly inexorable drift toward a surveillance society," said Barry Steinhardt of the American Civil Liberties Union, urging caution with respect to the technology at a hearing before the House Subcommittee on Commerce, Trade, and Consumer Protection.

"Soon we could have Big Brother and big business tuning into the same frequency, where not only will they know where you are, but what you're wearing," added Rep. Jan Schakowsky (D-Illinois).[a]

a. (Mark S. Sullivan, "Growing use of RFID technology draws privacy concerns and defense by retailers," Medill News Service, 15 July 2004).

Addressing RFID Privacy

Many avenues exist for furthering RFID privacy. They span (in no specific order of importance) the gamut of government legislation and guidelines, industry guidelines, self-policing by companies, consumer awareness groups, and technological enablers.

Government legislation

Many governments are currently debating legislation that would protect consumers from improper collection and use of RFID data in both the public and the private sectors. Whether special laws will be required to promote RFID privacy and security or whether these issues will fall under the umbrella of broader laws on privacy is not yet clear. Governments must carefully balance consumers' and citizens' privacy needs against the needs of corporations to collect marketing data and the benefits gained by society at large through efficiencies introduced into the supply chain using RFID technologies. Several bills related to data privacy, protection, and security were introduced during the 108th legislative session of the U.S. Congress. Representative Gerald D. Kleczka (D-Wisconsin) sponsored a bill that proposed requiring warning labels on consumer products containing RFID devices. The bill, H.R.4673, was introduced under the title "Opt Out of ID Chips Act."

In August 2004, California's state Senate passed a measure to set limits on the use of RFID technology by libraries, retailers, and other private entities. Known as SB1834, the bill prohibits businesses and libraries in California from using RFID tags attached to consumer products or using an RFID reader that could be used to identify an individual, unless they comply with certain conditions. The information collected using RFID can relate only to the items customers are actually buying or borrowing. That is, the information collected cannot be tied into customer and lifestyle information available on consumers. Obviously, this brings up enforcement issues, as later data mining could tie together pieces of information that were previously kept separate.

While reasonable laws could speed adoption of RFID by addressing citizens' concerns, overly aggressive laws may limit innovation by raising barriers in areas we don't yet understand.

> **NOTE**
>
> Here's an example of how laws can limit innovation. "Development of the automobile was retarded for decades by over-regulation: speed was limited to 4 mph (6.4 kph) and until 1896 a person was required to walk in front of a self-propelled vehicle, carrying a red flag by day and a red lantern by night."*

---

* "Development of the Automobile," *The Columbia Electronic Encyclopedia*, 6th ed. (New York: Columbia University Press, 2005), *http://www.factmonster.com/ce6/sci/A0856792.html*.

Government guidelines

Many national governments have prescribed guidelines for enhancing consumer privacy and security. These guidelines often serve to test the effectiveness of proposed remedies and tend to precede equivalent laws. For example, the European Union and member nations have adopted a comprehensive set of privacy policies that control how information may move between member nations and outside of the EU.

In the context of information systems that collect personal information from consumers, the Federal Trade Commission (FTC) in the United States listed four widely accepted principles in a 1998 report titled "Privacy Online: Fair Information Practices in the Electronic Marketplace."* These principles provide guidance on the collection, use, and dissemination of personal information. The following is a summary of the FTC's guidelines:

Notice

Data collectors must disclose their information practices before collecting personal information from consumers. This means that consumers should know what information is being collected, how it is being collected, and the purpose for which it is being collected. In the context of RFID systems, consumers should know if a product contains an RFID tag, what information is being stored on that tag, and what information about the consumer will be associated with the tag. The consumer should also know when, where, and why an RFID tag is being read.

Choice

Consumers must be given options with respect to whether and how personal information collected from them may be used for purposes beyond those for which the information was originally provided. Such choice would encompass secondary uses, such as putting them on marketing lists and selling or giving their information to other companies or entities. Consumers should be given the choice to opt out of information collection and of receiving marketing messages.

Access

Consumers should be able to access, verify, and contest the accuracy and completeness of data collected about them. This means that consumers should know that certain information that involves them has been collected and should be given access to the information and the ability to confirm its accuracy.

Security

Data collectors must take reasonable steps to assure that the data collected from consumers is accurate and secure from unauthorized use. There have been high-profile instances of e-commerce companies storing customer information, including their credit card numbers, without adequate security and hackers breaking into their web

---

* Federal Trade Commission, "Privacy Online: Fair Information Practices in the Electronic Marketplace," 25 May 2000, *http://www.ftc.gov/os/2000/05/testimonyprivacy.htm*.

sites and stealing the vital customer identity information. Customers' identity and pro-file information should be stored and managed with care.

These guidelines have enjoyed strong support from industry and have led to widespread adoption of "privacy policy" statements on web sites. Regulations for health care privacy and credit privacy may arguably be seen as having developed from FTC's guidelines.

AUSTRALIAN PRIVACY

The Government of Australia bases its privacy laws on a set of well-thought-out privacy principles.[a] The Australian National Privacy Principles cover aspects of information collection, use, and disclosure; data quality and security; access; and correction. These principles have specific provisions and exceptions for small businesses.

a. "National Privacy Principles (Extracted from the Privacy Amendment (Private Sector) Act 2000)," *http://www.privacy.gov.au/publications/npps01.html*.

Industry guidelines

While it is debatable whether government regulations are needed to address RFID privacy issues, it is important for industries and companies to note both consumer sensitivity to this issue and the possibility of abuse. Consequently, they should develop or adopt policies and procedures to ensure a high level of privacy and security for the data collected using RFID systems.

EPCglobal, like the Auto-ID Center before it, has consistently emphasized privacy as a key consideration in promoting RFID adoption. With this in mind, EPCglobal has provided the following guidelines* in order to establish a responsible basis for the use of EPC tags on consumer items. These guidelines map closely to the Fair Trade Practice guidelines outlined in the previous section, "Government guidelines." They are:

Consumer Notice
  This guideline requires that consumers be given a clear notice of the presence of EPC tags on products or their packaging. This notice will be given through the use of an EPC logo or identifier on the products or packaging.

* "EPCglobal Guidelines on EPC for Consumer Products," September 2005, *http://www.epcglobalinc. org/public_policy/public_policy_guidelines.html*.

Consumer Choice

This guideline requires that consumers be informed of their choices to discard, remove, or disable EPC tags from the products they acquire. It is anticipated that for most products, the EPC tags will be part of disposable packaging or will otherwise be discardable.

Consumer Education

Consumer education is key to dispelling some of the myths about RFID's benefits, capabilities, and limitations. ECPglobal, working along with its member companies, will strive to provide consumers with the opportunity to obtain accurate information about RFID and its applications, as well as information about advances in the technology.

Record Use, Retention, and Security

The EPC does not contain, collect, or store any personally identifying information. As with conventional bar code technology, data associated with an EPC will be collected, used, maintained, stored, and protected by the EPCglobal member companies in compliance with applicable laws. Companies will publish, in compliance with all applicable laws, information on their policies regarding the retention, use, and protection of any personally identifying information associated with their use of EPC.

Privacy/security thought leaders

Simson Garfinkel, Ph.D, from the Massachusetts Institute of Technology's Computer Science and Artificial Intelligence Laboratory, is one of the thought leaders on computer security. In a paper presented at the Ubiquitous Computing Workshop in 2002, he outlined a framework for RFID privacy policies that is based on the Code of Fair Information Practices listed earlier. In what Dr. Garfinkel called an "RFID Bill of Rights" for consumers, he proposed:

- The right of the consumer to know what items possess RFID tags
- The right to remove or deactivate the RFID tag once a product is purchased
- The right to products and services even if a consumer chooses not to use RFID tags
- The right to know where, when, and why an RFID tag is being read
- The right to know what information is being stored inside an RFID tag

Watchdog organizations

Before embarking on an RFID project, prudence dictates that you should find out what some of the well-established industry watchdog organizations are saying about this technology. Whatever your views may be on the specific organizations, it is worthwhile to be aware of the concerns they voice and the proposed remedies. Organizations of note include:

- CASPIAN: Consumers Against Supermarket Privacy Invasion And Numbering (*http://www.nocards.org*)
- Privacy International (*http://www.privacyinternational.org*)
- EPIC: Electronic Privacy Information Center (*http://www.epic.org*)

Privacy-enhancing technologies

Mechanisms and tools that restrict the surveillance capabilities of insecure or unauthorized RFID systems can enhance the effectiveness of privacy laws and guidelines. Some of the technologies proposed include EPCglobal's "kill tag" standard and RSA Security's "blocker tag."

The kill tag approach is conceptually the simplest and most appealing way to promote consumer privacy. In this approach, a consumer can direct a retailer to issue a kill command to the RFID tag embedded in a product after purchasing it. Assuming the consumers have the opportunity to verify the success of the kill command, this approach protects them from unauthorized radio frequency scanning of their possessions.

The main drawback of the kill tag approach is that it limits the usefulness of the RFID technology to the point of sale. If the product needs to be returned to the store later for any reason, the returns counter will need an alternate means of identifying the product and perhaps a means of retagging it. Killing the tag also means that smart appliances or recycling systems will not be able to recognize the item. For instance, in the future, a refrigerator might be able to inventory all of its contents automatically and place an order for milk and orange juice with your favorite online grocer. Killing the RFID tag would exclude these applications. Also, the practicality of consumers taking conscious measures to disable tags in every product they purchase is debatable, especially if doing so would involve standing in a line or spending more time at the checkout stands.

The blocker tag approach, proposed by RSA Security, uses a special-purpose tag called a blocker tag that is designed to passively jam the readers by preventing them from interpreting the backscatter from normal RFID tags. The blocker tag works by jamming a reader's anti-collision algorithm for a range of tag IDs. A blocker tag is capable of mimicking responses from tags, in effect "drowning out" real tags in its vicinity. A universal blocker tag would be capable of obscuring the complete range of serial numbers for a given type of RFID tag, while a partial blocker tag would obscure only tags with serial numbers in a certain range. Figure 10-2 illustrates this principle in action.

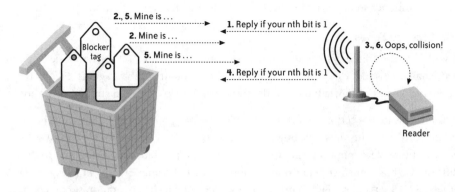

FIGURE 10-2. The blocker tag

While the blocker tag has been proposed to aid consumer privacy, it could also serve subversive purposes, such as hiding products at the store checkout or launching DoS attacks on readers.

The efficacy of this approach for enhancing consumer privacy is questionable. Because the new Gen2 protocol does not singulate by serial number, it partially defeats the blocker tag. Future readers may also use information from comparisons of signal strength or triangulation to overcome blocker tags.

RFID Security

The motto of Sun Microsystems, "the network is the computer," seems more true now then ever before. Today, our personal computers are almost always connected to the Internet. We are more mobile: we access email, surf the Web, and trade stocks even on our cell phones. Auto manufacturers are coming up with Internet-enabled cars. Increasingly, more high-end home appliances are web-enabled. As a corporate employee or a customer, you can access information from anywhere, on almost any device, at any time.

This increased access and mobility has brought forth a host of security-related challenges for corporations and consumers. As the network becomes our computer, it becomes more and more important for security to be as an integral part of every IT product and solution. Connectivity and access assume some level of trust, but when you open up access to your critical computing systems and connect to public networks, your security policy must begin with not trusting anyone.

RFID expands the boundaries of your corporate information systems to their very edges. Deploying RFID technologies in your existing supply chains is bound to introduce additional complexity to the edges of corporate IT. Tapping into the full granularity of data made possible by the RFID technology will expose you to an overwhelming flood of data. With RFID, some of your most sensitive data becomes airborne. This situation requires a carefully thought-out security policy that encompasses the periphery of your data centers. This section looks at the security aspects of the components introduced by RFID technologies and examines some of the implications of RFID-enabled information systems.

RFID Security Zones

As with any distributed system, to define a security strategy for RFID systems, we begin by treating all access requests as if they're coming from potential threat agents. Figure 10-3 shows a schematic of how a typical RFID system can be broken into distinct security zones.

Each zone assumes a certain amount of trust for the components that fall within that zone and mistrusts any outsiders. Starting from the bottom left in Figure 10-3, you can see that the tags and readers communicate using radio waves. The reader then connects to the RFID service bus, which contains one or more of the following: EPC event mangers, ONS servers, EPCIS servers, and RFID integration servers. The RFID integration server connects to other corporate information systems, both infrastructure-level (such as Directory, Identity Management, Messaging, and so on) and application-level (such as an Enterprise

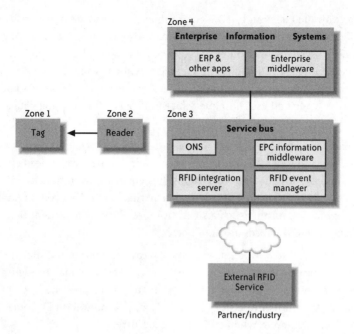

FIGURE 10-3. RFID security zones

Resource Planning, or ERP, system). The RFID integration server also connects to external RFID service providers, such as an industry's ONS and EPCIS servers or a partner's RFID integration servers. (Please see Chapter 2 for a detailed description of the overall architecture and its individual components.)

Zone 1: RF tags

Zone 1 covers the RF tags themselves.

Vulnerabilities. There are two main areas of vulnerability:

- Data on the tag is stored unencrypted. Adding encryption to tags requires additional space and circuitry on the RF chips. This means additional cost (in a retail/supply chain environment that is extremely cost-conscious), increased processing time, and also additional real estate on the chip, which in turn impacts its form factor.

- Without physical supervision, anyone on the premises with physical access to tags can remove a tag or switch one tag with another.

Threat agents. Threat agents include anyone with physical access to tags and the need, capability, and will to study and possibly alter their contents.

Example threats. Possible scenarios include the following:

- Someone with physical access to a tag can read its contents by analyzing it in a laboratory setting, using probes, x-rays, and the like. Note that as both physical access to the tags and a controlled laboratory-type environment are needed for attacks like these, they are difficult to carry out on a massive scale. Also, the threat of snooping is not unique to RFID systems—bar codes have human-readable labels, so their contents can easily be determined. The somewhat increased threat comes from the richer tracking information available with RFID systems. The threat becomes serious if someone obtains an EPC code and uses it to query an EPCIS server for tracking data associated with the code.

- A threat agent can simulate a valid tag (e.g., forcing a read while the product is missing/stolen) or switch an RFID tag to a higher-priced item from a lower-priced one. This type of threat is also not unique to RFID systems. It is equally easy, if not easier, to do the same switch with bar code tags. The difference perhaps is that bar codes require a supervised scan, which means that such a switch is more likely to get caught than it is in an RFID system, where the reads are automated.

- Someone with access to a warehouse can steal a case of widgets and stick the RF tag on another case. This remaining case will now have two tags and may be identified by readers as two cases. Since RFID systems rely on automated processes (possibly without human inventory counts/inspections), the theft may go unnoticed for some time and it will be difficult to pinpoint when and where it occurred.

- Unauthorized modifications of the information stored on a rewritable RFID tag may occur.

Possible countermeasures. There are several possible countermeasures, which include:

- Providing proper access control for the physical premises
- Implementing surveillance of the RFID-tagged merchandise
- Requiring strict access control to information derivable from an EPC code
- Separating the EPC code from any information that is sensitive to the corporation or the consumers, introducing an extra level of information that would have to be breached in order to make use of the EPC codes
- Using rewritable tags only where appropriate and with proper access control (physical or encryption)

Zone 2: RFID readers

RFID readers are normally connected to an internal Ethernet network using either wired or wireless connections.

Vulnerabilities. Vulnerabilities include the following:

- The data traffic from tag to reader is not encrypted.
- Readers do not authenticate the tags.

The derived vulnerabilities include spoofing, DoS attacks, and protocol attacks.

Threat agents. Threat agents include anyone connected to the same network (like any node connected to a network, a reader is open to all the network threat agents), and someone with a wireless sniffer device and knowledge of the reader protocols.

Example threats. Possible scenarios include the following:

- If a reader sits on a wireless network, it is vulnerable to a rogue node that is able to access the wireless access point. Both wired and wireless readers are open to network-based attacks. The most likely network threat is a denial-of-service attack.

- Someone with an RF sniffer and an understanding of the reader protocols can monitor the communication between readers and tags and spy on the movement of inventory. The communication from the reader to the RFID tag is called "forward channel," whereas the echo back from the RFID tag to the reader is called "reverse channel." Generally speaking, the forward channel uses much more power and has a longer range (up to 10 meters) than the reverse channel (around 3 meters). Someone could monitor the forward channel more easily than the reverse channel. Table 10-2 shows the relationship between read range and tag technology.

TABLE 10-2. RFID read ranges

	Passive tags	Active tags
Net read range	Up to 3 meters	100 meters
Required signal strength	High	Low
Forward channel signal range	10 meters	100 meters or more
Reverse channel signal range	3 meters	Depends on the power available—normally around 100 meters

- A DoS attack can occur wherein an intruder jams the communication between the reader and the tag by introducing random noise.

- A universal blocker tag can also be used to launch a DoS attack.

- As a means to defeat the radio waves, someone can hide an item by putting it between metal liners or concrete blocks.

- By identifying individuals according to items they carry, someone can monitor the whereabouts of those individuals. When this information is tied to other items also mapped to various locations, the snoop can build a very detailed profile of the buying behavior, health, and lifestyle of the individuals being tracked.

Possible countermeasures. There are a number of possible countermeasures:

- Communication between readers and tags can be encrypted. This is easier said than done at present, though, as tags need additional circuitry to handle encryption/decryption, which drives up their costs. Advances in semiconductor technologies coupled with economy of scale are needed to keep the costs low.

- A simple, yet effective authentication mechanism between the tags and readers might be needed for certain types of applications. As described in Chapter 4, the Gen2 protocol adds a "bitmask" to obfuscate communications on the forward channel, keeping costs down by not requiring masking of the reverse channel.

- Readers should require proper authentication and authorization to allow access to their services.

- If deployed on wireless LANs, careful consideration must be given to the security of wireless access points.

- If the network sits on the Internet, the internal network should be prevented from Internet-based attacks through the use of standard firewalls, intrusion detection systems, network sniffers, and so on.

- Anti-collision protocols that make it difficult for someone to track items' EPC codes by monitoring forward-channel traffic can be used.

- A shielded enclosure could reduce the possibility of eavesdropping on the forward channel, but this would probably be an extreme approach in most applications.

Zone 3: RFID service bus

The RFID service bus is a grouping of middleware components that includes the Object Naming Service, the EPC event manager, the EPCIS server, and the RFID integration server.

Vulnerabilities. Components of the RFID service bus communicate with the internal enterprise information systems (over LANs or WANs) and with partner and industry systems (over the Internet).

Threat agents. Threat agents include corporate spies, espionage agents, and intruders.

Example threats. Possible threats include the following:

- As with any enterprise middleware, the RFID service bus is vulnerable to intruders, internal and external spies, and saboteurs.

- By identifying individuals according to items they carry, someone can monitor the whereabouts of those individuals. When this information is tied to other items that are mapped to various locations, the snoop can build a very detailed profile of the flow of goods and information in the enterprise.

- Using the EPCIS, Manufacturer A is querying the EPCIS of Retailer B for the inventory of Product X in store Y. Unless this query/response is protected, a competitor of either Manufacturer A or Retailer B could potentially intercept and mine this data source.*

- Someone (maybe even a competitor) "pretends" to be Manufacturer A and sends a valid EPCIS query to Retailer B, who responds with the results of the query.

---

* Graham Gillen, "RE: RFID Essentials," 22 June 2005, personal email.

Possible countermeasures. Several countermeasures may be taken:

- Adequate network access control may be implemented, using firewalls, intrusion detection systems, network sniffers, and so on. Physical access control mechanisms may also be put in place to restrict access to the premises.

- EPCglobal has a Security Working Group (part of the Software Action Group), co-chaired by VeriSign and ConnecTerra, that is working on specifications to help secure EPCIS communications. It is expected that the recommendations of this group will include already available technologies for the purpose of encrypting Internet communication pipes (such as SSL/TLS) or for encrypting and signing distinct message payloads (WS-Security standards, WS-I interoperability guidelines, AS/2 secure transport protocol). EPCglobal hopes to publish these guidelines in conjunction with the EPCIS specifications in the second half of 2005.*

- EPCglobal is working on a security infrastructure that will define which "Network" participants will be authenticated. This will most likely involve the widely used concept of digital certificates issued from a trusted authority. This is common today in most B2B frameworks, such as RosettaNet and UCCNet. In addition, the ONS is an "authoritative" directory of manufacturer information services that can be consulted to ensure that an EPCIS query is coming from a trusted source.

Zone 4: Enterprise information systems

Enterprise information systems include corporate systems such as Directory, Identity Management, Access Control, and Messaging systems, as well as all the backend systems that will be consumers of RFID data. Backend systems include the ERP systems.

Vulnerabilities. The transaction and data volumes RFID systems require may overwhelm the existing network infrastructure. Companies may be faced with the need to store unexpectedly or potentially sensitive information.

Threat agents. Threat agents include corporate spies, intruders, and pranksters.

Example threats. Two example threats are:

- Individual item tracking could lead to the acquisition of information more valuable than what the storage infrastructure is designed to protect. Information in one system might be useful for tracking individuals if tied to information in other systems. Intruders may value this information more highly than a company realizes, and the company may underinvest in security because of this misperception.

- Enterprise information systems are likely to be exposed to much higher transaction and data volumes with RFID systems than with bar code systems. For example, using a typical bar code system and batch-level tracking, registering the arrival of a case of shaving razors

---

* Ibid.

would probably be tracked as a single transaction containing a single row of data. This transaction might look like: add <quantity> <product bar code id>. Using an RFID system and item-level tracking, the sheer transaction volume between the reader, EPC event managers, and EPC information servers will be vastly increased. If a case contains 100 razors, the system will perform at least 100 transactions of the type: add <EPC Code>.

Possible countermeasures. One area of countermeasures exists:

- Adequate network access control should be implemented, using firewalls, intrusion detection systems, network sniffers, and so on. Physical access control mechanisms may also be put in place to restrict access to the premises. Access control measures must be based on a careful consideration of how data assets might be abused.

Summary

The privacy and security issues discussed in this chapter can be summarized as follows:

- If you are building applications, privacy and security considerations should be central. Making informed and responsible choices will require input from both privacy advocates and efficiency and accountability advocates, in equal measure. Effective education and an ongoing, reasonable dialog among the public and decision makers is the only way to ensure that individual rights and safety are not put at risk in the service of efficiency and also that important opportunities to improve the delivery of goods and services don't run into unnecessary roadblocks.

- Even though the consumer privacy issues surrounding RFID systems seem to get the most press, there are other aspects of security that are equally important. Whereas RFID privacy concerns mainly involve what, when, where, and how much consumer data is being tracked by a third party without the consumer's permission or even knowledge, RFID security focuses on securing RFID systems from pranksters, spies, thieves, and other unauthorized entities.

- When beginning a new RFID project, place privacy and security high on the list of non-functional requirements and track negative public perception as a risk to the project.

- As with any other mission-critical system, it is important to consider and to plan to mitigate threats to the availability, integrity, and confidentiality of your RFID system.

- Security needs differ for different systems. Determine yours early on and develop a master security plan.

- Privacy and security need more than technologies and tools. People and processes play an important role in ensuring that the technologies are used effectively.

- Make a point of joining security mailing lists such as Crypto-Gram,* and follow the debate carried on between industry, government, and organizations such as EPIC. What you don't know can hurt you.

---

* *http://www.counterpane.com/crypto-gram.html.*

CHAPTER ELEVEN

The Future

DR. ALAN KAY ONCE SAID, "The best way to predict the future is to invent it." This is truer now than ever. New and competing RFID technologies emerge almost daily, some of which are refinements to existing systems and some of which are significantly different. Businesses are, for the most part, holding back and waiting for the dust to settle before deciding what, if anything, to do with RFID. The people working in the EPCglobal and ISO groups to forge standards are taking Dr. Kay up on his challenge and choosing to define the future rather than attempting to predict which way it will go. This chapter discusses the trends in standards, technology, and business that are emerging from this effort.

Standards

The development of standards for RFID has been complicated by what Ken Traub described as "a unique application of the standards process," in which the standards are actually seeding a new industry rather than describing existing technologies and practices. "I don't think anyone going in understood that it would take about two years per standard, and so people are frustrated that it is taking time, but if you really step back for a moment and look at what we are doing it's a pretty remarkable accomplishment."*

---

* From a phone interview in March 2005 with Ken Traub, co-founder and CTO of ConnecTerra, co-founder of the EPCglobal Software Action Group, and principal author of many of the EPC standards and specifications, including the EPCglobal Architecture Framework, the EPCIS specification, and the ALE specification.

In addition to the usual challenges of opening up a new field, patent and licensing issues have threatened to slow the process still further. Differing regulations for radio spectrum from country to country have been a challenge as well, not just for EPC standards but also for ISO standards such as those for livestock and companion animal identification. What can we expect from EPCglobal in the near future? What about the ISO? And what standards will China, the largest exporter of manufactured goods in the world, support?

EPCglobal Road Map

With the publication of the Gen2 standard and the ALE specification in early 2005, EPCglobal has begun to complete the picture sketched by the EPCglobal Architecture Framework. Leaders at EPCglobal expect to see a "complete suite of standards in the areas of object exchange, data exchange, and infrastructure by the end of 2005," with support for "very complex multi-party supply chain interactions where you need some central indexing or discovery services to find all the data" in 2006.*

In late 2004 and early 2005, a patent debate began when Intermec surprised the industry by taking a hard line on patents it claims cover important portions of the EPCglobal Gen2 specification. Fortunately, a compromise reached by mid-2005 seems to have left Gen2 relatively unscathed. However, by raising the possibility of license fees for EPC standards, the Intermec patents increased concern that China, already sensitized to license fees by its objections to those for DVD technology, would be less likely to adopt the new standards.

Convergence

Convergence is the act of coming together, and if the theme of 2004 for RFID standards was chaos, the theme for 2005 seems to be convergence. After much uncertainty, the various governments and standards bodies involved seem to be making a genuine effort to cooperate to produce global standards.

ISO/EPCglobal

In February 2005, the EPC UHF Gen2 specification was formally approved at an EAN.UCC forum in Brussels, and it has since been submitted to the ISO. This will hopefully lead to a resolution of some of the conflicts between the previous ISO approach and the EPCglobal approach. The press and pundits seem optimistic that the standard may be rapidly adopted by the ISO.

China

In late 2004, reports warned that China might adopt completely different RFID standards than those proposed by the ISO or EPCglobal. This led to even more uncertainty in what was already a very volatile standards environment. Qiang Bai, the CTO of uniView Technologies and the organizer of the Chinese Association of Science and Technology (CAST)

---

* Ibid.

pavilion at RFIDWorld in Dallas, Texas, said that he thought China would support a global standard, but that it was not interested in licensing proprietary intellectual property (IP) to do so. He cited the IP licensing costs of DVD standards, which have increased the cost of DVD players manufactured in China compared to those manufactured in other countries. He suggested that China might insist upon modifications to the standards to remove anything that might be encumbered by patents.

Although this may not seem like convergence, it represents a dramatic shift toward the adoption of shared standards rather than toward a completely independent RFID standard for China. As one of the world's leading manufacturers, China is in a good position to dictate what kind of identification will be applied to goods at the point of origin. To balance this, Wal-Mart currently buys about $15 billion worth of goods each year from China, and Wal-Mart has, thus far, strongly supported the EPCglobal standards. The influence flows both ways, though, and China's strong interest in a standard unencumbered by license fees is likely to play an important role in shaping global RFID standards.

Technology

Smarter, smaller, cheaper, and faster are the recurring trends in computer-related technologies, so it doesn't take much courage to predict the same for RFID. But what is likely to come of the development of smarter, smaller, cheaper, and faster RFID devices? Our expectation is that this will lead to more-varied sensors and more-active tags making up more-manageable and more-interconnected systems. Most importantly, we also predict (as have others*) that RFID will produce some "killer app" within the next three to five years that will be as unexpected and groundbreaking as the introduction of the World Wide Web in 1990. Let's examine these predictions in order to get an idea of what the future may hold.

More-Numerous and More-Varied Sensors

A person in a crowd is just a person in a crowd, easily ignored. Once we know that person's name, he becomes much more significant. We want to know more, if only to help us place this new identity into our framework of people we recognize. Knowing that Jane owns several bakeries, graduated from the University of Oklahoma, and is very involved in the City Council helps us to remember Jane and understand how she might impact our lives. The principle applies to inanimate objects as well. As we identify more and more things at the edges of our networks, the next, natural step is to want to know more about those things. What is the greatest temperature this fruit has endured? Has this container ever been opened since shipment? Where exactly on the factory floor is that portable wire feed welder right now?

---

* Steve Meloan, "Toward a Global Internet of Things," 11 November 2003, *http://java.sun.com/ developer/technicalArticles/Ecommerce/rfid*.

One of the challenges of dealing with this growing wealth of information is building systems and applications that are capable not only of recording the presence of something and, perhaps, its temperature today, but also of understanding new sensors that may be added in the future. Abstractions around events, which we described along with the ALE specification in Chapter 7, are specifically designed to simplify support for a wide variety of sensors by representing the data from any of them as messages about events submitted in a standardized format and following a common, flexible protocol.

More Active Tags

Although the current wave of RFID adoption has been focused largely on passive tags, this is not likely to remain the case if the cost of active tags drops sufficiently. Advances in the production of chips, antennas, and batteries are steadily reducing the cost of active tags. The EPC road map includes Class IV and Class V tags and assumes they will be active. Real Time Location Systems (RTLSs) can use RF tags, among other technologies, to perform (with a few antennas and some triangulation) tasks that would require a large number of antennas for passive tags. For now, the cost of active tags offsets their tremendous flexibility, with the most expensive component being the batteries. Printable, biodegradable batteries are a particularly promising technology already in use that may greatly reduce the cost of active tags in the near future as well as help to revolutionize the way we think about computing in general. For more on these topics, see the "Printable batteries" and "Ubiquitous and amorphous computing" sections that follow.

EPC Class IV and Class V tags

While EPCglobal's focus recently has been on EPC Class 0, Class I, and Class II tags, which are all passive, the standards describe future tag classes that will instead be active. Class III tags will have an internal power source to power faster processors, more memory, and built-in sensors, but they will still use passive backscatter for communications. Class IV tags will essentially form a wireless peer-to-peer network. These tags won't even need a reader to communicate with other Class IV tags. Class V tags will be readers themselves, capable of powering and reading Class I, Class II, and Class III tags, as well as communicating with Class IV and other Class V tags. To get a sense of how Class IV and Class V tags might work and what they may accomplish, see the "Wireless mesh" and "Ubiquitous and amorphous computing" sections later in this chapter.

Real Time Location Systems

Since an active tag is capable of transmitting a relatively strong signal in comparison to the reflected signal of a passive tag, active tags may be used as locator beacons and placed in two- or three-dimensional space using triangulation. This means that with only two or three antennas, a reader can determine the location of each tag in a roomful of tags. Figure 11-1 shows how this could change our smart shelf example from Chapter 2. Notice the two antennas mounted high on the walls. With only these two antennas, we can determine the locations of the active tags attached to each of the items shown on the shelves.

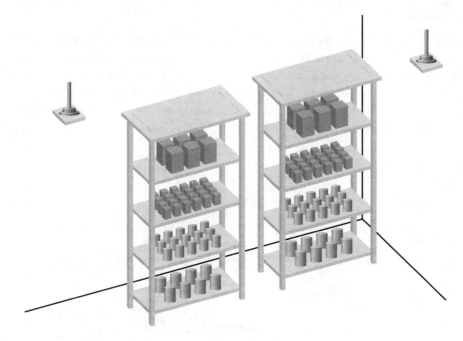

FIGURE 11-1. An RTLS in action

In our earlier example from Chapter 2, each shelving unit had multiple antennas to recognize the arrival and departure of passive tags. Using active tags, the entire sales floor might require only two antennas for coverage. Figure 11-2 shows how the same signal from an active tag arrives at the two antennas at different times.

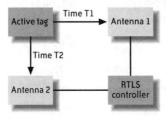

FIGURE 11-2. Using triangulation to locate items in two dimensions

By precisely measuring the time the signal takes to travel from the active tag, the controller is able to determine that the item is four meters from Antenna 1 and two meters from Antenna 2. This places the tag in a two-dimensional coordinate system. If the item then moves from that location, rather than sending these measurements to an application, the reader and ALE server conspire to make this very different technology generate exactly the same events as a passive smart shelf application. An item leaving a shelf is, after all, an item leaving a shelf regardless of how you recognize it.

Printable batteries

Computer printers are amazing devices. They take something represented in bits and turn it into atoms. An ink jet printer follows a template in memory and precisely sprays small droplets of ink until the design made of bits in memory is transferred to paper. Now, if the printer sprays one ink containing zinc, another ink that is an electrolyte such as a salt water gel, and a third ink containing manganese dioxide, together the layers of these inks will form a battery. Figure 11-3 shows the layers.

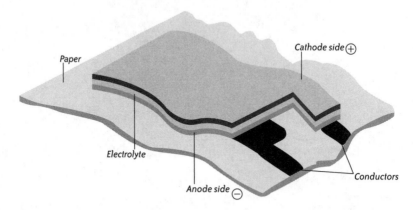

FIGURE 11-3. A battery printed on paper (image courtesy of Power Paper)

These batteries, which are already in use for disposable medical equipment such as digital thermometers and in novelty school supplies such as folders with built-in calculators and games, coupled with thin, flexible, and efficient circuits also printed in place, can turn something as simple as a business card into an interactive application for only a few cents each. Speaking more directly to our concerns here, active tags no larger than passive smart labels are already available using this technology.

More Manageability

As discussed in Chapter 9, manageability and extensibility are key concerns for RFID systems. These two properties of a system are, not coincidentally, also the most affected by the need for standards. With a system of numerous individual devices widely dispersed over a large area and deployed in rough conditions, new devices are likely to be added in addition to and in place of old devices. If the management infrastructure is proprietary, the types of new devices supported could be very limited. Even a new manufacturer for a temperature probe otherwise identical to the one it replaces might lead to significant code changes. Fortunately, because these concerns also affect other types of systems, such as manufacturing and building automation systems, standards that will become increasingly important for RFID systems in the field are already available.

IEEE 802.15.4 (ZigBee)

ZigBee is an emerging standard for a network layer based on the Institute of Electrical and Electronics Engineers (IEEE) standard 802.15.4. It is a low-power, always-on, physical and media access control protocol designed specifically for low-power, low-latency communication with sensors and control devices. This simple protocol can be implemented on inexpensive hardware, requires very little power, and can support a large number of sensors and controllers with very little latency. Expect to see ZigBee compatibility in many devices around the home and in RFID readers in the near future. In addition, active RFID tags may themselves be ZigBee-enabled, allowing them to interoperate with generic management systems designed for other building automation, home automation, and manufacturing purposes.

Jini

Jini is a technology developed by Sun Microsystems that allows devices to dynamically discover each other and work together on a network. A simple example is probably more suited to our purpose here than a long discussion of remote invocation and Java spaces. The classic example is a Jini-enabled car and cell phone. The phone, upon entering the car, searches for devices that describe themselves as having speakers. The phone then downloads interface software from a speaker that allows the phone to use that speaker when a call comes in. When the phone is removed from the car and brought into a home, it searches for a device with a speaker in the new location and finds speakers on the home entertainment system.

This is nice with a cell phone. It's a critical requirement for a sensor network. Systems will have to support the addition over time of new sensors that may not have even been invented when the systems were designed. Also critical to a system in a harsh environment is the capability to "route around" failures. One sensor may fail, requiring the system to find an alternate source of data in real time. Jini offers the basic toolset for this kind of dynamic system. Many of the trends and opportunities described in the following sections are a result of advanced technologies such as Jini.

More-Interconnected Systems

All computing systems, not just RFID systems, are moving toward becoming more connected—connected with each other, with the Internet, and with us. The same technologies that support this trend in other systems are important to the future of RFID as well. For many years, the Internet Protocol, Version 6 (IPv6) has slowly but inexorably extended in deployment and has been routing more and more traffic on the Internet. With recent mandates, this technology is close to the critical mass necessary to make it the default protocol. New topologies may also change the way RFID systems are deployed. Sensor networks may evolve into mesh networks composed of many peers rather than a star arrangement with a central "hub" and many "spokes." Even further into the future, expect to see the materials from which we build relatively mundane objects include, along with properties such as color or tensile strength, a new property: computing power. Smart materials and amorphous computing offer the promise of a network of objects serving double duty as physical objects such as walls and floors and processors for information. Wild as it may seem, the first working prototypes are already in the labs.

IPv6

The protocol computers (or more properly, networks) use to communicate on the Internet (remember, it means inter-network) is the Internet Protocol, Version 4 (IPv4). This decades-old protocol routes packets for everything from web browsing to Voice over IP (VoIP) phone calls and, increasingly, peer-to-peer applications such as BitTorrent. Consider a phone call. Each end of the call has a number, an address. Without getting too far into the details, IPv4 is able to support a maximum of about 3.7 billion addresses (actually, more like 500 million for Class C, as the addresses were originally assigned). This made sense when the protocol was designed, as it was only intended to route between a few hundred thousand, or possibly a few million, points. Early growth led to a "classless" scheme for assigning numbers. This increased capacity, but the explosive growth of the Internet in the 1990s threatened to overwhelm the limited number space nevertheless.

In 1994, the Internet Engineering Task Force (IETF) proposed a new Internet Protocol called IPv6 or IPng (for IP Next Generation) with a greatly increased address space. As the following examples show, IPv6 has a much larger address space than IPv4:

```
IPv4 Localhost
127.0.0.1

IPv6 Localhost
0000:0000:0000:0000:0000:0000:0000:0001

IPv6 Localhost (shortform)
::1
```

It's been more than 10 years since the introduction of IPv6, and an anonymous wit has described IPv6 as "a protocol that will always be just two years from widespread adoption." Sometimes touted as the cure-all for the Internet's mobility, security, and ad-hoc addressing challenges and other times derided as an unneeded and expensive waste of time, IPv6 is one of those polarizing topics like religion and politics best not brought up in polite conversation. But, at long last, the protocol may be seeing some life. The U.S. Department of Defense has recently committed to an IPv6 transition for all networked systems by 2008. Japan is currently following an even more ambitions plan as part of the e-Japan Priority Policy Program.

What does this have to do with RFID? Well, for one thing, IPv6 supports an address space large enough to serve in the place of EPC codes for RFID tags. Of course, no one is seriously arguing that these numbers—which are, remember, addresses for packets—should be used to identify bars of soap. But what about television sets? If a television is able to stream video over the Internet, it will obviously need an IP address (either IPv4 or IPv6).

There are many more televisions in the world than personal computers, but IPv4 could still probably handle them all with some creativity. But what about mobile phones, or active RFID tags capable of serving web pages?

As the "Internet of Things" extends to more and more types of objects that have not traditionally been connected, the address space needed to route packets between them becomes greater and greater. IPv4 may be able to handle two billion addresses, or possibly even three billion. But what if five billion people had VoIP cell phones? What if for every person on the planet there were a hundred networked sensors monitoring everything from air quality to pacemakers? Chances are, this estimate is conservative. Sensor networks and RFID may be the final impetus to push adoption of IPv6.

> ## NOTE
> For more details on IPv6, you should check out RFC 2460 (available at *http://www.ietf.org*) or read *IPv6 Essentials*, by Silvia Hagan (O'Reilly).

Wireless mesh

A satellite wouldn't be of much use if it had to plug into a wall socket. As sensors spread into ever harder to reach corners of our environment, we will find it more and more difficult to connect them to a wired network. Even traditional wireless networks pose problems, since each sensor may not have a clear line of sight to a wireless hub. Adding repeaters can help, but this means added cost for devices that will essentially do nothing but forward packets. Wouldn't it be nice if each sensor (and other device) in the network could act as a hub, a repeater, or an end point, depending on the need?

Wired and even wireless networks are often configured according to a star, ring, or linear topology. That is, all of the nodes connect to one central hub in a star pattern, or they connect to one or two neighbors to form a ring or line. These topologies are rigid and reliable but brittle. One lost node can bring down a network, because each node is always in a particular place in the topology and communicates only with its preassigned connections. A mesh network, in contrast, is a messy emergent thing where nodes connect to each other willy-nilly and pass packets around like juicy gossip from one node to another until they happens to reach the right nodes, seemingly by chance. This is a floppy, unreliable way to connect things together, but it is extremely resilient, since the loss of any single node has little impact on the network. Mesh networks also overcome line-of-sight problems, because a node may be able to forward a packet to a neighbor who then forwards it to another neighbor who happens to have visibility to the final destination.

For the purists, a mesh network is a network where each node is connected to more than one other node. What we will talk about here is what is known as a wireless, ad-hoc, partial mesh. This is a topology where the nodes are connected and disconnected from time to time and each node connects to some, but not all of the other nodes. Figure 11-4 shows how a wireless mesh network can "see around" an obstruction.

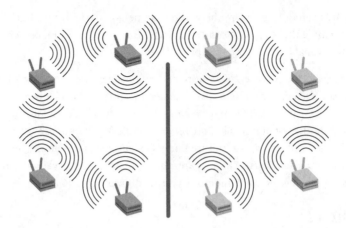

FIGURE 11-4. Wireless mesh network

The obstruction—a wall, in this case—blocks the line of sight from nodes on the right to nodes on the left. A single node beyond the wall has visibility to some of the members of each group and, as is the nature of a mesh network, this node automatically routes communication between the two separate groups. An RFID system made up of readers, passive tags, active tags, and other sensors might be deployed as a mesh network, allowing components to be added and removed with a minimum of disruption and reconfiguration. Mesh products are available now from the usual suspects as well as new vendors with a focus on mesh technology. In addition, just about any device that currently supports wired or wireless Ethernet networks can participate in a mesh network.

Ubiquitous and amorphous computing

Mark Weiser is often called the "Father of Ubiquitous Computing." What he proposes is that, in order to make interacting with computers more efficient, productive, and natural, devices with computing power should be everywhere in our environment, interacting with each other (ubiquitous) and with us in ways that are as intuitive and as inconspicuous as possible (amorphous). Imagine an office where the walls are displays and input devices, a place where a person can interact with the room itself—the walls, the desk—using touch, voice, and gestures. The workspace becomes a set of smart tools with no one thing in the room that might be identified as "the computer." You can probably imagine how the sensors and mesh networks discussed previously might make some of this possible, but where will the processors be? How could a whole wall display work without costing a fortune? The secret might be in the paint.

Each year, a consumer's money buys more and more computing power per dollar. This has contributed to a trend in software and systems to depend on increasingly powerful hardware. The reason for this is that buying more hardware is cheaper than optimization. Since 1998, however, the Defense Allocations Research Project Agency (DARPA) and the MIT Artificial Intelligence Lab have been working on a concept called *amorphous computing*. Just as mesh networks challenge some of the ideas behind conventional network topologies, amorphous computing shakes up what we think of as a computer. The entire effort is based on a simple idea: What if we built systems using the smallest and cheapest computing devices possible and used many of them together to solve some of the same problems that a single, more expensive computing device might solve?

Along with the idea of using cooperative "mobs," "motes," and "smart dust" or "smart paint" to perform calculations, amorphous computing offers the opportunity to include processing power very close to sensors and even in the individual pixels of a display. Amorphous computing takes for granted that the individual units in a smart material may have only sporadic and failure-prone communication. Individual elements may become unavailable due to motion or failure, but this should not interfere with computation. Figure 11-5 shows one concept of how each individual computing device might be embedded in a medium that provides both power and communication. Each unit communicates only with a few of its nearest neighbors, as we described in the "Wireless mesh" section, earlier in this chapter. The antennas represent one possible sensor attachment.

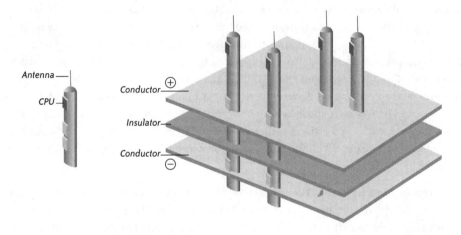

FIGURE 11-5. Amorphous computing

Future active RFID tags capable of tag-to-tag communication, such as the proposed Class IV and Class V EPC tags, may present an opportunity for amorphous computing as a side benefit of the presence of computing devices with the capability to communicate. Amorphous and ubiquitous computing are complementary approaches to enabling the fundamental shift in computing out to the edge of the network, to the "Network of Things." Because of amorphous computing's flexibility (both literally and figuratively), it may be possible to manufacture a "computational substrate" in bulk and cut it with a pair of scissors to fit your space. Massive computational power could someday be bought in sheets like wallpaper or painted onto surfaces like latex semi-gloss. Computational power, as we mentioned above, would then become another property of a material, like its color and weight. But with all of this power for use at the edge of the network, how will it be allocated to tasks? Who will have permission to program the walls of your office, your home, or the White House?

RFID may again be a key technology in making amorphous and ubiquitous computing practical. A person may carry an RFID tag containing an encryption key that allows her, upon entering an office or entertainment room, to authenticate herself to the systems embedded in the walls and furniture with an additional password and biometric scan. The RFID tag then becomes the "something you have" in the security triad of "something you know, something you are, and something you have."

Candidates for the "killer app" can usually be identified only in retrospect. The killer app for Apple II was the VisiCalc spreadsheet; the jury is still out on whether email or the web browser has been the killer app for the Internet. But even in the misty past prior to 1990, there were those who suggested that hypertext might be pretty important someday. With their luck in mind, we will try here to peer into the future of RFID and describe what we see. Both of the sections below describe applications for which prototypes already exist.

Micro payments

As mentioned before, RFID could be a key enabler for ubiquitous computing. We talked about how it could be used to provide IDs for authentication, but there are other ways RFID could be critical to making these technologies work. Not long ago, driving home from work, you wouldn't have been likely to call home to let your family know when to expect you. Too much time and effort would have been required to locate a pay phone, pull over, and dig for change. Now, with more ubiquitous phone service, many of us make calls we would never have made before. Imagine calling home in 1980 to let your spouse know that you were "at the street corner a block away on the pay phone." These days it's not unheard of to use a cell phone rather than the doorbell! "Hello? I'm here, just outside. Meet me in the driveway."

What changed our behavior? The ubiquity of mobile phones is the most obvious answer, but that's not the whole story. The cost of making a call was also reduced, not just by reducing the time and effort necessary to make the call, but by reducing the actual per-minute charge. Most of us remember when calls from a pay phone cost a dime. More recently they were a quarter, and then thirty-five cents. Per-minute charges on the worst cell plan are nothing near that expensive. With the cost of the conversation reduced and telephones always at our fingertips, we are willing to engage in conversations with less perceived value. This concept applies to other forms of communication as well. Compare bulk mailings to email spam. Email spam is such a plague because the incremental cost to spammers of sending their little gems of artifice is negligible.

Now, instead of free talk-time or free email, apply that same reasoning to computing power. If computing power were almost free, individuals or groups might take advantage of it, running massive calculations that would, ironically, leave others without enough computing power to complete their necessary tasks. An example might be an unscrupulous group that used the entire computing power of a small city to crack the encryption of financial transactions. What makes this particular exploit unfeasible now is the cost of acquiring so much computing power; if computing power was cheaper, the disincentive to abuse it would also be reduced. One solution might be to provide users with IDs that are attached in some way to any running "jobs" in the system. The systems might have accounting features that "charge" either real fees or credits in some system of allocation that limits users to varying levels of resource consumption.

A convenient way to handle these IDs would be to put them into RFID tags. Using a centralized account for storing user credits would be prohibitively expensive and would cancel out much of the value derived from the distributed, locally defined amorphous computing approach. This problem could be solved by having the active RFID tag actually act as a "smart wallet," storing credits that are deducted as they're used and "recharged" when the user terminates running jobs. More issues and questions are raised by this idea than we have room here to discuss, but it's not the most bizarre use of RFID we may see in the near future.

Augmented reality

Using a portable projector combined with an RFID reader, researchers at Mitsubishi Electric Research Labs have invented a way to project labels directly onto objects identified by RFID tags. This is more than a new user interface; it also involves a completely new idea for tag singulation.

Using a reader with a built-in projector, a user can find items by waving the reader in their general direction. The projector will adjust for motion and position and project a mark on the item or items of interest. The system works by first sending out an RF pulse that energizes the passive tags. The projector then projects a pattern over the general area, scanning around until the photo sensor on a tag recognizes the pattern. The tag informs the reader that it is currently illuminated, and the projector then projects whatever images are appropriate, oriented according to a calculation based on which tags report being illuminated and, possibly, other location information. Figure 11-6 shows how this might look.

The projected image can be arbitrarily complex, so the device could be used to outline a part on a shelf or to recognize the presence or absence of specific components on a workbench. The device could then display video and graphics, complete with arrows projected on the parts themselves to show how to assemble them.

A variation of this device could use invisible infrared light to singulate the tags and orient itself. It could then project the markings not onto the items but directly into the user's eye, thereby creating a private "heads-up display" oriented with and overlaid onto the physical world. The projection of such a display is called "augmented reality." Systems already exist to provide augmented reality to pilots, technicians, surgeons, and even bulldozer operators. What the Mitsubishi researchers have done is apply this idea to the "Network of Things" and thus allow people to actually visualize and more easily manipulate how items are connected to information through RFID tags.

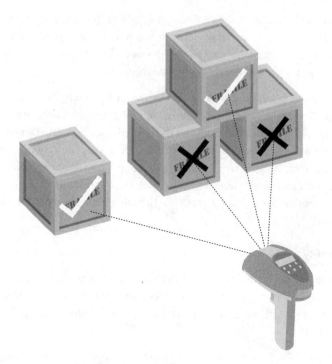

FIGURE 11-6. RFID-facilitated augmented reality

Business

We've peered into our crystal ball for this chapter, but when it comes to the future of business, we leave the scrying to the professionals. On a panel at the 2004 EPCglobal U.S. Conference, Sarah Friar, Vice President of Goldman Sachs and Company, said that mentioning RFID was the "easiest way to get on a CIO's agenda." But she agreed with her fellow panelist, Reik Reed, Director and Senior Analyst for Robert W. Baird Company, when he said that in 2005 we should "expect suppliers to meet mandates, but do so at minimal cost." Friar added, however, that she believes we can expect major implementations in 2006.

Summary

As businesses carefully test the waters, standards and technology are catching up with the potential applications at an accelerating rate. Somewhere out there, someone may be developing a specific use for RFID that will be the "killer app" that makes a global network of things a reality in the very near future. Then again, maybe that person is you.

We hope this book has given you a firm foundation in RFID and prepared you to participate in one of the technologies that, along with other "edge" technologies, may affect business, society, and culture as much as or more than the invention of the telegraph. If the best way to predict the future is to invent it, you are in a unique position to know the "shape of things to come." Get to work.

EPC Identity Encodings

THIS APPENDIX DESCRIBES THE HEADERS, PARTITION TABLES, AND FIELDS used to encode EPC identities to 96-bit binary strings, as defined in Version 1.1, Revision 1.26 of the EPC Tag Data Standard. To help explain the meanings of the fields, each encoding includes a practical example of how to convert a bar code to an EPC and then to a bit string. For an explanation of partition tables and the encoding process, see Chapter 4. EPCglobal has indicated that it will support even more encodings in the future, so be sure to check Appendix B for information on how to stay up to date as these new encodings become available.

As a reminder, the general algorithm for creating the bit string is:

1. Find the appropriate header for the identity type.
2. Look up the partition value based on the length of the Company Prefix.
3. Concatenate the 8-bit header, 3-bit filter, and 3-bit partition fields.
4. Append to this the Company Prefix and other fields appropriate to the identity (for example, Item Reference and Serial Number for an SGTIN).
5. Calculate the CRC and append the EPC to the end of the CRC.

GS1 SGTIN Encoding

The SGTIN is an extension of the GS1 Global Trade Item Number (GTIN) that assigns Company Prefixes and Item References for use in identifying a particular class of object. The common 12-digit UPC and 13-digit EAN bar codes are a subset of the GTIN. These types of codes are being merged with the 14-digit GTIN in 2005 by prepending zeros to the existing codes. The GTIN doesn't have an individual item Serial Number, so the SGTIN appends a Serial Number, the value of which is assigned by the General Manager.

Figure A-1 shows a typical UPC bar code. To convert this UPC into an EPC and store it on an RFID tag, we must first convert it to a GTIN. This bar code has an Indicator Digit (0), a Company Prefix (12345), an Item Reference (54322), and a Check Digit (7). To convert this to a GTIN, we take the entire code as a string and add two zeros to the beginning, yielding a GTIN of 00012345543227. Notice that our Company Prefix has now become 00012345, an 8-digit number. We will then convert the GTIN to an SGTIN, which allows us to track individual items, by adding a Serial Number (4208).

FIGURE A-1. UPC bar code

To represent a pure identity, the EPC uses a URI expressed in the URN notation. For an SGTIN, this notation is:

    urn:epc:id:sgtin:CompanyPrefix.ItemReference.SerialNumber

This notation includes only the information necessary to tell one item from another; it does not include the GTIN check digit or a filter value. The Item Reference here is actually the Indicator Digit plus the Item Reference from the GTIN (Figure A-2). Our example would thus be encoded as:

    urn:epc:id:sgtin:00012345.054322.4208

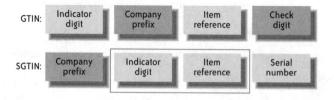

FIGURE A-2. Conversion of GTIN to SGTIN

To express an identity encoded as SGTIN-96, a value dependent on the tag type, the EPC uses a different format for the URN:

    urn:epc:tag:sgtin-96:*FilterValue*.*CompanyPrefix*.*ItemReference*.*SerialNumber*

Using this notation, our example would be encoded as:

    urn:epc:tag:sgtin-96:2.00012345.054322.4208

Table A-1 shows the possible values for an SGTIN-96 partition. In each case, the 44 available bits are partitioned with different lengths for the Company Prefix and Item Reference. From the table, we see that our 8-digit Company Prefix belongs to partition 4, which allows 8 digits (27 bits) for the Company Prefix and 5 digits (17 bits) for the Item Reference. (The Company Prefix will become our General Manager Number in the EPC, and the Indicator Digit plus the Item Reference will become the Object Class.) The check digit is discarded.

TABLE A-1. SGTIN-96 partition values

Partition	Company Prefix		Item Reference	
	Bits	Digits	Bits	Digits
0	40	12	4	1
1	37	11	7	2
2	34	10	10	3
3	30	9	14	4
4	27	8	17	5
5	24	7	20	6
6	20	6	24	7

Tags store binary representations of the EPC codes. Since we are building an SGTIN-96, the standard header value is 0011 0000, or 30 hex. (Table A-2 shows the possible SGTIN header values.) Building the SGTIN-96 is simply a matter of concatenating bits, starting with the header as the most significant bit (MSB), followed by the bits for the filter (3 bits), the partition (3 bits), the Company Prefix (27 bits in our case), an integer value made by appending the Item Reference to the Identifier Digit (17 bits in our case), and the Serial Number (38 bits). The GTIN checksum is discarded. This yields an SGTIN-96 (in hex) of 305000181CB50C8000001070. This value is then stored in the tag along with a 16-bit CRC (CCITT-CRC), which would be FFF1 in this case. The value with CRC would be FFF1305000181CB50C8000001070.

TABLE A-2. SGTIN header values

Type	Header
SGTIN-96	0011 0000
SGTIN-64	10

GS1 SSCC Encoding

Serial Shipping Container Codes (SSCCs) uniquely identify individual shipping containers, such as the ATA shipping containers used for air cargo and the ISO containers used aboard container ships. An SSCC is an 18-digit code that contains an Extension Digit, a Company Prefix, and a Serial Reference, which must be unique for 12 months. A modulo 10 check digit is added at the end to ensure data integrity. Figure A-3 shows a typical SSCC code.

(00) 00801234999999997

FIGURE A-3. An SSCC as a UCC-128 bar code

The code begins with an optional Application Identifier, "(00)," which is not strictly a part of the code but is often used. This is not converted for the EPC. The next digit is the Extension Digit (more about that later), which is followed by a zero that, as with the GTIN identifiers discussed previously, may be added to a UCC Company Prefix to change it into a Company Prefix for an SSCC (here, making 801234 into the Company Prefix 0801234). The next field is the Serial Reference, which in this case is 999999999. An Extension Digit of 0 between the Application Identifier and the leading zero of the Company Prefix means that the Serial Reference may actually be represented as 099999999. The last digit, 7, is a modulo 10 check digit.

The SSCC pure identity can be encoded using the URN notation for SSCC:

urn:epc:id:sscc:*CompanyPrefix.SerialReference*

In our example, this would be:

urn:epc:id:sscc:0801234.0999999999

This would be encoded for a 96-bit tag as the URN:

urn:epc:tag:sscc-96:*FilterValue.CompanyPrefix.SerialReference*

For our example, this would be:

urn:epc:tag:sscc-96:2.0801234.0999999999

Company Prefixes in SSCCs, as in SGTINs, are of variable length, and the SSCC-96 encoding uses partition numbers similar to those used in encoding SGTINs. Table A-3 shows the partition values for SSCC-96.

Partition	Company Prefix		Serial Reference and Extension Digit	
	Bits	Digits	Bits	Digits
0	40	12	18	5
1	37	11	21	6
2	34	10	24	7
3	30	9	28	8
4	27	8	31	9
5	24	7	34	10
6	20	6	38	11

The physical realization of the SSCC-96 begins at the MSB with the header 0011 0001 (8 bits) and concatenates the filter value (3 bits), for which we will again use the value 2. Next comes the partition value (3 bits). For our example, this value would be 5. The Company Prefix is next (24 bits), followed by the Extension Digit plus the Serial Reference, encoded in 34 bits. The check digit is discarded, as in the SGTIN. The value is then padded to 96 bits by adding 24 trailing zero bits. The hex value for our example would thus be 315461CE90773593FE000000; with the CRC it is 7E57315461CE90773593FE000000.

GS1 GLN/SGLN Encoding

The Global Location Number (GLN) is an identifier introduced in January 2004 that contains a Company Prefix and a Location Reference in 12 digits, followed by a single check digit. The Location Reference field can identify a specific location such as a cabinet or warehouse gate, or it can identify an aggregate location such as a factory or a hospital. A GLN can also represent a logical entity, such as a region or department. The way GS1 describes this is that the GLN can represent any legal, functional, or physical entity. EPCglobal only uses this code as it refers to a specific physical location, indicated by the Application Identifier "(414)." At some point, EPCglobal will add a Serial Number to the GLN, creating a proper Serialized GLN (SGLN). This field should not be used for now, although for the purposes of our example we will populate it with zeros as a placeholder.

As we have seen with other encodings, we can change the UCC Company Prefix into a Company Prefix by adding a leading zero. In Figure A-4, the UCC Company Prefix was 012345. Adding a leading zero makes it 0012345. The Location Reference is 00002, and the check digit is 7. The "(414)" is the Application Identifier.

The SGLN pure identity can be encoded using the URN notation for SGLN:

    urn:epc:id:sgln:*CompanyPrefix*.*LocationReference*

In our example, this would be:

    urn:epc:id:sgln:0012345.00002

(414) 0012345000027

FIGURE A-4. A GLN encoded as an EAN-13 bar code

This would be encoded for a 96-bit tag as the URN:

    urn:epc:tag:sgln-96:FilterValue.CompanyPrefix.LocationReference

For our example (assuming again a filter value of 2), this would be:

    urn:epc:tag:sgln-96:2.0012345.00002

Encoding an SGLN to a 96-bit tag using SGLN-96 again requires a partition table.
Table A-4 describes the partition types available for SGLNs. From this table, we can see
that our example would have a partition type of 5.

TABLE A-4. SGLN partition values

Partition	Company Prefix		Serial Reference and Extension Digit	
	Bits	Digits	Bits	Digits
0	40	12	1	0
1	37	11	4	1
2	34	10	7	2
3	30	9	11	3
4	27	8	14	4
5	24	7	17	5
6	20	6	21	6

The physical realization of the SGLN-96 begins at the MSB with the header 0011 0010 (8
bits) and concatenates the filter value (3 bits), for which we will again use the value 2.
Next comes the partition value (3 bits). For our example, this value is 5. The Company
Prefix is next (24 bits), followed by the Location Reference (encoded in 17 bits). The check
digit is discarded, as with GTINs and SSCCs. Lastly, we append 41 bits set to zeros as a
placeholder for the future Serial Number field. The hex value for our example would thus
be 325400C0E400040000000000, which, with the CRC, is
823D325400C0E400040000000000.

GS1 GRAI Encoding

The Global Returnable Asset Identifier (GRAI), also known as Application Identifier "(8003)," allows trading partners to track transport equipment and packaging that may temporarily change possession from one partner to another. These items should have enough intrinsic value that the owner expects them to be returned and may even charge a fee or a deposit for their use. They could be anything from reusable packaging to pallet-jacks and trailers. Any logistical asset that may be rented or loaned out with the expectation of its return would make a good candidate for a GRAI. The code contains a Company Prefix (formed as described previously, by taking the assigned Company Prefix or adding a leading zero to a UCC Company Prefix), followed by an Asset Type and an optional Serial Number. The EPC is only capable of encoding GRAI Serial Numbers that have no leading zeros, although the GRAI specification itself does allow for Serial Numbers with leading zeros.

The bar code in Figure A-5 represents a GRAI in which the Company Prefix is 0614141. The Asset Type is 12345, and the modulo 10 check digit is 2. The Serial Number is 543210. The "(8003)" that precedes the Company Prefix is an Application Identifier, which indicates that this bar code is a "UPC/EAN Number and Serial Number of a Returnable Asset." The zero that precedes the Company Prefix is a static part of the GRAI code.

(8003) 00614141123452543210

FIGURE A-5. A GRAI as a UCC-128 bar code

The GRAI pure identity can be encoded using the URN notation for GRAI:

    urn:epc:id:grai:*CompanyPrefix.AssetType.SerialNumber*

In our example, this would be:

    urn:epc:id:grai:0614141.12345.543210

This would be encoded for a 96-bit tag as the URN:

    urn:epc:tag:grai-96:*FilterValue.CompanyPrefix.AssetType.SerialNumber*

For our example (assuming again a filter value of 2), this would be:

    urn:epc:tag:grai-96:2.0614141.12345.543210

Encoding a GRAI to a 96-bit tag using GRAI-96 again requires a partition table. Table A-5 describes the partition types available for GRAIs. From this table, we can see that our example would have a partition type of 5.

TABLE A-5. GRAI partition values

Partition	Company Prefix		Asset Type	
	Bits	Digits	Bits	Digits
0	40	12	4	0
1	37	11	7	1
2	34	10	10	2
3	30	9	14	3
4	27	8	17	4
5	24	7	20	5
6	20	6	24	6

The physical realization of the GRAI-96 begins at the MSB with the header 0011 0011 (8 bits) and concatenates the filter value (3 bits), for which we will again use the value 2. Next comes the partition value (3 bits). For our example, this value would be 4. The Company Prefix is next (27 bits), followed by the Asset Type (encoded in 17 bits). The check digit is discarded, as it was in the previous encodings. Lastly, we encode the Serial Number as 38 bits. The hex value for our example would thus be 3354257BF40C0E40000849EA, which, with the CRC, is 4FF73354257BF40C0E40000849EA.

GS1 GIAI Encoding

The Global Individual Asset Identifier (GIAI), also known as Application Identifier "(8004)," provides a unique identifier for assets. Whereas GRAI numbers identify assets that may be loaned or rented out, the GIAI identifies assets that typically do not leave the possession of the owner. For example, a lathe might have a GIAI number for program maintenance and warranty tracking, or an office chair might be identified with a GIAI for enterprise resource planning.

The GIAI is composed of the usual Company Prefix followed by an Individual Asset Reference. In Figure A-6, "(8004)" is the Application Identifier for GIAI, the Company Prefix is 007654321, and the Individual Asset Reference is 12345. Note that there is no check digit.

(8004) 0076543211 2345

FIGURE A-6. A GIAI encoded as a UCC-128 bar code

The GIAI pure identity can be encoded using the URN notation for GIAI:

```
urn:epc:id:giai:CompanyPrefix.IndividualAssetReference
```

In our example, this would be:

urn:epc:id:giai:007654321.12345

This would be encoded for a 96-bit tag as the URN:

urn:epc:tag:giai-96:*FilterValue.CompanyPrefix.IndividualAssetReference*

For our example (assuming again a filter value of 2), this would be:

urn:epc:tag:giai-96:2.007654321.12345

Encoding a GIAI to a 96-bit tag using GIAI-96 again requires a partition table. Table A-6 describes the partition types available for GIAIs. From this table, we can see that our example would have a partition type of 3.

TABLE A-6. GIAI partition values

Partition	Company Prefix		Individual Asset Reference	
	Bits	Digits	Bits	Digits
0	40	12	42	12
1	37	11	45	13
2	34	10	48	14
3	30	9	52	15
4	27	8	55	16
5	24	7	58	17
6	20	6	62	18

The physical realization of the GIAI-96 begins at the MSB with the header 0011 0100 (8 bits) and concatenates the filter value (3 bits), for which we will again use the value 2. Next comes the partition value (3 bits). For our example, this value would be 3. The Company Prefix is next (30 bits), followed by the Individual Asset Reference (encoded in 52 bits). The hex value for our example would thus be 344C074CBB10000000003039, which, with the CRC, is 38AC344C074CBB10000000003039.

References

THE GOAL OF THIS BOOK Is to give you an overview of the essential components of an RFID system. In this appendix, we have provided some of the references we found useful to help you learn more. Even in this list, we can't possibly cover every publication and company in the field. If we have missed a resource here that you think we should have included, please contact us at this book's web site, where we will keep a growing list of RFID resources along with news and updates:

Web site: *http://www.rfidessentials.com*
Contact: *http://www.rfidessentials.com/contact*

Organizations, Standards, and Specifications

There are many organizations whose standards and specifications define one or more components of an RFID system. These are some of the most important global standards organizations. You should also check with appropriate regional and national standards organizations and other RFID-oriented organizations, which serve as a great place to meet others in the field. Here are just a few to get you started.

AIM Global RFID

The Association for Automatic Identification and Mobility (AIM) is a global trade association comprised of providers of components, networks, systems, and services that manages the collection and integration of data using information management systems. As part of its mandate, it produces specifications and standards for RFID, RTLSs, and other technologies.

Web site: *http://www.rfid.org*
Contact: *info@aimglobal.org*

EPCglobal, Inc.

EPCglobal is the organization developing standards for the Electronic Product Code (EPC) and for RFID systems to store and manage EPCs. This organization is a collaboration between RFID technology vendors and major customers and integrators. It is sponsored by GS1, the organization that manages existing bar code standards. Over the last few years, EPCglobal has been the organization to watch for some of the most important standards in RFID.

Web site: *http://www.epcglobalinc.org*
Contact: *http://www.epcglobalinc.org/contact_us/contact_us.html*

GS1

The European Article Number and Uniform Code Council groups, formerly known as "EAN.UCC," chose the new name "GS1" in 2005. *GS1* is not an abbreviation but instead stands for "one global standard, one global system and one global organisation." This organization is responsible for establishing global bar code, data interchange, and (through EPCglobal) RFID standards.

Web site: *http://www.gs1.org*
Contact: *http://www.gs1.org/index.php?http://www.gs1.org/members.html&2*

International Organization for Standardization (ISO)

The ISO is a leading international standards body that is behind some of the most influential standards in almost every area of technology and manufacturing. The ISO also has specific standards for RFID.

Web site: *http://www.iso.org*
Contact: *http://www.iso.org/iso/en/xsite/contact/contact.html*

Internet Engineering Task Force (IETF)

The IETF is an international group open to anyone interested in helping to define the standards and practices that allow the Internet to work. IETF documents are created through the Request for Comment (RFC) process. For example, the IETF Mission Statement is documented in RFC 3935. This is the organization that defined the IPv4 and IPv6 protocols described in Chapter 11.

One of the RFCs of most interest here is RFC 2460 ("Internet Protocol, Version 6 (IPv6) Specification"), by S. Deering and R. Hinden.

Web site: *http://www.ietf.org*
Contact: *http://www.ietf.org/secretariat.html*

RFID Tribe

From the RFID Tribe web site: "RFID Tribe, a global organization with local chapters, is a radio frequency identification (RFID) collaboration forum. The group of industry experts collaborates on RFID and sensor technology, standards, venture capital, products, solutions, industry trends, people and events. RFID Tribe serves as an engine for ideas, people and capital." This organization, founded by Mark Johnson, has a very innovative incentive program for participation, which may be part of the reason it's so successful. This is a really good place to meet investors, customers, developers, and experts in the field.

Web site: *http://www.rfidtribe.com*
Contact: *info@rfidtribe.com*

Important Papers on RFID

- Gagne, Martin. "Identity-Based Encryption: A Survey." *RSA Laboratories CryptoBytes* 6, no.1 (2003): 10–19.

- Garfinkel, Simson. "The Trouble with RFID." *The Nations,* 16 February 2004, *http://www.thenation.com/doc/20040216/garfinkel/.*

- Hill, John. "Automatic Data Collection Perspective." *Esync,* 2003, *http://www.esync.com/whitePapers.asp.*

- Hill, John. "RFID: A Roadmap Now and for the Future." *Esync,* 2003, *http://www.esync.com.*

- Juels, Ari and Ravikanth Pappu. "Squealing Euros: Privacy Protection in RFID-Enabled Bank Notes." *Financial Cryptography '03,* (2003): 103–121.

- Juels, Ari, R.L. Rivest, and M. Szydlo. "The Blocker Tag: Selective Blocking of RFID Tags for Consumer Privacy." ACM Press, 2003.

- Miyako, Ohkubo, Suzuki Koutarou, and Kinoshita Shingo. "Cryptographic Approach to 'Privacy-Friendly' Tags." NTT Laboratories.

- Palmer, Mark. "Seven Principles of Effective RFID Data Management." *Enterprise Systems Journal,* 3 August 2004, *http://www.esj.com/enterprise/article.aspx?EditorialsID=1076.*

- Palmer, Mark. "Event Stream Processing Advances Web Services and RFID." *InfoWorld,* 1 August 2005, *http://www.infoworld.com/article/05/08/01/31FEinnovator6_1.html.*

- Palmer, Mark. "Event Stream Processing—A New Physics of Software." *DM Direct Newsletter,* 29 July 2005.

- Rakesh, Kumar. "Interaction of RFID Technology and Public Policy." RFID Privacy Workshop, Massachusetts Institute of Technology, November 2003.

- Sarma, Sanjay E., Stephen Weiss, and Daniel Engels. "RFID Systems and Security and Privacy Implications." Auto-ID Center, Massachusetts Institute of Technology, 2002.

- Sarma, Sanjay E., Stephen Weiss, and Daniel Engels. "Radio Frequency Identification— Security Risks and Challenges." *RSA Laboratories CryptoBytes* 6, no.1 (2003): 1–9.

- Sozo, Inoue and Hiroto Yasuura. "RFID Privacy Using User-Controllable Uniqueness." Kyushu University, 1 November 2003.

- Stapleton-Gray, Ross. "Would Macy's Scan Gimbels? Competitive Intelligence and RFID." RFID Privacy Workshop, Massachusetts Institute of Technology, November 2003. *http://www.stapleton-gray.com*.

- Weiss, Stephen, Sanjay E. Sarma, Ronald Rivest, and Daniel Engels. "Security and Privacy Aspects of Low-Cost Radio Frequency Identification Systems." First International Conference on Security in Pervasive Computing, 2003.

- Weiss, Stephen. "Security and Privacy in Radio-Frequency Identification Devices." Department of Electrical Engineering and Computer Science, Massachusetts Institute of Technology, 9 May 2003.

Related Books

Klaus Finkenzeller's *RFID Handbook* (John Wiley & Sons) is the book to read if you want to know more about the physics behind RFID. This book also has a web site at *http://rfid-handbook.de*.

David A. Chappell's *Enterprise Service Bus* (O'Reilly) is a great book on how to integrate enterprise applications and services. This book is just as applicable to integrating edge devices. The author's web site is *http://www.oreillynet.com/pub/au/207*.

Silvia Hagan's *IPv6 Essentials* (O'Reilly) is a quick and easy-to-read introduction to IPv6, and it has a snail on the cover.

Periodicals

In the past five years many new RFID magazines, journals, and web sites have appeared. We list here just a few that we happen to read regularly.

RFID Journal

Established in 2002, *RFID Journal* is a leading source of RFID news and information, which it publishes online. It also sends out a free newsletter and publishes a bimonthly print magazine.

> Web site: *http://www.rfidjournal.com*
> Subscription: online and print, $189.00/year

RFID Operations

This new magazine seems to focus primarily on industry case studies, new RFID products, and legislation affecting RFID. It sometimes carries stories you won't see anywhere else.

Web site: *http://www.rfidoperations.com*
Subscription: online and print, $185.00/year

Transponder News

Transponder News is described on its web site as "A news service reporting on developments regarding the use of radio-based tagging transponder systems for commerce and scientific applications. Covering RFID and EAS technologies as well as magnetic/electric field coupled techniques…" This South African publication offers a slightly quirky alternative view of RFID compared to the EPC-centric perspective that has become so common recently.

Web site: *http://transpondernews.com*
Subscriptions: free (online only)

RFID Weblog

This blog is written by Anita Campbell, a serial entrepreneur whose main business interests are information technology, the small and mid-size business market, and RFID.

Web site: *http://www.rfid-weblog.com*
Subscriptions: *http://www.rfid-weblog.com/index.rdf*

History

The long history of RFID can be a fascinating subject. There are many web sites out there with information about the history of RFID. We'll mention some of the best here.

The Signals Collection '40–'45

Created and maintained by Paul Bodifee, this site has some great photos and information about allied radio and radar equipment from WWII. This is where RFID started. Make sure you check out the RAF Eureka/Rebecca units.

Web site: *http://www.qsl.net/pe1ngz/*
Contact: *pbodifee@dds.nl*

Eagle's Nest

Created and maintained by Jim Eagle, an experienced RFID engineer, this site has a wonderful, quirky overview of RFID's early years as well as links to even more information.

Web site: *http://members.surfbest.net/eaglesnest/rfidhist.htm*
Contact: *jimeagle@surfbest.net*

Free Tools

Nothing beats hands-on experience when learning a new technology, and free tools can help make that possible even on a limited budget.

epcTranslator

The Avicon epcTranslator is a set of Java classes that can convert EPC codes to and from other encodings. The tool is free for personal use.

Web site: *http://www.epctranslator.com*
Contact: *http://www.avicon.com/contact.htm*

Radioactive Project

The Radioactive Project hopes to produce a suite of open source RFID software that is compliant with EPCglobal standards as certification becomes available.

Web site: *http://www.radioactivehq.org*
Contact: *contact@radioactivehq.org*

Singularity Project

Singularity is another open source suite of RFID middleware designed to "support RFID enabled Supply Chain Management, integration to the enterprise, and EPCglobal. It includes edge services for device management, event filtering, workflow, as well as integration components."

Web site: *http://www.radioactivehq.org*
Contact: *contact@radioactivehq.org*

Glossary

Abbreviations

ALE   (Application Level Events)

EPCIS   (EPC Information Services)

ISO   (International Organization for Standardization)

RFID   (Radio Frequency Identification)

RTLS   (Real Time Location System)

Terms

Alert   A message from a reader to a host indicating a change in reader health or containing a scheduled update of reader health information.

Backscatter coupling   A form of coupling that uses the reflected energy of the reader to power tag communications.

Command   A message from a host to a reader that causes a change in state or reaction from the reader; also, a message from a reader to a tag that causes a change in state or reaction from the tag.

Coupling   The way a circuit on the tag and a circuit on the reader influence each other to send and receive information or power.

Capacitive coupling   A form of coupling in which the reader and tag each have conductive patches that form a capacitor when held exactly parallel to each other without touching.

Inductive coupling   A form of coupling in which the reader powers tags by generating a magnetic field with a coil antenna. The field drives current through a coil on the tag by induction, in much the same way that a transformer transfers energy between two coils.

Edge device   A device deployed in close proximity to physical operations and end users. Examples include desktop systems, printers, and RFID readers.

Electronic Product Code (EPC)   An identifier based on the standards established by EPCglobal, Inc.

Event   An observation with meaning in a particular context, such as the arrival of a pallet in the context of an inventory control system.

Filter   As used in this book, a filter is a rule that rejects some events while allowing others to pass.

Host   An application or middleware component that communicates with readers.

Identity   A unique name for an object, usually in the form of some digital representation of letters and numbers.

Keying   Describes which attributes on an analog carrier may be modulated to represent the ones and zeros of a digital message.

Observation   A record of some value somewhere at some time. An example might be a temperature in a particular curing oven at some timestamp, or the appearance of ID tag 42 at dock door 5 at 16:22:32 on July 23, 2005.

Reader   A sensor that communicates with tags to observe their identities and then communicates those observations to a host. In the case of a passive or semipassive tag, the reader also provides power to the tag.

Sensor   A device able to detect qualities of the physical world and represent data concerning those qualities as a machine-readable signal.

Tag   A data carrier that attaches data to a physical object.

Transport   A communications mechanism used by readers and hosts to communicate with each other; also may more generally refer to any communications mechanism.

H

I

J

organizations (*continued*)
    future benefits of RFID for, 5
    related to RFID, 239–241
    RFID mandates for, 1
    sharing RFID information between, 32,
        177, 183
    using RFID information within, 31, 183
Orwellian society, concerns about RFID
    technology leading to, 202
Output subsystem, Reader layer, 128

P

pallet and carton tracking applications, 13
Palmer, Mark
    "Event Stream Processing – A New Physics
      of Software", 241
    "Event Stream Processing Advances Web
      Services and RFID", 241
    "Seven Principles of Effective RFID Data
      Management", 241
Pappu, Ravikanth ("Squealing Euros: Privacy
    Protection in RFID-Enabled Bank
    Notes"), 241
partition, SGTIN encoding, 85
passive tags, 31, 35
    power source for, 58
    privacy concerns regarding, 202
password for disabling tags, 79
patches for edge devices, 193
patterns for grouping, ALE specification, 155
payments, micro, 226
performance, design considerations for, 49
pets (see animals)
pharmaceutical industry
    anti-counterfeiting measures by, 103
    B2B sharing of RFID data by, 32
    privacy issues regarding, 201, 202
    RFID initiatives for, 2
    uses of RFID for, 2, 5, 14, 24, 179
phase-shift keying (PSK), 61
Physical Markup Language (PML), 183
Physical Realization of an Encoding, 81
PML (Physical Markup Language), 183
PML service, ONS result set, 183
polling (see synchronous approach for
    notifications)
polling mode, ALE specification, 151
portal arrangement of antennas and
    readers, 113
power source for tags, 35, 58
pragmatism, applying to new technologies, 22
primary servers, 181
"print and apply" devices, 111
printable batteries, 220

printers (see RFID printers)
privacy
    balancing privacy concerns with
      benefits, 201
    concerns from specific RFID features, 201
    defining, 201
    design considerations for, 48
    government guidelines regarding, 204
    government legislation regarding, 203
    impact of RFID on, 3, 197–201
    industry guidelines for, 205
    tag features for, 102–104
    technologies for, 207
    thought leaders opinions regarding, 206
    watchdog organizations views
      regarding, 206
Privacy International, 206
"Privacy Online: Fair Information Practices in
    the Electronic Marketplace" (FTC), 204
processing capacity of tags, 67–71
Proprietary era of RFID, 6, 7
protocols, 77
    (see also reader protocols; tag protocols)
provisioning, 193
PSK (phase-shift keying), 61
public perception, privacy and, 200
publications
    "Automatic Data Collection Perspective"
      (Hill), 241
    "Cryptographic Approach to 'Privacy-
      Friendly' Tags" (Miyako, Koutarou,
      Shingo), 241
    Enterprise Service Bus (Chappell), 242
    "EPCglobal Guidelines on EPC for
      Consumer Products", 205
    "Event Stream Processing – A New Physics
      of Software" (Palmer), 241
    "Event Stream Processing Advances Web
      Services and RFID" (Palmer), 241
    "The Great CRC Mystery" (Ritter), 80
    "Identity-Based Encryption: A Survey"
      (Gagne), 241
    "Interaction of RFID Technology and Public
      Policy" (Rakesh), 241
    IPv6 Essentials (Hagan), 223, 242
    "The Jargon File" (Raymond), 77
    list of, 241–243
    "National Privacy Principles" (Government
      of Australia), 205
    "Privacy Online: Fair Information Practices
      in the Electronic Marketplace"
      (FTC), 204
    "Radio Frequency Identification – Security
      Risks and Challenges" (Sarma, Weiss,
      Engels), 242

ABOUT THE AUTHORS

BILL GLOVER has been writing software since 1981 and has worked as a programmer, lead developer, or architect on systems of all sizes, from small, automated systems controlling dams and feedmills up to a complete redesign and reimplementation of one of the world's busiest travel web sites. Bill first worked with RFID in 1995, tracking individual cattle using ear tags. He is currently a Senior Java Architect with Sun Microsystems, Inc. and works with Sun's RFID consulting practice and RFID Test Center.

HIMANSHU BHATT heads the U.S. RFID Practice and Software Technology Lab for Sun Microsystems, Inc. As a Practice Manager for Sun Microsystems's Enterprise Web Services group, Himanshu was responsible for business development, software technical sales, and professional service sales and delivery in emerging areas of technology, including Java, J2EE, J2ME, SOA, and Sun's Java Enterprise System product family. Prior to assuming the Practice Manager role within Sun, Himanshu spent over 10 years working on the architecture and development of distributed, multitier systems using Java, C++, Smalltalk, and Eiffel for various Fortune 1000 companies. Himanshu has spoken at industry conferences such as JavaOne and the LoneStar Symposium and is a published author of articles on Java/J2EE technology. Himanshu has an MS in computer science and an MBA in finance and international business.

COLOPHON

MENDEDESIGN DESIGNED AND CREATED the cover artwork of this book. The cover fonts are Akzidenz Grotesk and Orator. The text font is Adobe's Meridien; the heading font is ITC Bailey; and the code font is LucasFont's TheSans Mono Condensed.

Better than e-books

Buy *RFID Essentials* and access the digital
edition FREE on Safari for 45 days.

Go to www.oreilly.com/go/safarienabled
and type in coupon code HPM5-5TRM-HVVE-NGMD-2Z6V

Search
thousands of
top tech books

Download
whole chapters

Cut and Paste
code examples

Find
answers fast

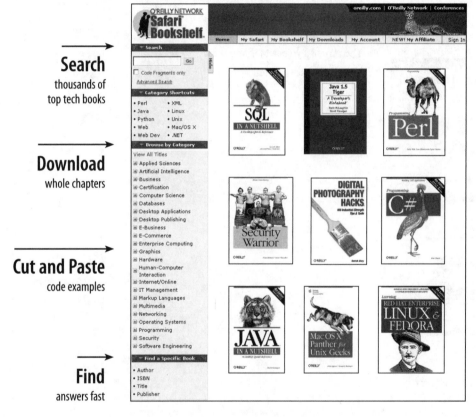

Search Safari! The premier electronic reference
library for programmers and IT professionals.

Related Titles from O'Reilly

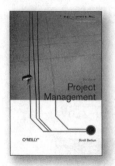

Software Development

Applied Software Project Management

Designing Interfaces

Essential Business Process Modeling

Enterprise Service Bus

Head First Design Patterns

Head First Design Patterns Poster

Practical Development Environments

Prefactoring

The Art of Project Management

UML 2.0 in a Nutshell

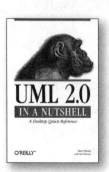

O'REILLY®

Our books are available at most retail and online bookstores.

To order direct: 1-800-998-9938 • *order@oreilly.com* • *www.oreilly.com*

Online editions of most O'Reilly titles are available by subscription at *safari.oreilly.com*